DENNIS FRIEDMAN

INHERITANCE

A PSYCHOLOGICAL HISTORY
OF THE ROYAL FAMILY

D1275734

SIDGWICK & JACKSON

First published 1993 by Sidgwick & Jackson Limited

a division of Pan Macmillan Publishers Limited
Cavaye Place London SW10 9PG
and Basingstoke

Associated companies throughout the world

ISBN 0 283 06124 3

Copyright © 1993 Dennis Friedman

The right of Dennis Friedman to be identified as the
author of this work has been asserted by him in accordance
with the Copyright, Designs and Patents Act 1988.

1 3 5 7 9 8 6 4 2

A CIP catalogue record for this book is available from
the British Library

Typeset by Cambridge Composing (UK) Ltd, Cambridge
Printed and bound in Great Britain by
Mackays of Chatham PLC, Chatham, Kent

For Rosemary, our family, and future generations.

'Things are not necessarily lovely behind the façade and so it is with human beings, too.'

Sigmund Freud

CONTENTS

SUSAN HILL

researched and contributed to the
writing of this book.

ACKNOWLEDGEMENTS

I have taken the British Royal Family from Queen Victoria to Charles, Prince of Wales to illustrate the universality of family behaviour.

Published material including biographies and letters has been the sole source of information for the study. No member of the Royal Family or any of their confidants has been interviewed and all hearsay, including unsubstantiated rumour, has been excluded from comment. All interpretations are my own.

My publisher, William Armstrong, has had faith in the project from its inception and has taken a keen personal interest in it. Hazel Orme has brought the added dimensions of a historian's approach to her skilled copy-editing and intuitive understanding of the subject matter. The photograph of the author is by Dennis Toff.

Thanks are also due to my wife, Rosemary, for her advice and help with the manuscript, and to Debbie Lennard who has patiently and painstakingly typed and retyped it as events overtook its progress with bewildering rapidity.

PROLOGUE

In 1861, a Prince of Wales, son of Queen Victoria and Prince Albert, and a future King, strayed from the royal path by having a clandestine affair with an actress.

In 1936, a Prince of Wales, son of King George V and Queen Mary, abandoned the throne for the only woman he felt would really understand him.

In late 1992, the marriage of a Prince of Wales, son of Queen Elizabeth II and Prince Philip, disintegrated when it came to light that both he and his wife had compromising friendships.

Can it be that a fatal flaw runs through the Royal Family like the San Andreas fault, contaminating relationships and severing marriages? Were the first rumblings of this felt in the nursery of Queen Victoria? Did it continue to affect her descendants – hostages not to fortune but to ancestral patterns – as they played out their psychodramas against a privileged background of English palaces and Scottish castles?

Could hints of this have been detected one hundred and fifty years ago when Prince Albert looked for a mother in Queen Victoria and she for a father in her consort? Was it their unresolved conflicts that made them unwittingly neglect the emotional needs of their children, passing on to their royal descendants an ever-widening chasm of psychological problems? *Inheritance* examines the complex interpersonal relationships of the Royal Family from the time when the ten-year-old Victoria on hearing she would be Queen promised, 'I will be good', and her cousin Albert, her future husband, confided to his diary at almost the same time, 'I intend to train myself to be a good and useful man.' The result of the rigid upbringing of these two children, with its emphasis on duty rather than on love, has been to produce in the Royal Family – just as in other families – generations of loveless adults destined to seek compensation in alternative forms of gratification including such risk-taking activities as extramarital relationships, overt gambling – casinos and horse-racing – and more recently involvement in dangerous sports.

Through the dynamics of the Royal Family, other families will recognize the significance of their own psychological inheritance. Family members will come to realize how a loving grandparent, an absent parent, a supportive teacher, or an antagonistic sibling may influence their own emotional development and their eventual choice of life partners.

CHAPTER ONE

Victoria and Albert

'The hand that rocks the cradle . . .'
JOHN O'LONDON'S *Treasure Trove*

Queen Victoria and her consort, Prince Albert,* were both psychologically disadvantaged in that neither was brought up by *two* caring parents: Queen Victoria's father, the Duke of Kent, died when she was only eight months old, while the four-year-old Albert was deprived of his mother, Duchess Luise of Saxe-Coburg-Saalfeld, when she was banished from the court following her illicit relationship with an army officer. As a result, both Victoria and Albert left legacies of emotional damage, handing down through the generations their unresolved conflicts and disturbed behavioural patterns together with the crown.

Several of Queen Victoria's descendants have been either seriously depressed, compulsive gamblers, or alcoholics. Some have had difficulties in making and maintaining commitments, and others in bringing up their children. In three out of the five generations, from Queen Victoria to the present Prince of Wales, certain family members have been confused about their sexual orientation, and at least one has turned for solace to illegal drugs. Every generation has experienced marital crises, reflected particularly in recent events which many people feel have brought the future of the monarchy into question.

Victoria and Albert, two deprived children born within three months of each other, were destined to seek attention and love to compensate for the absence of the parent of the opposite sex.

---

* Franz August Karl Albert Emanuel was the younger son of Ernst, Duke of Saxe-Coburg-Saalfeld, who later became Duke of Saxe-Coburg-Gotha. His mother, Duchess Luise, was the daughter of August, Duke of Saxe-Gotha.

Destiny also played a role in their betrothal and subsequent marriage.

Princess Victoria was born in 1819, the only child of an arranged marriage between Prince Edward, Duke of Kent, and Princess Victoria Mary Louisa of Saxe-Coburg-Saalfeld.* Prince Edward's parents, George III and Queen Charlotte, had produced thirteen children, yet the succession was a matter of concern. Their eldest son, George (the Prince Regent), was unlikely to have further children with Caroline of Brunswick, whom he hated – his only legitimate daughter Charlotte died in childbirth in 1817 – so his younger brothers were encouraged to produce legitimate offspring.

Edward, Duke of Kent, was living in Belgium with a French-woman – Julie, Madame de St Laurent – who was slightly older than he. At the age of forty-eight, and with some initial reluctance, he terminated this long-standing relationship and married the thirty-year-old Princess Victoria of Saxe-Coburg-Saalfeld. (Although the relationship was not, at first, a romantic one, Edward and Victoria later grew fond of one another.) The couple settled into apartments in Kensington Palace, which had been grudgingly offered to them by the Prince Regent, where Victoria, their only child, was born ten months after the marriage. She was delivered by Fraülein Siebold who, coincidentally, also delivered her cousin Albert three months later.

The Princess was christened in June but several of her parents' chosen names were rejected by the Prince Regent. He did not, however, object to the name Alexandrina, after the Tsar of Russia, Alexander I. Victoria was called by the diminutive Drina until she was twelve. Within the Royal Family any first name closely associated with a dynasty has been regarded as the 'property' of the most superior person to have been given that name. This has led to the widespread use within the family of diminutives and middle names, a practice which may well have caused Victoria some confusion and concern over her identity. Although the Duke of Kent may have been hoping for a son, he was not displeased by the arrival of his daughter – 'The decrees of

* Princess Victoria had a half-brother, Charles, born in 1804 and a half-sister, Feodore, born in 1817. Her mother, Victoire, was the widow of Prince Erich Charles of Leiningen. She became Regent of that state when her husband died.

Providence are at all times wisest and best,' he wrote – and he had no reason to suppose that Princess Victoria would accede to the throne. He, after all, had brothers who might yet produce sons and Victoria's mother was still relatively young and fertile.

By the end of the year, Victoria's parents were considering returning to Germany, where life would be cheaper and the atmosphere warmer. The Prince Regent, who was still distraught over the death of his daughter Charlotte, not only regarded Victoria as an intruder but also resented the continuing presence at court of her uncle Prince Leopold, who was also Charlotte's widower and a constant reminder to her grieving father of his beloved daughter's death. Before deciding on their move to Germany, however, the Duke of Kent took his wife and just-weaned daughter to Sidmouth, in Devon, for Christmas. By the sea he caught a cold which developed into pneumonia. On the advice of Dr Stockmar, a young friend of Prince Leopold, the Duke made his will. Among his executors was his equerry, Sir John Conroy.

The Duke died on 23 January 1820, six days before his father George III. Accepting the generosity of a small allowance from her brother Leopold, the Duchess of Kent and Princess Victoria returned to Kensington Palace where Victoria grew up without a father and with a mother who was not only a poor relation of the Royal Family but also a foreigner. The only two men in her life were her uncle Leopold and Sir John Conroy.

King Leopold of the Belgians, brother of the Duke of Kent, was born in 1780, Prince of Leiningen, the son of Francis, Duke of Saxe-Coburg. He had married Charlotte, the cherished daughter of the Prince Regent, in 1816, against her father's wishes. That the Duke of Kent had encouraged the courtship may partially explain Leopold's later fondness for Victoria. He remained on the fringes of the English court after Charlotte's death and, until accepting the crown of Belgium in 1830, was a frequent and welcome visitor at Kensington Palace, although he was absent for four years following his accession.

Victoria responded warmly to this flamboyant uncle: Elizabeth Longford tells us that he sported a wig, three-inch soles to his shoes and a feather boa – this outward effeminacy primed the Princess to feel comfortable with such men and an attraction to the effeminate, the man dressed as a woman, remained with her for the rest of her life. Leopold displayed consistent kindness and generosity towards Victoria and her mother and his affection for them both contrasted sharply with the *froideur* accorded the Duchess by George IV (who appeared to think it was something of an impertinence for her to have given birth to the heir to the throne and associated this, again all too painfully, with the death of his own daughter). That he had never liked Leopold made it inevitable that he would feel hostility to those with whom his son-in-law was aligned. On her uncle's departure for Belgium, however, Victoria wrote, 'I look up to him as a Father, with complete confidence, love and affection. He is the best and kindest adviser I have. He has always treated me as his child and I love him more dearly for it.'

By contrast, Captain John Conroy, whose influence over her mother increased after Leopold's departure, seemed a scheming, ambitious intruder. Upon her accession Victoria banished him from Court and at his death in 1854 she wrote to her mother, '. . . I will not speak of the past and of the many sufferings he entailed upon us by creating divisions between you and me which could never have existed otherwise . . .'

An Anglo-Irishman, Conroy was married to Elizabeth Fisher, a relative of the Duke of Kent's former tutor, which connection might have led to his appointment as the Duke's military equerry in 1817. After the Duke's death Conroy took it upon himself to serve his widow with particular diligence. He moved, with his family, into Kensington Palace where he became Comptroller of the Duchess's Household and was knighted in 1827.

If Conroy had ambitions to establish and wield influence over Victoria, by now clearly destined to be Queen, through her mother, he failed. Victoria referred to his 'personal affronts', 'slights and incivilities' and to her 'hatred' of him. Her dislike of Sir John certainly contributed to her later estrangement from her mother whom she perceived as being overly close to him. Later, she was ruefully to refer to the 'enmity' that had existed between the Duchess and herself at the time.

Victoria and her mother had a curious mutually dependent relationship. The Duchess owed her place at Court to the existence of Victoria, and Victoria needed her mother's approval and the reassurance of her presence. They slept in the same bedroom until Victoria was eighteen.

The Duchess of Kent's mothering of Victoria alternated between extreme protectiveness – until she had become Queen, Victoria was not allowed to walk downstairs without someone holding her hand – and zealous expectation.

Victoria collected male and female dolls, unconsciously compensating for her lack of brothers and sisters, and children of her own age to play with. (Fond as she was of her two half-siblings, Victoria always thought of herself as an only child and Feodore and Charles were more occasional playmates for her than family.) She quickly learned to respect both authority and the importance of duty. Writing in her fifties, Queen Victoria described her earliest memory, that of being admonished as a two-year-old: she had been crawling on a yellow carpet at Kensington Palace and was warned that if she made a noise her uncle Sussex (Augustus, Duke of Sussex) would punish her. Early memories have a particular significance: memory encapsulates feelings and attitudes never forgotten and which current behaviour continues to reflect.

Victoria continued to suppress her own needs and never ceased trying to please authority, and remained for ever dependent on the approval of her ministers and of the public. She was dedicated to duty, and family life inevitably took second place. Her early years were both over-controlled and lacking in childhood pleasures. Later, with little or no experience of happiness herself, she had little to offer her children.

Victoria, indeed, thought of giving birth with distaste. 'I think, dearest Uncle,' she wrote to Leopold – by now King of the Belgians – with ill-concealed impatience, 'You cannot really wish me to be the *"mama d'une nombreuse famille"* . . . men never think, at least seldom think, what a hard task it is for us women to go through this very often.' Her dislike of pregnancy and babies, whom she thought 'frog-like', was not conducive to a benevolent attitude towards young children. 'Having children is the only thing I DREAD,' she remarked, soon after her first pregnancy threatened to disturb her newly married idyll with Albert. All but the last of her nine children endured their childhoods while their mother was in that state of pregnancy which she found so disagreeable, or in its aftermath, when she showed little interest in her new baby.

Children learn early on to suppress feelings they sense will be unacceptable, because they fear the loss of parental approval upon which they are entirely dependent. Disapproval, expressed in body language – the warning finger, the stern glance – may come to be as threatening as anything verbally expressed. Victoria's need to please her mother through compliant behaviour, was, as with all children, based upon fears of being abandoned, which would have been strong in Victoria since she had already lost one parent. Victoria's celebrated remark 'I will be good', reflects both a precocious sense of duty and a need for the approval of the parent upon whom she was still heavily dependent. When parents impress on their children the importance of duty and obedience rather than showing them unconditional love, all negative feelings in the child are obliged to be suppressed, only to reappear inappropriately in adulthood. Such children over-emphasize pleasing at the expense of acquiring self-esteem and self-confidence, and adopt assertive behaviour.

If Victoria felt threatened by the attention her mother showed Sir John Conroy, she was happy in the company of Fraülein (later Baroness) Louise Lehzen. The daughter of a Lutheran pastor, Lehzen was brought from Germany when Victoria was five to be her companion and governess, and had previously taught Feodore. While Lehzen's presence maintained her charge's familiarity with things German, she was diligent in her efforts to interest Victoria in British history. Victoria had lessons from numerous teachers, but it was her relationship with Lehzen that most shaped her character. Although severe, Lehzen was loyal and protective, and Victoria understood that her reprimands did not imply diminished devotion. One of Lehzen's habits was to pin a sprig of holly to Victoria's collar, so that her small, sloping chin would always be raised. Had Victoria not been fond of her, some complaint about this might have been found in the daily diary that Lehzen herself had encouraged her to keep.

As Victoria grew into womanhood, she retained affection and respect for Lehzen. Even as Queen, she wrote in her journal 'Walked with my ANGELIC, dearest Mother, Lehzen, who I do so love! . . . the most estimable and precious treasure I possess and EVER SHALL POSSESS.'

Perhaps, in the light of such freely expressed affection, it is not to be wondered that Prince Albert resented Lehzen's continuing presence in the royal household, and in particular the influence

she had on his wife. In 1842 she finally left the household and
returned to live in Germany on a pension of £800 a year. Lehzen's
departure was engineered by Albert. He described the governess
as 'a crazy, common, stupid intriguer, obsessed with lust of
power . . .' Victoria deferred to him in Lehzen's dismissal, having
found her 'other half' in her husband and therefore being less in
need of a surrogate parent. She continued to correspond with
Lehzen, though, and visited her until the Baroness's death in
1870.

For the young Victoria it must have been distressing to have
had a mother who bonded with her during breast-feeding, but
who had probably given this up abruptly on the death of her
husband. This would have been her first experience of the pain of
separation which reappeared so dramatically on the death of her
husband. A more gradual separation from her mother and breast
feeding would have allowed her to cope better with the losses,
forty years later, of her mother and husband. Her confusion
would have been compounded by the presence of Fraülein Lehzen,
another 'mother', who was not only affectionate, but who imbued
her with a strong sense of self and impressed upon her her place
in history. From her biological mother Victoria learnt 'negligent
mothering', but from her surrogate mother she learnt how to
be a queen. In the event because of her remoteness and her
melancholy aura during her bereavement she became the mother
that her people wanted rather than the one whom her children
needed.

Queen Victoria's grief when her biological mother died in
March 1861, was greater than she might have anticipated. After a
period of estrangement shortly after Victoria's accession, mother
and daughter had grown closer as Victoria's family increased and
discussion of her children's progress was mutually enjoyed. It is
not surprising that Victoria felt regret that her mother's affection
for her had not been acknowledged by the Duchess. Victoria had
told Lord Melbourne, 'I don't believe Ma ever really loved me.'
After the Duchess's death, she was moved to find many fond
references to herself among her mother's papers, which would
have caused her to feel both remorseful and guilty about her
interpretation of her mother's behaviour. On Albert's birthday in
August – normally a day to be celebrated – and four months
before his unexpected death, Victoria wrote, 'Alas! so much is

9

different this year, nothing festive . . . I am still in such low spirits . . .' She also wrote to her aunt Augusta of her 'immeasurable loss and grief', which caused her loss of appetite, headaches, irritability and what Lord Clarendon referred to as a 'morbid melancholy' – or what we would now term 'depression'. Finally, Albert heard of reports circulating in Germany that the Queen was being attended by several doctors. He denied the 'horrid, vile rumours' but set about persuading Victoria to end her mourning for her mother and return to some semblance of public life. But shortly afterwards he too was dead, from typhoid fever, leaving Victoria a widow at the age of forty-two. In 1861 Victoria experienced one loss too many, and she remained the picture of melancholy for the rest of her life.

The death of Victoria's father had led her mother to try to play the role of both parents for her daughter. That this had not worked for Victoria was demonstrated by her continuing dependency on her mother until her marriage to Albert. Unconsciously she had hoped Albert would come to replace her father but in reality she needed him to be both father and mother to her – her mother may have felt herself a good parent but Victoria's perception of her would have been influenced by the Duchess's reaction to her bereavement when Victoria, as a tiny baby, was entirely dependent on her. That both her mother and her husband died in the same year reactivated Victoria's dependent needs.

In 1848, she had lost Viscount Melbourne who died six years after his stroke. Victoria had relied upon him as she would on a father and he had spent much of his time at Windsor acting as her private secretary and mentor as well as her first prime minister. Happily, at the time Albert was able to take his place.

Victoria's feelings had always to be suppressed. Her earlier losses were denied but this defence eventually broke down at Albert's death. The Queen's sadness was as much to do with unexpressed, and now inexpressible, childhood griefs (since there was now no one to whom she could relate), as it was for the loss of a mother whom she now felt she may have misjudged and a husband on whom she had been heavily dependent.

Victoria had grown up a lively and spirited child. She was not intellectually gifted but was full of curiosity and imagination. Like other members of the Royal Family down the generations, she drew well, had an ear for music, a gift for mimicry, and she enjoyed the make-believe world of ballet, theatre, and opera. However, when it became clear that she would eventually become Queen, new responsibilities meant that she had much less time for the things she enjoyed doing especially when she embarked on a series of tiring journeys around Britain. These provided visible evidence to the populace that the monarchy was continuing but at the end of one tour she wrote, 'Here is the end of our journey, I am happy to say. Though I liked some of the places very well, I was much tired by the long journeys and the great crowds we encountered.' Her travelling companion and only friend was Lehzen and communication from her mother was largely admonishing; she exhorted her daughter to 'Avoid stepping out of your room an unknown and untried person . . . shew a promise of character – let the People hope for something worth having, free from all the faults of former reigns.'

It was a great joy for her to be reunited with Uncle Leopold in 1835, after the four-year separation. Letters, however kindly and frequently exchanged, were not as satisfactory as meetings. 'What happiness was it for me to throw myself in the arms of that dearest of Uncles who has always been to me like a father . . .' she wrote in September. King Leopold had married Louise of Orléans who became at once 'very dear' to Victoria.

Because Victoria's childhood and adolescence almost totally lacked the companionship of her peers, she never learnt how to communicate with children, and was understandably to become drawn to animals as soon as she had outgrown her dolls. Her favourite pet, a King Charles spaniel called Dash, came into the household, ironically as a present for her mother from the loathed Sir John Conroy. Victoria commandeered the little dog, giving him presents at Christmas and dressing him in little jackets and trousers. Dash in his turn was devoted to her, refusing even to leave her room when she was ill.

The dog can be seen as a transitional object, an extension of Victoria's mother, something that she could openly cherish and pet in the absence of fulfilling human contact. Horses, too, symbols of strength, power and masculinity, were important to her all her life, from the ponies she rode as a child, to the great beasts upon which Landseer and others painted her, dressed in her widow's weeds, the bridle frequently held respectfully by a gillie.

The Princess was given firm lessons about the significance of the Crown – and her destiny to uphold it – and her own importance. By the time she was twelve she merited a twenty-four-hour bodyguard, and was very much aware that when her uncle William IV died, she would be the Queen. She was addressed as 'ma'am', treated with deference by courtiers as well as servants and the breadth of her education stressed the magnitude of her future role. Victoria was pleased to observe in her own features a resemblance to those of the King, and had been inconsolable when the Duchess of Kent decided that her daughter should not attend his coronation: it had been decreed that Victoria's royal uncles should take precedence over the Heir Presumptive. The child was a state treasure yet lacked family life, and grew to be wilful. The diarist Charles Cavendish Fulke Greville, who was as spiteful as he was amusing, described her as 'hard-hearted, selfish and self-willed.' If this was so, much can be attributed to the baffling paradox which confronted her. While being trained for the throne, she was denied the unqualified 'personal' acceptance from loving parents, which would certainly have made her a better mother and would scarcely have made her a lesser Queen. When she complained that years later William Gladstone addressed her as if she were a public meeting, it was perhaps an unconscious declaration that, rather than being seen as a person, she symbolized an institution.

Comfort eating is a well-known phenomenon. Those who eat to excess are expressing a wish for gratification hitherto denied them. The food they choose is usually a symbolic reminder of unfulfilled childhood needs. Sweets and puddings represent what they feel life owes them. At the age of seventeen, Victoria was barely five feet tall but weighed almost nine stone. Shortly after she became Queen, it was reported that she was ordering her dresses a size larger. According to Elizabeth Longford, she resolved to eat only half a biscuit at lunch and then, later, to miss the meal altogether. These resolutions were broken, however, and Victoria may have taken comfort from Lord Melbourne's remark that the best figure for a woman was 'fine and full with a fine bust'. Soon after, however, he told her that she was in danger of becoming very fat, but he sweetened the pill by attributing her weight to her age. Victoria's weight gain may be interpreted as compensation for insufficient emotional nourishment from her mother and a prelude to another frustrated appetite – the sexual – which became apparent later.

William Lamb, Viscount Melbourne, Victoria's prime minister at her accession, was to become as important to the young Queen as her uncle Leopold had been to her as a princess. He was not merely a scholar, consummate politician and wit, but was attractive, charming and affectionate to Victoria, whose regard for him was not limited by his having scraped through two scandalous divorces. Their devotion was entirely mutual, and in Melbourne Victoria found the support, kindly advice, and almost flirtatious regard that she might have wished for from a father. He dealt expertly with all her self-doubts, reassured her that her nervousness denoted 'high and right feelings', and even comforted her when she bemoaned her short stature and the shape of her nose. Her height, he said, was 'great enough', and people with small features 'never did anything'. To have Melbourne at her elbow, guiding her invisibly, eased Victoria's transition from Princess to Queen.

Two of Melbourne's favourite names for girls were Alice and Louise, and Victoria duly gave these names to two of her daughters. She was highly entertained by his waggish epigrams: of wife-beating, he remarked, 'It is almost worthwhile for a woman to be beat, considering the exceeding pity she excites,' and of cheating, 'No people cheat like the English.' His influence might have been of dubious value, although amusing, but he treated Victoria as a person and a woman, as well as his Queen, and she responded accordingly.

It was just as well that Victoria was able to confide in her prime minister, and that he was sympathetic and wise. When she admitted to him that she had become lazy about dress, Melbourne replied, 'That's the feeling of a sensible person, but I shouldn't encourage you.' She disliked getting up in the morning, took her bath last thing at night instead of before dinner, so that she could cut down on the time spent dressing and undressing, and even disliked brushing her teeth. Melbourne reminded her of the Four Commandments enumerated by a prominent politician's wife to her children: 'Fear God. Honour the King. Obey your parents. Brush your teeth.'

It may be that Victoria's lack of interest in washing and dressing can be attributed to her dislike of the Mistress of the Robes, the Duchess of Sutherland, but it is more likely that the depression which was to affect her throughout her life was beginning to show itself. Because she could not face the day she neglected both her appearance and her personal hygiene. In the light of her childhood losses, new responsibilities, political press-ures, and the burden of duties for which she was only half prepared, a change in behavioural patterns was inevitable.

Lord Melbourne became one of Victoria's few trusted confi-dants. She leaned on him, relied on him, and felt able to be herself in his presence. When Melbourne resigned, albeit temporarily, in 1839 she despaired: 'All my happiness is gone! that peaceful life destroyed, that dearest kind Lord Melbourne no more my Minis-ter,' she wrote in her journal on 7 May. She wept at the idea of either the Duke of Wellington or Sir Robert Peel forming an adminis-tration. However, her spirits lifted when Melbourne unexpectedly formed a new government, and Sir John Conroy resigned from her mother's household. (She found herself able to dance until a quarter to four at a ball held for the visiting Russian Tsarevitch.)

Victoria dreaded the thought of marriage at this time in her life and wrote to her uncle Leopold, whom by now she knew desired a match between herself and her cousin Albert, requesting that Albert's proposed visit be cancelled. The King of the Belgians was shrewd enough to remain calm, and persuaded Victoria to agree that Albert's visit should not be forgotten but merely delayed for a few months. On 18 April 1839, after a discussion during which Lord Melbourne had advised against marrying a foreigner or a commoner, marriage seemed to have been staved off. She wrote in her journal, 'Why need I marry at all for 3 or 4 years? did he see the necessity? I did not think so, still this & certainly the present state is dreadful; always, as he says on the verge of a quarrel; I said I dreaded the thought of marrying; that I was so accustomed to have my own way, that I thought it was 10 to 1 that I shouldn't agree with anybody.' The 'dreadful' state to which Victoria alluded was her uncomfortable relationship with her mother. Until and unless she married Victoria would remain stifled by the Duchess's suffocating presence.

Victoria had first met her cousin Albert in 1836 when he and his brother had visited London. She was then unaware that this was an early move in Leopold's long-cherished plan to see his niece and nephew married, and was no more impressed with Albert than she had been with other glamorous European male cousins who had been presented to her.

As a frequent visitor in court circles, Leopold was better placed than anyone to see the political benefits of a match between Albert, younger son of his brother Ernst (Duke of Saxe-Coburg-Saalfeld), and his niece Victoria. His long-nursed wishes were realized late in 1839 when the brothers visited Victoria again. Mindful perhaps of the infancy and thus fragility of his own dynasty, Leopold was keen to replicate through his nephew and niece the union between the houses of Hanover and Coburg that his own first marriage had represented. After her cousins' first visit Victoria dutifully and probably unconsciously colluded with Leopold's plans by writing of Albert to her uncle in terms certain to please him: 'He possesses every quality that could be desired to make me perfectly happy. I have only to beg you now, my dearest Uncle, to take care of the health of one, now so dear to me . . .'

Yet the eighteen-year-old Victoria's admiration of Albert did not prevent her from delaying a return visit for three years. That she experienced one of history's great *coups de foudre* when she saw Albert again speaks of several things: her wish to be freed from her mother's lowering influence and to replicate in her personal life the power she had come to enjoy as Queen, Albert's startling loss of weight since 1836 and the lean beauty which was consequently clear, and her helpless desire to please her uncle.

After Albert's mother, Duchess Luise, had been banished from court, she had subsequently married her army officer. In the seven years before her death, Albert never saw her again. Although his father was kindly he was also remote, and Albert came to lean heavily on his older brother, also named Ernst. He grew up without the influence of women, and it is likely that he was not only ignorant and suspicious of them, but also hostile towards them. It was inevitable that, as an adult, he would unconsciously try to replace the irreplaceable, and seek a woman who understood his loss. No seeking was necessary, though. Albert knew that his marriage was preordained and that he had little choice in the matter. 'I intend to train myself to be a good and useful man,' he wrote uncannily reiterating his cousin Victoria's vow to be good.

Albert was as assiduous a diarist as Victoria, although he mainly recorded details of his illnesses. His preoccupation with loss, unlike Victoria's, showed itself in hypochrondriasis. Illness and a fear of death, the ultimate separation, echoed anxieties relating to the loss of his mother. Having been deprived of the source of life at the age of four he inevitably remained concerned about loss of life through illness. The renewal of life through birth was important to both of them but it was *life* they sought, not children. Albert, like Victoria, had looked to a series of tutors for companionship and 'mothering'. One in particular, Herr Florschütz, known to Albert as 'Thus', provided him with an emotional prop. As a youth in Venice, plagued by an abscess on a tooth, he wrote of his longing for Thus's comfort '. . . but nowhere could I find my beloved Thus to sob out my pain in his arms . . .'

At the University of Bonn, Albert's interests were artistic and intellectual. He studied natural sciences, languages, music and painting. He fenced, developed a deep love of the beautiful but melancholy music of Mendelssohn, and played chess, often against himself. He seems to have been a natural scholar but had difficulty in relating to others: he was content in solitude, and neither sought nor encouraged friendship. This did not seem to trouble him – loneliness was a way of life for him. Thrown upon his own resources at an early age he had had limited opportunities to rely on others or to trust them: his mother, after all, would have had little time for him while she was involved with her lover before Albert was four and after that he never saw her again.

Albert's shyness affected his behaviour when he returned to England in 1839. He knew almost no one and was hampered in conversation by his heavy German accent. After the all-male society of the university, and knowing that he was to be judged by a young queen – not to mention her court – he vowed that he would not be 'corrupted'. In German, the word meaning 'to corrupt', *bestecher*, may also be translated as 'bribed': a strange reaction to a proposed commitment to a woman. But his first commitment, that to his mother, had ended badly for him and it seems likely that he would have reservations about involvement with another woman. It was clearly his duty to marry but a one-to-one relationship with a female was not something he was looking forward to: Melbourne noted that he showed a marked reserve with ladies, and made tactless and premature remarks about 'moral codes'.

From the moment that Victoria indicated her enthusiasm for their marriage in 1839, Albert was denied any wish to return to his studies, his music, or his Rhineland. His life was determined for him but, by nature shy and withdrawn, it was not easy for him to adapt to it. One of his few diversions was his talent for mimicry, which was shared by his wife: role-playing often reflects an uncertainty about one's own role in life.

Victoria was perhaps fortunate that her attraction to 'beautiful people' such as Lord Melbourne was not shared by Albert. Resigned to his fate, and probably indifferent to it, Albert was not put off by her plumpness or homeliness, and anyway, it is possible that since she was in love she had acquired the radiance that love can bring to the plainest of women. We are told by Elizabeth Longford that at times Victoria was worried by Albert's quiet wistfulness, particularly during occasions which were supposed to be social. 'When she introduced him to her ladies for the first time he found it very tiresome and could not remember which was which.' In General Grey's account of Albert's early life, written with Victoria's approval and published in 1867, it is asserted that Albert 'never took kindly to great dinners, balls, or to the common amusements of the fashionable world'. Victoria was enchanted by his appearance and seems to have been sexually attracted to him. 'Albert's beauty is most striking, and he is so amiable and unaffected – in short, very fascinating . . .' she wrote during his second visit. Albert's 'beauty' (a term more usually held in association with women) rather than his 'good looks' appealed to Victoria, probably because once more she had found a father in a 'woman'. But her infatuation with him stopped short of leaving him in any doubt as to who would be the senior partner in their marriage. Victoria always wore the trousers, just as her mother before her. After their betrothal, Albert mooted plans for a long honeymoon but his fiancée replied, adoringly but firmly, 'You forget, my dearest Love, that I am the Sovereign and that business can stop and wait for nothing.' Later on, in the early days of their marriage, Victoria recorded that, after she had dealt with some State papers, 'Albert helped me with the blotting paper when I signed.'

Paradoxically it had been at the Queen's insistence that the word 'obey' was retained at their wedding service. Her resolve to delay marriage had dissolved during Albert's autumn visit. Victoria proposed to him within three days of his arrival and they were married on 10 February 1840.

The diarist Charles Greville alluded to the superficiality of Albert's physical desire for his bride when he observed that the couple walked early in the morning after their wedding night. 'Strange that a bridal night should be so short; and I told Lady Palmerston that this was not the way to provide us with a Prince of Wales.' Yet Albert's need to be reunited with a lost 'mother' was quickly satisfied by Victoria's first pregnancy and the birth of their daughter Victoria (known firstly as Pussy and then as Vicky), and by eight further pregnancies over the next sixteen years. Since Albert had never felt loved by a woman in his childhood, he welcomed the birth of his daughter. He adored her – but, more importantly, he expected her to adore him.

No child should be expected to please a father by filling the vacuum created by an earlier bereavement. In certain circumstances, a daughter may gradually come to replace a wife, with all the inevitable incestuous and damaging consequences to the child. It is improbable that the 'replacement' of Albert's mother with his daughter led to sexual abuse, and in any event Albert would have been unlikely to have found physical contact with a woman particularly agreeable since his early life experiences would have ruled against it. Vicky would, nonetheless, have been emotionally exploited if Albert's demands of her were such that the normal parent/child transaction was distorted. (Albert's affection for Vicky was not repeated with any of his other children, and, at times, it was a source of friction between him and his wife.)

When Vicky (married to Prince, later King, Frederick, 'Fritz', of Prussia) was pregnant for the first time, and about to present a shortly-to-be-reunited Germany* with the future Kaiser Wilhelm, Victoria admitted that she resented pregnancy because it

* Germany was then a network of linked but independent principalities of which Prussia was the most powerful.

came between her and Albert. This would suggest that Albert avoided his wife sexually during this time, and probably also in the post-natal period. Albert had, once again, satisfied his need (to create another 'mother'), but Victoria, having enjoyed the physical union with him, regretted its consequences, namely the children. She described herself as being 'wretched', 'low' and 'depressed' during and after her pregnancies. However, 'Can I have no more fun in bed?' was her response to news from one of her doctors that her ninth pregnancy must be her last. The remark adds weight to the suspicion that Albert's sexual attentions were procreational rather than recreational and that Victoria now anticipated, reluctantly, fewer approaches from her husband. Victoria must have suffered from Albert's sexual indifference and the transfer of her resentment to the infants, who had resulted from his need to make a mother of her, was sad but understandable. She would have envied them having a father, since she had not had one herself.

Early in their marriage, Victoria and Albert restored and enlarged Osborne House, an Italianate villa on the Isle of Wight. More intimate than a palace and relatively informal, it became their favourite residence; Victoria hung their bedroom with paintings of male nudes (perhaps instinctively hoping that her husband would find them visually erotic).

Albert and Victoria were certainly united by bonds other than parenthood. Victoria, delighted with her husband, gradually conferred upon him the status reserved for men she loved and trusted. As Albert became a father figure as well as a husband, Lord Melbourne's influence gradually faded.

Soon after their marriage Albert had complained to Prince William of Löwenstein that he was 'the husband, not the master of the house'. 'I alone must be her adviser,' he wrote to Melbourne in the politician's declining years. Victoria was happy, or at least willing to defer to Albert, as she did over Lehzen's dismissal. But it was she and not he who had been trained to be a monarch. Although she worshipped Albert, regarded him as head of the family, gave him access to the red dispatch boxes, and gazed at him adoringly in every official portrait, unsurprisingly, it was not enough for him.

Albert seldom gave vent to his helplessness: there were few people in whom he could confide. On one occasion, however, after he and Victoria had quarrelled over Lehzen's influence in

Pussy's nursery, he wrote to Baron Stockmar, 'Victoria is too hasty and passionate for me to be able to speak of my difficulties. She will not hear me out but flies into a rage and overwhelms me with reproaches of suspiciousness, want of trust, envy, etc., etc.' His dissatisfaction with life at home, his lack of friends at court, a persisting language barrier, and ongoing frustrations concerning his lack of official purpose, led him to take upon himself an advanced and scientific concern in industrial and agricultural matters. He had many interests, travelled widely and achieved much, but, by addressing himself to Britain's problems rather than to its people, he earned respect but little affection.

One of Albert's concerns was the state of the drains and sewerage at Osborne, Windsor and Balmoral. Advances in technology in the royal palaces helped to improve public health generally in that people became aware that disease could be caused by inadequate plumbing. But this and other crusades failed to make Albert popular. He noticed that the hundreds of candles in Buckingham Palace were snuffed half burned, and discarded – perhaps because a low-glowing candle casts an unflattering light on a lady's throat. Albert however saw no reason why so much candle-wax should be wasted every year and put a stop to the practice. His motives might have been commendable, but generations of palace servants had seen the half candles as an extra source of income, and Albert's economy provoked an indignant reaction below stairs.

With time on his hands, and satisfying his obsessional needs, Albert took it upon himself to catalogue, restore, and hang the many valuable pictures which lay stacked and neglected in the royal archives. Like Sir Anthony Blunt, a hundred years later, he became Keeper of the Pictures. He worked hard both socially and politically, and although the British people might later have had good reason to thank Albert for his Teutonic diligence and precision, at the time they evinced little interest. He was embraced neither by society nor by the nation, but only by the plump arms of his wife, and by the trusting Vicky, the one woman he loved for herself, who in return was expected to love him for himself. Albert was lonely and unhappy for much of his life. William Gladstone's comment upon his 'stillness and chillness' suggests depths of internalized misery and frustration. He was friendless at court, intellectually thwarted, sufficiently insecure to resent his wife's enduring affection for Baroness Lehzen and for some of her prime ministers, and able to communicate only in a disciplinary way with most of his children.

Feared by them, disliked at court, and misjudged and misunderstood by the British people (even though he contributed to an industrial and cultural flowering that significantly improved millions of lives), Albert adopted distanced behaviour as a defence against his feelings of rejection and turned to the familiar past: Germanic music, customs from home (including the Christmas tree which he introduced to Britain), the celebration of nature in the woods around Balmoral, the 'Swiss Cottage' he had constructed in the grounds of Osborne, and the intimacy of conversations in German with his wife. As he grew older, Albert identified more and more with those who supported unpopular moral stands, and he felt at one with minority opinions. By the age of forty-three Albert must have felt completely isolated. Even his only friend, Baron Stockmar, had returned to Germany and was now geographically closer to beloved Vicky than Albert would ever be.

Although Victoria and Albert were united in their disappointment with their son and heir, Prince Albert Edward, born on 9 November 1841, they were divided by quarrels and disagreements about him. At first, his birth was celebrated: the Queen had produced the desired male heir, and he was a strong, attractive baby. Before long, however, Albert displayed his preference for Pussy, and Victoria showed marked indifference to the son who was to succeed her.

Between the nurseries and the Queen's apartments at Buckingham Palace lay a mile of chilly corridors. Although Victoria could have altered these arrangements, she chose not to do so. A belated interest in him on the part of both his parents must have come too late for Edward. He spent much of his adult life attempting to deal with the consequences of having been dismissed by his mother almost as soon as he was born. Since neither Albert nor Victoria was temperamentally suited to parenthood, it is ironic that they had such a large family. As we have seen, both of them had underlying motives for this, but neither a genuine love of children nor a wish to create a secure, warm and loving environment was among them.

Victoria's age was one in which children were expected to be seen and not heard. They had to 'earn' parental love if they were to receive it, and conveniently for exploitative and uncaring parents, children's memories were considered to be short.

Albert was not the first husband to find his wife more agreeable in her absence. Nor was he the last member of the Royal Family to find it easier to express his devotion to her on paper. In 1844 he returned to Coburg to attend his father's funeral and on the first day of his journey wrote, 'My own Darling – I have been here about an hour and regret the lost time which I might have spent with you . . . You are even now half a day nearer to seeing me again; by the time you get this letter, you will be a whole one – . . .' Similarly, later that year Victoria wrote enthusiastically about the family idyll that in theory was so appealing to her. 'The children again with us, and such pleasure and interest! Bertie and Alice are the greatest friends and always playing together . . . Oh! if I could only exactly describe our dear happy life together!'

Vicky, their first-born, was intelligent and intuitive; she sensed her father's need for love and responded to it. But the friction between her parents as a result of Vicky's affection for him was obvious in the months preceding her marriage to Crown Prince Frederick of Prussia in 1858. Vicky had been groomed by dining à trois with her parents, and Victoria recorded in her diary, 'We dined with Vicky who generally leaves at 10, and then I have the rare pleasure of being alone with my beloved Albert.' Prince Albert, however, had criticized his wife about her 'worries' at their forthcoming separation from Vicky, 'whom', he wrote, 'you are thankful to be rid of'.

Later, when Vicky was married and pregnant, she was bombarded by as many as four letters a day from her mother. Replying to the letters was exhausting her, and she asked Albert to make her mother desist. Victoria picked up her pen and wrote to her daughter that 'Papa has snubbed me several times on the subject and when one writes in spite of fatigues and trouble, to be told it bores the person to whom you write, it is rather too much!' It is probably true that it was not simply the number of letters but the nature of some of them that upset Vicky. Victoria clearly envied the love that Vicky was giving to her husband Frederick, just as earlier she had envied her relationship with Albert. Victoria, pregnant with her last child as Vicky prepared to give birth to her first, wrote to her daughter with a disagreeable frankness: 'What you say of the pride of giving life to an immortal soul is very fine, dear, but I own I cannot enter into that; I think much more of our being like a cow or a dog at such moments; when our poor nature becomes so very animal and unecstatic.' These remarks indicated that in any competition for motherhood Victoria would always know best. They were also a triumphant reminder to Vicky that her mother was still receiving Albert's attentions.

Ironically Albert had lost Vicky, his favourite child, to the 'mother' country to which he had always dreamed of returning. Making Victoria a mother, yet again, was poor compensation for his twofold deprivation.

Although Albert's well-meaning efforts at social reform had hitherto been received in Britain as haughty and meddling, the triumphant success of the Great Exhibition of 1851, of which he was chief architect, earned him a grudging respect. As the Queen deferred to her husband more and more however, the influence of her ministers weakened, and Albert was regarded with suspicion and hostility. Despite Victoria's undisputed devotion, she did not give him the official status that would have made his life easier. Although it was well within her power to do so earlier, she did not make him Prince Consort until 1857, when the realization that the Prince of Wales would take precedence over his father made her take action. She withheld status from Albert because she wanted to keep all available power to herself. That strong sense of sovereignty would not yield, even to her 'dearest Angel' outside the family. (Albert, conversely, was able to take over from Victoria when she was indisposed during and after pregnancy.) He received the title Prince Consort in the same year as his wife's final pregnancy, as if Victoria, somehow knowing that his reign in the nursery was soon to end, decided that Albert should be compensated for his diligence in carrying out his obligations as a husband and securing the succession. But her dilatoriness can also be construed as a reflection of her earlier resentment of her father for abandoning her, and her wish to 'punish' him.

Victoria and Albert had been married for twenty-one years when in 1861, shortly after the birth of their ninth child, Albert contracted typhoid fever and died. Ill and feverish, he had asked to be buried in Germany, but the woman at his side was to deny him his last wish, just as his mother in leaving him had denied many of his earlier ones.

Albert had spent over twenty years in emotional isolation, imprisoned by his obsessional needs just as his daughter-in-law Alexandra was later to be by her deafness. He had not embraced the British people, only their problems. The child who had kept a diary of his aches and pains yearned always for his mother. Perhaps Albert hoped that he would return to her in the afterlife in which he so deeply believed. 'We do not know', he had written, 'in what state we will meet again; but that we shall recognize each other and be together in eternity I am perfectly certain.' (So strongly did Victoria concur with the notion that their spirits would be reunited that she attempted to communicate with Albert through mediums after his death.)

His marriage to Victoria could not have been very happy, despite the desperate attempts at communion through sex. He had been withdrawn and introverted throughout his adolescence but he was drawn to Victoria, as she to him, out of a need that they shared for emotional fulfilment. He was crushed by the affections of a woman on whom he depended but whom he could not have loved – because dependence and hostility go hand in hand – and from whom he was unable to escape other than by dying.

Queen Victoria virtually beatified Albert both within their marriage and after his death. His monument in Kensington Gardens, the plans for which she approved, has him seated beneath a sharply steeled spire – pointing him, as it were, to heaven – and surrounded by ecclesiastical architectural features.

Victoria's demeanour during the thirty-eight years of her widowhood, and especially the first decade, suggested to her children and grandchildren that little mattered without her spouse. Her children were a painful reminder to her of Albert's absence, and even less important to her now than they had been before. But for Victoria, too, the marriage must have been less than satisfactory. Hungry for love, she had married a man of probably confused sexual orientation with a fixation on his mother's passion for another man. This would have made of him a partner who fulfilled her 'expectations of neglect' based on the absence of her father and subsequent ineffectual mothering.

Women with cold or distant husbands often direct their emotional energies into their children or work. Victoria did neither. She did have some insight and knew that there was room for improvement in her behaviour – she encouraged Albert to write reports to her on her progress. Nevertheless it was she who proposed marriage, it was in her palaces that they lived, and it was her crown which symbolized the balance of power in the relationship.

Victoria was the first queen regnant of England since Anne. From the insecurities of her childhood had come the certainty that she, as guardian of the Crown, could, like her forebear, demand love and loyalty. She 'assumed' she had Albert's love, just as she expected love from her children. She was happy with Albert, and she expected him to be happy with her. Victoria believed that her children were fortunate to have such a perfect man as their father, but by the time of his death, much psychological damage – unrecognized by either parent – had already been passed on, most notably to their heir, Albert Edward, who had become an angry and emotionally impoverished young man.

At the time of Edward's birth, his sister Vicky was ill and Victoria may have experienced an early pang of jealousy at her husband's concern for their little daughter. Because of her need for Albert, she would have had difficulty in blaming him for this so her resentment would have been displaced on to her new baby whom she saw as yet another rival for Albert's love. It is significant that Victoria referred to Edward as 'the Boy' until her next child, 'Fat Alice', was born. Such dismissive and depersonalizing nicknames are hurtful, derogatory and humiliating. The woman whose name has become synonymous with the virtues and values of family life was unable to express affection for her children until long after they needed it most.

There are many portraits of Queen Victoria painted during and immediately after her child-bearing years. In most of these she is depicted as melancholy despite being surrounded by her apparently adoring husband, who stands, or leans, by her side, and children who gather, like puppies, around the folds of her skirt. A listless hand will touch the ruffled shoulder of a younger child, but the seated Queen never smiles, and the eyes are glazed behind the bulbous stare and above the drooping chin.

Victoria had always been parsimonious. She knew that the Crown represented the ultimate source of national wealth and she was careful not to squander it. Having been given so little parental love as a child, she had a profound sense of inner poverty. She inherited her mother's debts and insisted that these be paid off out of her own allowance. Living mentally in her past, she was slow to pay for the modernization of her homes and gas and electricity were not installed in Buckingham Palace or Balmoral until 1846. Single bulbs dimly illuminated vast rooms as if to underline the Queen's reluctance to expose cracks or stains in the fabric of her castles. Paradoxically, in her role as Empress of India, the Queen upheld a large staff of Indian chefs and servants to prepare the curry that was invariably served as an alternative at dinner and which was almost never sampled. She deplored decadence but had a bottle of whisky brought to her room every night. This was seldom touched, but in its reassuring and potentially comforting presence the bottle at least might have been a ghostly reminder of the maternal nurturing she had been denied.

The Queen, who had always been fat, began putting on even more weight in her widowhood, but compulsively satisfying oral needs could hardly make up for her losses. William Gladstone noted in 1863 that the Queen weighed over eleven stone. Today this would be regarded as obese for a woman of less than five feet in height. After Albert's death, she became depressed for some years, virtually retiring from public life until her Golden Jubilee in 1887. For her children this seclusion was another reminder that she had always been more concerned with their father than she had been with them. Her prolonged grief reaction included the discouragement of any kind of pleasure within the family, and a determination that Edward in particular should be married as quickly as possible to a suitable princess. Victoria expected to be dead within a year of Albert's demise and had informed King Leopold of this conviction. Years later, in 1888, having been deprived of a rapid reunion with Albert, she told Vicky that she had contemplated suicide. Something, however, had restrained her. 'A voice told me, for His sake – no, Still Endure.'

As a child Edward had disappointed his parents with his lack of scholastic achievements and even with his looks. He was now, in addition, being used by his mother as a scapegoat for her deep and lasting distress at the death of his father. In January 1862 his mother wrote to Vicky: 'I doubt if you could bear the sight of the one who was the cause; or if you would not feel, as I do, a shudder . . . I feel daily, hourly, something which is too dreadful to describe. Pity him I do . . . But more you cannot ask. This dreadful, dreadful cross kills me!' Perhaps belatedly experiencing guilt about the distanced mothering that her upbringing had compelled her to adopt with her own children, Victoria treated her grandchildren more kindly. She was demonstrative and affectionate with them, and took an extraordinary interest in the progress of each one. The depth of her concern was to be queried and resented by her daughter-in-law, Alexandra, who knew, both directly and indirectly from Edward, what a bad mother Victoria had been.

The paradoxes of Victoria's marriage to Albert are manifold. Despite her avowed devotion to him, her many references to 'I and Albert' reflect vanity and conceit which were defences against feelings of inferiority and worthlessness. An arrogant self-sufficiency, the legacy of her dead father, covered her sense of being unworthy of love. The curious association of veneration with domination which characterizes Victoria's relationship with her husband epitomizes similar patterns found in later manipulative women in the Royal Family, such as Queens Alexandra, Mary and Elizabeth the Queen Mother, Wallis Simpson and even the current Princess of Wales.

We know that both Victoria and Albert had difficulty in verbally expressing their feelings for each other. On paper, Victoria also found possible an intimacy with Vicky after her marriage which is unlikely to have developed had they remained in the same house. Such communication might have been somewhat artificial and distant but at least a fondness existed and was expressed. The same cannot be said of Victoria's feelings towards her eldest son.

As a widow Victoria resumed her lifelong search for the kindly man of authority. The three she lighted upon were Benjamin Disraeli, who was effeminate, John Brown, her gillie, who wore the kilt, and her Indian servant, the Munshi, who dressed in long androgynous robes, all of them reflections of the original care giver, the mother who had to be both mother and father combined. Before her marriage Victoria had relied upon the affection and advice of older men, notably her first prime minister, Lord Melbourne, and King Leopold. During her marriage her husband came to meet almost all her emotional needs. One important result of this was that she was able to perceive her politicians with an objectivity that would hitherto have been impossible, and thus to develop political opinions and diplomatic skills which have yet to be surpassed by any British monarch.

In widowhood, Victoria formed new attachments. Her beloved Albert was no longer available to guide her and the Queen reverted to the patterns of her youth. The men she chose to advise and support her were all of an age that reflected her need for a father figure, even if by now she was older than they were.

Victoria's relationship with John Brown, her chief gillie, is the most widely speculated upon. Years before his death Albert had appointed Brown to take particular responsibility for the Queen's ponies when she was at Balmoral. Therefore after Albert's death, as Brown had received the blessing of the beloved deceased, so he came to represent a continuity with Albert himself. Brown was allowed to address Victoria as 'wummun', chided her if she was inappropriately dressed for a chilly ride, and laced her tea with whisky from time to time. It was not long before this servant's presence was required at Osborne where the Queen was in danger of becoming a permanent recluse.

Within five years of the Prince Consort's death Brown's salary had increased five-fold, he had been given a cottage at Balmoral and 'Esquire' rank, which raised him far above any ordinary servant's status. The Queen's dependency upon him even led to rumours that they had married. Yet despite fondly addressed New Year greetings and an affectionate remembrance of him in her will, there is no evidence that Queen Victoria had any more, or any less, than the most innocent emotional dependency on this uncultured Highlander. Her people and, indeed, her family might not have appreciated fully how much John Brown had helped the Queen to cope with the loss of her husband and gradually to return to the public life which she might have otherwise eschewed.

Upon Victoria's death the new King, Edward VII, ordered that all the busts and other relics that his mother had collected after Brown died in 1883 should be destroyed. The former Prince of Wales would have resented displays of trust and affection towards a gillie when his mother had been unable to show them to him.

Victoria had first met Benjamin Disraeli in 1844 and disliked him. By the time he became her prime minister in 1868 Victoria saw him in a kinder light. He was married to an older woman, and related to women in a seductive and flirtatious manner. He seemed to need the approval of an older woman, and referred to the plump and plain Victoria as his 'Faery Queen'. He sent her early copies of his novels and when, in 1868, the Queen privately published her *Leaves from the Journal of Our Life in the Highlands*, he referred to Victoria and himself as 'we authors'.

Disraeli explained his rapport with the Queen by saying that he spoke to her as a woman. As astute with his monarch as he was with politicians, Disraeli hoped that the widowed Queen would respond to his approach far more readily than she had to some of her previous ministers. Victoria would have had little notion of the implications of effeminacy in men or lack of conventional femininity in women. She took her 'Dizzy' at face value – as a man who made her smile, treated her with respect and yet had the confidence to advise her when her opinions were questionable.

The importance of John Brown and Benjamin Disraeli in Victoria's life contributed to her recovery from her ongoing bereavement reaction. For years she had shown no sign of interest in her family, her people or her empire, but she was encouraged back into public life by the attentions of these men. Brown and Disraeli might have gained personally from their relationship with her but the greater gain – that of the re-emergence of the Queen as an active leader of her people – might have ensured the continuation of the monarchy.

The third and last of Queen Victoria's most devoted servants was known as the Munshi. His name was Abdul Karim and he came into her service around the time of her Golden Jubilee, aged twenty-four. His father, he said, was a doctor in Agra, but others in the Queen's household at pains to dispute his origins tried in vain to challenge his story. The Queen, however, appointed him as her secretary to help her with papers and documents relating to matters in India, gave him a cottage at Windsor, and a staff of his own, and resisted plots to discredit him as a spy.

He clearly treated her with a fondness and respect she did not receive from her children. She would not listen to their criticisms or those of political advisers who were concerned about her association with a 'black man' – a phrase Victoria abominated. None of the suspicions of espionage against the Munshi were ever supported. When he died, however, the new King, Edward VII, arranged for all his papers to be burnt. This act, which echoes Edward's order that all evidence of his mother's attachment to John Brown should be destroyed, suggests the jealousy he felt towards the few friends she had made. No one could blame him for scapegoating others who had received the kindness and loyalty from his mother that she had denied to him.

Victoria reigned for sixty-four years. She involved herself in the complex diplomacies of the Crimean War, the long-drawn-out unification of Germany, and the escalation of hostilities in Ireland. She was as well, if not better, informed than any previous monarch about affairs of state, and had simultaneously dealt as best she could with the demands of a large family and a husband who was often melancholy.

In allowing her seventeen-year-old daughter to live in Germany after her marriage to Prince Frederick, having, indeed, agitated for the alliance with Prussia, Victoria was yielding to both personal and political expediency and therefore exploiting Vicky. No amount of tearful remorse as the day of Vicky's departure drew nearer could alter the fact that her main rival for Albert's affections was shortly to be removed and that Victoria was not displeased at this. Equally, it was desirable for England that the inevitable unification of the disparate German states should be achieved under the leadership of Prussia and that a close bond, created by marriage, should foster British interests.

The match between Vicky and Frederick had been encouraged by Albert for slightly different reasons. If his favourite child resided in his homeland he would, vicariously, be there too. Albert wanted to strengthen the links between his birthplace and his adopted country and as early as 1851, when Vicky was only ten, had promoted the idea that his daughter would eventually marry his cousin. Frederick was ten years her senior but in 1855, when Vicky was not quite fifteen, he was invited to spend the summer at Balmoral. To her parents' delight, she accepted his proposal.

As a 'Victorian' the Queen lent her name to a new valued lifestyle, and an expansive industrial age. As a woman she loved her husband but failed to understand him. As a mother she produced nine children but failed to communicate with them. She indulged her own griefs but was unable to tolerate the problems of others.

In a revealing letter to her seventeen-year-old granddaughter, Princess Vicky – warning her against same-sex friendships – the now elderly Queen hinted at sexual liaisons between women which in those days were rarely acknowledged. 'You are right to be civil and friendly to the young girls you may occasionally meet, and to see them sometimes – but never make friendships: girls' friendships and intimacies are very bad and often lead to mischief . . .'

Victoria had a 'blissful' marriage, a large family, world power, and an empire. Not one of these, however, could compensate her for her primary loss. Through the absence of a male role-model she had learned only to relate to distant men, such as Albert, and authority figures, such as her uncle King Leopold. The full burden of Victoria and Albert's emotional problems was to be passed on to the next runner in the royal relay race, their eldest son, Albert Edward, Prince of Wales, eventually to be King Edward VII.

CHAPTER TWO

Edward, Prince of Wales:
His Childhood and Adolescence

'Tis better to have loved and lost . . .'
TENNYSON

Edward VII, as he became, was named after his father, but always known within the family as Bertie. He was the first heir born to a reigning British monarch for eighty years and his arrival was widely celebrated. His life was to be dictated by his search for the love that childhood had denied him, which led, amongst other proclivities, to his promiscuity, compulsive eating, and gambling.

Edward was born prematurely. He was, however, a large baby and Victoria had a difficult confinement. Before his birth his mother was already depressed and Edward's arrival did nothing to lift her spirits. Her beloved Lord Melbourne was out of office, and had had a severe stroke, leaving him paralysed and unavailable to her. Also trouble was brewing in the nursery: Pussy was unwell. Lehzen had advised Victoria not to worry unduly about her daughter but Albert accused her of neglect. A furious row broke out. Albert wrote to his wife, 'Dr Clark has mismanaged the child and poisoned her with calomel and you have starved her. I shall have nothing more to do with it; take the child away and do as you like and if she dies you will have it on your conscience.' He wrote to his friend, Baron Stockmar, that 'Lehzen is a crazy, common, stupid intriguer, obsessed with lust of power, who regards herself as a demi-god . . .' Victoria was 'naturally a fine person but warped in many respects by wrong upbringing'.

Victoria displayed her usual contrition in the face of Albert's anger but the tensions between husband and wife led to Lehzen's return to Germany and, more significantly, illustrate how Victoria, in striving to recapture Albert's approval, was showing more concern at the well-being of her daughter than at that of her new baby.

Albert had stayed with Victoria during her confinement. She was pleased to have produced the male heir for which the country had been waiting since the death of George III, but the delivery had exhausted her. She handed over the baby to the wet-nurse, Mrs Roberts, and did not see him again for six weeks. After Vicky's birth Victoria had been depressed and the arrival of Edward again provoked this response. (It recurred after the births of all her children.) He was a placid baby, caused no trouble, making few demands upon his mother. When this 'good baby' grew up to become a 'bad child' it must have come as some surprise to his parents, unaware that a passive, undemanding, docile infant is unknowingly colluding in its own emotional deprivation. Had Edward been more demanding, or Victoria more nurturing, his life might have been happier and healthier.

Few opportunities were given to Edward to develop that trust which is based on the certainty of freely available affection. If he seldom cried in his mother's presence, there was no need for her to comfort him. If he slept most of the time, she was not required either to soothe him with lullabies or to stimulate him with baby-talk. It is ironic that the child's failure to make his presence felt contributed to his parents' failure to communicate with him. Negligent parenting is tragic in any family; in one in which the children are expected to secure royal dynasties, the repercussions will echo through the generations.

The tensions which existed within the royal household during the heir's first weeks, coupled with Albert's unequivocal worship of his older sister, would have left Edward with the conviction that his father loved Vicky more than he loved him, and that his cold, distant and indifferent mother cared for him not at all. It was not until he was a grown man and had affairs with a succession of loving women that he was in a position to redress the balance. That his lovers were mainly married women with children fulfilled his earlier need for a mother's love as well as allowing him to take his revenge on their husbands (scapegoats for his own neglectful father), by robbing them of their wives.

The kindest words that his mother could find to say of 'the

Boy' after his christening at Windsor, were that at least 'he now had his dear father's name'. But he was for ever denied the honour of using the hallowed name and always known in the family by the diminutive 'Bertie'. And although he resembled his father a little, he did not have the same delicacy of feature. His appearance was *lumpen*, and he was slow by nature. Despite all of the recent ructions, harmony was restored in the household and by July of that year Victoria was again pregnant, and gave birth to 'Fat Alice' in April 1843, simultaneously dislodging Edward from his status as baby of the family after only seventeen months.

When Edward had outgrown the ministrations of his nurses, his mother felt that 'the Boy' would more easily acquire his father's virtues if he were supervised by a person of more noble character: someone of superior standing was required to look after the future King of England, and Edward was assigned to the care of Lady Lyttelton, one of the Queen's ladies-in-waiting, the first in a long line of tutors.

Edward's life was burdened from the start both by the millstone of his destiny, and his awareness that his sister Vicky was preferred by his parents. Later he was to suffer from the inequality of the treatment received by his younger siblings. It was not that they escaped the harsh punishment meted out by Albert, but it was Edward who seemed to bear the brunt of it: the others were spared the pressures of the high expectations placed upon the shoulders of the heir to the throne. Nursery sounds disturbed Prince Albert and he would frequently use corporal punishment on his children. Among other 'crimes' which invited his attention were disobedience and laziness. Edward, for whom higher standards had been set, was punished more often and more severely than the other children although Albert saw no harm in whipping them – his daughters as well as his sons. Charles Wynne Carrington, who became a true friend to Edward, wrote of his early acquaintanceship with Prince Albert when, as a boy, he was one of a very few youngsters selected as suitable companions for the royal children. Albert seemed 'a proud, shy, stand-offish man, not calculated to make friends easily with children. I was frightened to death of him . . .' But Frederick Gibbs, one of Edward's tutors, later noted in his diary that he agreed with Albert, who advocated the boxing of ears and the striking of knuckles with a stick should Edward fly into one of his rages.

Albert deplored the laziness and untidiness he observed in the younger children, and would bind their hands together in punishment for minor transgressions. The use of physical restraints was recommended by the German paediatrician D. G. M. Schreber as a means of controlling the 'wilfulness' of children. He had introduced various harnesses and braces to encourage them to sit upright at the table and to correct their posture; Albert would seem to have followed the advice given in Schreber's notorious book *The Harmful Body Positions and Habits of Children, Including a Statement of Counteracting Measures*, published in German in 1853. He seems to have carried restraint even further than Schreber, whose dangerous advice was to influence more than one generation of German parents; as each generation of child victims grew up, they became the persecutors of the next generation and could have contributed to Teutonic authoritarianism and the rise of Nazism. Views like this were spreading throughout Europe: control and restraint, directed towards the breaking of a child's spirit, were recommended as an essential ingredient in encouraging compliancy. Victoria attributed God-like qualities to her husband. In so doing she was echoing Schreber's advice that fathers must be as 'gods in the family' and that children should be devoted to God's divine authority. Schreber believed that if the child's father is his God, then the father's power over the son increases. On 26 August 1857, Victoria wrote, 'You may well join us in thanking God for joining us all to your dearest, perfect Father . . . None of you can ever be proud enough of being the child of SUCH a Father who has not his equal in this world – so great, so good, so faultless. Try, all of you, to follow in his footsteps and don't be discouraged, for to be really good in everything none of you, I am sure, will ever be. Try, therefore, to be like him in some points, and you will have acquired a great deal.' She might have directed this exhortation to all her children, but it was certainly Edward who felt its full weight.

By the time Edward was four, he had developed a stammer. Lady Lyttelton who was firm, but not unkind, was forced to report that he was 'uncommonly averse to learning, not like his sister'. Edward quarrelled with Pussy and bullied his younger brother and sister. When he was six, Victoria wrote that he was backward compared with his elder sister.

Labelled as stupid, he was punished for his parents' failure to respond to his early signals, such as crying and wanting to be picked up, which would have made learning easier for him and allowed his intellect to develop. He was forced to fit into a mould of their devising, with no recognition of his individuality and finer qualities: helpless, furious, and miserable, the child was fated to become the adult whose appetites were never satisfied.

'The Plan', which was systematically to govern the heir's education and moral development, had been worked out by Victoria and Albert, with the help of Baron von Stockmar (who had come to England as Albert's companion upon his marriage to Victoria). In January 1848, the diarist Charles Greville wrote, 'the hereditary and unfailing antipathy of our Sovereigns to their Heirs Apparent seems thus early to be taking root, and the Q. does not much like the child.' It was unfortunate for Edward that Lord Melbourne no longer exerted strong influence on the Queen: 'Be not over solicitous about education,' he wrote, in December 1841 when the Prince was only weeks old. 'It may be able to do much, but it does not do as much as is expected from it. It may mould and direct the character, but it rarely alters it.'

Even six years after Melbourne had made his remarks hope still remained that Victoria and Albert intended their son to learn about affairs of state and come to understand his destiny. 'We talked about Vicky and Bertie, Albert saying the latter ought to be accustomed early to work with and for us, to have great confidence shewn him, that he should early be initiated into affairs of State . . . the more confidence we shew him the better it will be for himself, for us and the country,' wrote the Queen, in her journal on 12 December 1847. Not long afterwards, she began to fear that Bertie would never be fully capable of dealing with his future responsibilities. Several tutors had been engaged for particular subjects but Edward's education was supervised first by Henry Birch and then by Frederick Gibbs, the first of whom the boy came to like and trust, the second less so. Lessons in French and German continued; religion, music, arithmetic, geography, history and English were included in his curriculum. But many of the masters could not easily adapt to the shifting domestic arrangements of Victoria's court and so, despite the continuity of Birch and Gibbs, and his parents' wish that he should study almost every day, Edward was deprived of the chance of forming the relationships with his masters that might have made learning seem less of a chore. By the time he was eighteen, in April 1859, she felt gloomy enough to write to Vicky, in Germany: 'Oh dear, what would happen if I were to die next winter! One trembles to think of it. It is too awful a contemplation . . . And all from laziness! Still, we must hope for improvement in essentials; but the greatest improvement, I fear, will never make him fit for his position. His only safety – and the country's – is his implicit reliance in everything on dearest Papa, that perfection of human beings!'

Despite the rigours of Edward's education, nothing was to convince Victoria that her 'backward' heir had progressed. She may have felt that she encouraged Bertie when she wrote to him in praise of his father, but it is more likely that the boy was disheartened by remarks which could only suggest an unfavourable comparison. Despite Henry Birch's unfortunate name, redolent of vicious corporal punishment, and Edward's initial dislike of him, he was a kind man to whom his pupil later became attached. Birch revised his first impression of a boy 'impertinent, lazy, inconsistent, moody, selfish and ignorant', and came to see Edward's qualities of humour and enquiry. The Prince of Wales, according to Birch, did not respond well to the devising of his lessons because 'he was so different on different days'. This may have been a euphemism for the rages and dumb insolence which the Prince exhibited. Birch, anxious to be fair, also remarked that he 'always evinced a most forgiving disposition after I had occasion to complain of him to his parents, or to punish him'.

It is likely that Edward's parents regarded Birch as an inadequate disciplinarian, for they were not satisfied with his progress. A new tutor was engaged, Frederick Gibbs, who was stricter and more formal. Gibbs recorded that the Queen had noticed that the Prince would hang his head in contrition, only, within a short time, to have 'one of his fits of nervous and unmanageable temper'.

Two other tutors formed differing views. Dr Voisin, who attempted to teach Edward French, warned Gibbs, 'You will wear him out too early . . . Make him climb trees! Run! Leap! Row! Ride! . . . In many things savages are much better educated than we are.' His German master, Dr Becker, also recognized the Prince's honesty: '. . . a great straightforwardness and a sense of truth . . . as I scarcely ever witnessed in a child of his age'. Dr Becker went further and suggested that the strains imposed on the Prince by the severity of his educational regime could cause 'a nervous condition of total prostration and collapse'. These views went unheeded, but Gibbs even failed to recognize or nurture any of Edward's intellectual capabilities such as his gift for languages.

By the time he was thirteen, Edward became even more unhappy at his brother Alfred's departure to Royal Lodge, in Windsor Great Park. Initially their parents had been pleased to have the two boys brought up together, but now they considered separation more desirable given Edward's special educational requirements as heir to the throne. Edward's loneliness was further compounded when he was sent with Gibbs for a two-month intensive study period at Balmoral, but he continued to disappoint his parents academically, and to irritate them in other ways: he argued, interrupted adult conversation, and was still prone to tantrums and rages.

By 1852, so worried were his parents at the flaws they perceived in Edward's character that they felt the answer must be to step up his lessons to seven hours a day; six days a week and to ensure that he was exhausted by an even more rigorous programme of physical exercise. Ever obedient, Frederick Gibbs obliged. The Queen had noted of her son that 'First he hangs his head and looks at his feet, and invariably within a day or two has one of his fits of nervous and unmanageable temper. Secondly, riding hard, or after he has become fatigued, has been invariably followed by outbursts of temper.' She had also observed that Edward had a strained relationship with his elder sister and was crushed by her clever articulate dismissiveness.

The Prince of Wales suffered from a lack of friends and companionship, especially after he had been parted from his favourite brother, further reinforcing his awareness of human inconstancy. (He was never as close to the other six younger siblings.) Moreover, his parents had stressed that there was a difference between 'companions' and 'friends' and that princes could not expect to enjoy the latter. It was, perhaps, perspicacious of them to warn the royal children about the attentions of sycophantic courtiers, and realistic to point out that the friendships available to others would be hard for them to make. It made it difficult for their children to feel, however, that they were capable of being loved for themselves.

While warning them of the dangers of 'friendship', Victoria

and Albert at the same time instilled into their offspring that they were not superior to other children. Against the background of this conflicting advice, however, a companion, Charles Wynn-Carrington, later Marquess of Lincolnshire, was engaged for Alfred, but also played with the other royal children at Buckingham Palace or at Windsor.

Having been ignored throughout his infancy, Edward began to draw attention to himself as an adolescent. The 'good baby' had long been the 'bad child' and his parents used ever more forceful measures to suppress his outbursts. He began to rebel against the tyranny of his upbringing, and to express negative emotions – including jealousy of his siblings – that had been suppressed in the nursery. He gave vent to his anger at being ignored by his care-givers, and his resentment at being humiliated and victimized by his parents. Soon he would be getting his own back by taking 'mothers' away from 'fathers', seeking a substitute for love through sex, food, and cigars – under the illusion that they could replace it – and taking risks at the gaming tables to provide himself with the stimulation he had not received from Victoria and Albert as a child. Few children pass through puberty without feeling misunderstood. Bertie's bewilderment was compounded by his receiving no approval or encouragement from his parents, who seemed blind to his strengths, or from his teachers who disagreed about his potential. In a rare admission of Prince Albert's severity (with which she invariably colluded), the Queen wrote to Vicky in 1861 that, 'You say no one is perfect but Papa; but he has his faults, too. He is often very trying in his hastiness and over-love of business . . .' Prince Albert, conversely, complained that 'the disagreeable office of punishment' had always fallen on him even though his wife had been anxious that the errant child be reproved.

Things began to improve a little for the Prince of Wales when he was fifteen. He was allowed to choose what he would eat from items in a prescribed diet; until now, his needs, even for food, had always been controlled by his parents. Suddenly to be allowed to satisfy a long forbidden appetite would have encouraged over-emphasis on his appetite not only for food but also for other 'life enhancers'.

Yet before long, even more drastic measures were deemed necessary to improve Edward's character, including another new diet which, it was hoped, would also stimulate his brain. A light breakfast of bread and butter and the occasional egg was prescribed; lunch of meat and vegetables and selzer water, and a slightly more substantial dinner with a little claret or diluted sherry. Any beneficial effects were not immediately obvious.

When Edward was seventeen Gibbs left and was replaced by a 'governor', Colonel Robert Bruce. Edward was not to leave the house without explaining where he was going and why, and Colonel Bruce chose his friends for him throughout his short stays at Oxford and Cambridge. Even now that he was away from home, Victoria, usually able to express affection on paper, could still bring herself to write only of Edward's shortcomings: his head was too small, his nose too large, his chin receded as did his hairline; he was too short and too stout. In the manner of those who criticize in others the faults of which they are aware in themselves, this catalogue of her son's physical imperfections could equally have been applied to herself.

Always having been solitary, even preferring in games of chess to play with himself (a solitary self-gratificatory activity, seen only too often in those who are products of a lonely childhood), Albert had no understanding of 'team spirit' or of being a 'good sport'. Edward could not have learned from his father how to relate to others, since companions had been discouraged and even his brother had been sent away in spite of their closeness. He had not the least idea how to be a 'good loser'. At the gaming tables, he put his fate in the hands of 'Lady Luck' who – as his mother had earlier – very often disappointed him.

When Edward was taken to Paris in 1856, he was enchanted by Empress Eugénie who turned down his request to be allowed to stay a little longer, telling him that his parents would be unhappy without him. Any hopes that the Prince might have entertained about the truth of her remark would have been dampened had he seen a letter written by his mother to the Queen of Persia in October of that year shortly after his visit. '. . . when Albert is away all day long, I find no especial pleasure or compensation in the company of the elder children . . . only very occasionally do I find the rather intimate intercourse with them either easy or agreeable . . .' Once again Victoria was demonstrating that she believed it the child's duty to please the parent, not that of the parent to care for the child. But Bertie's life continued to brighten somewhat. He now had a personal allowance and was permitted to choose his own clothes. After the Paris trip, he travelled to the Rhine and to Switzerland with courtiers, and these new freedoms brought out the best in him. One of his companions, Colonel Henry Ponsonby, described him as 'one of the nicest boys I ever saw, and very lively and pleasant'.

Edward wore his hair in an 'effeminate' way, to which his mother objected, and began to develop an idiosyncratic style of dress. He had come to believe that females (from the example of his sister Vicky) were favoured. By adopting a hairstyle more appropriate to a woman, Edward was taking the first step towards envy of all things female. Although his features were never delicate, he was described in 1857 as being slim and handsome by Prince Metternich, who entertained him in Austria. Most boys of his age with a personal allowance and some limited freedom of choice would assert individuality, even express rebellion, through appearance and would want the cut of their suits and their hair to differ from their fathers'. However, 'A gentleman does not indulge in careless, self-indulgent, lounging ways . . . He will take nothing from the fashions of the grooms or the gamekeeper, and whilst avoiding the frivolity and foolish variety of dandyism, will take care that his clothes are of the best quality . . .' Prince Albert's advice could scarcely have made more inevitable his son's liking of countryman's clothes for shooting and stalking, and fashion-setting details for his more formal wardrobe.

In 1858 his mother could still write to Vicky that 'I feel very sad about him. He is still so idle and weak.' Later that year, in another letter to Vicky, the Queen lamented, 'Unfortunately, he takes no interest in anything but clothes, and again clothes. Even when out shooting he is more occupied with his trousers than with the game!' Vicky however disagreed with her mother about Bertie's 'dullness': 'He is lively, quick and sharp . . .' she wrote – before, perversely, going on to enumerate his shortcomings. She had been deputed to help her parents find a suitable bride for Edward and was probably anxious to stress his good points before acknowledging his lesser ones, about which she generally agreed with her mother. The years of tension in the nursery were not conducive to sibling solidarity between them. However, Vicky played her part and it was she who suggested Alexandra of Denmark as a possible wife for her brother.

'The Boy' was overweight and, had he been the scion of another family, would not have been regarded as much of a catch. But he had become proficient in three languages, had some knowledge of economics, science, drawing, riding, and – oddly – bricklaying and carpentry. His expanding girth was not entirely his own fault: at Oxford, forbidden to live in college as he would have preferred, he maintained a household, Frewin Hall, outside the town where, at his father's insistence, he was required to host regular dinners for selected academics, fellow undergraduates, and distinguished visitors to Oxford. A first-class chef had been engaged to prepare the food, and, after years of being forced to eat from a restricted range of unappetizing foods, Edward over-indulged. His father, as yet unaware that his son would receive moderately good results from Oxford, was ready to criticize him to Vicky, castigating Edward for enjoying 'rich and indigestible foods', and adding, in another letter, 'I never in my life met such a thorough and cunning lazybones . . . it does grieve me when it is my own son, and when one considers that he might be called upon at any moment to take over the reins of government in an Empire in which the sun never sets . . .'

Edward's introduction to the Empire, however, was a triumph. In 1860, shortly after his time at Oxford and Cambridge, he toured Newfoundland, Canada, and then went to the United States. To the surprise of his parents, he displayed a charm and diplomacy which endeared him to the people. Like many another unloved child, Edward had developed techniques designed to encourage positive responses. Charm, like seductiveness, is used to manipulate others to provide concern and interest which it is believed would not otherwise be available.

Edward's short periods at university and the promise he displayed gave his parents the inaccurate impression that he could have been the scholar they had wished for: when he joined the Grenadier Guards in Ireland, his ever-hopeful father expected that the Prince would learn the duties of an army officer within ten weeks. In this unrealistic plan he was to perform in every regimental rank, being promoted every two weeks so that he would take charge of a battalion after ten. This process would normally take some years, even for unusually able and ambitious soldiers. Edward was indeed allowed to wear a colonel's uniform at the end of the ten weeks but complained that he was only expected to perform the duties of a subaltern.

Just before leaving Ireland, he had a short relationship with a young camp follower, Nellie Clifden, rumours about which began to circulate in London shortly afterwards. In November 1861 word of his son's indiscretion reached Prince Albert, who realized that if it were made public it would jeopardize the proposed plans for Edward's marriage to Princess Alexandra of Denmark. Family pressures made it inevitable that, once again, the young Prince of Wales would be accused of a 'crime' – his infatuation with the young actress – and castigated for this youthful lapse by his parents for the rest of their lives. It was more likely that Albert's horror at learning of Edward's sexual adventure was less to do with politics than with his own sexual prejudices. Most fathers at that time would have welcomed their son's initiative and, had he not taken such a course, might well have introduced him to a brothel. Albert behaved more as if a beloved daughter had lost her virginity or a son been caught *in flagrante delicto* with another man. Certainly, overt premarital heterosexuality seemed to outrage him unduly.

Although Albert was suffering from a feverish illness, he went to Cambridge to discuss the sorrowful and chastizing letter which he had already written to his son. He arrived at Madingley Hall, where Edward had been lodged to keep him out of harm's way. The weather was cold and damp, but father and son walked for several hours (largely because Edward got lost), until Albert felt confident that he had shown Edward the folly, danger, and moral turpitude of his behaviour. He then returned to London and resumed work, but his health deteriorated. Victoria was reassured by his doctors who told her that there was no cause for alarm but it soon became clear that Albert's condition was critical. On Friday 13 December 1861 the Prince Consort died from typhoid fever.

Queen Victoria always maintained that her eldest son had caused her husband's death, and she never forgave him for it. A leading expert of the day confirmed 'that great worry and far too hard work had led to his death'. Although the probability is that Albert was already in the early stages of the disease when he visited Edward at Cambridge, Victoria chose to believe that the long conversation in the damp and chill air of their walk was the direct cause of his death. Edward spent the next forty years underemployed and under a cloud.

Plans for the Prince of Wales's marriage now proceeded with increased urgency. The Prince had been in no hurry and had insisted that he wanted to be sure he was in love before any marriage took place. Victoria, feeling perhaps that Bertie had forfeited his right to be consulted, was not prepared to let him dither. What other scandals could be lurking which would demolish the chances of such a suitable match? It was not only that the Queen thought that marriage would be stabilizing and character-forming for Edward but her conviction that her son was to blame for her husband's death and her desire to see him as infrequently as possible.

Victoria spent the first few months of her bereavement at Osborne. She expected and perhaps hoped to die within the year and was anxious that Edward's life should be under control when he succeeded her. She wrote to Vicky of Edward's misdemeanour, who passed on to Alexandra's parents Victoria's message that Edward had been encouraged by 'wicked wretches' and had had something of a scrape, but that both his parents had forgiven him, lest there be any suggestion that Alexandra did not know exactly what she was taking on. It was Vicky, also, visiting Coburg with her brother at the same time as the Danish Royal Family, who effected the introduction between him and Alexandra. Tactfully she left before her brother, leaving him to his duty and his destiny. Edward knew what his duty was – and how he might redeem himself in his mother's eyes. He proposed to Alexandra and was accepted with alacrity in September 1862.

There were few things to cheer Victoria in the months after her husband's death although she managed to take some gloomy pleasure in her son's betrothal. Before the marriage, in March 1863, Alexandra spent ten days with the Queen, at Osborne. Victoria would have preferred a longer visit, but Alexandra wanted to be with her own family for her eighteenth birthday celebrations. Victoria found her future daughter-in-law enchanting, with most of the qualities the Queen regarded as necessary for the wife of the heir: beauty, a good nature, and what Victoria perceived as 'character'. She would have wished Edward's bride to have had a better education and a little more culture, but

Alexandra was young enough to learn – and certainly young enough to be indoctrinated and influenced.

The Queen could not bring herself to sit in the main part of St George's Chapel, Windsor, where the wedding took place. She watched the ceremony from the little gallery above the altar, known as Katharine of Aragon's Closet, managing only a wintry smile for Beatrice, her youngest daughter. Afterwards, she ate alone in her apartments, then visited her late husband's mausoleum rather than join her son and daughter-in-law and their guests for the wedding breakfast.

The day should have been one of optimism for Edward, on which he might have hoped for the past to be forgiven, but it had been blighted, once again, by his mother who, from the moment he was born, had made her priorities clear: that her husband was more important than her children.

CHAPTER THREE

Edward and Alexandra

'A rose by any other name'
SHAKESPEARE

'No one who knows the character of the Queen and of the Heir Apparent can look forward to the future without seeing troubles in that quarter . . .' wrote Sir James Clark in 1865.

Alexandra Caroline Marie Charlotte Louise Julie of Schleswig-Holstein-Sonderburg-Glücksburg was born in Denmark in December 1844. Like many other women who have since married into the Royal Family, she was, in comparison with her husband, poverty-stricken and obscure, but the British people have always had a soft spot for Cinderellas or, better still, commoners. Princess Alexandra was, in fact, neither of these, but her background was different from her husband's.

Her father, Prince Christian, was not in direct line to the throne until his elder brother contracted a morganatic marriage which constitutionally precluded him from reigning, and, decades later, made poor relations out of the Teck branch of the Danish royal family. (Victoria took pity on them, bestowing on them grace and favour accommodation in London, and, upon the marriage of May of Teck to the future George V, the dukedom of Cambridge.)

Alexandra, in contrast to Edward, had been brought up with warmth and informality. Until the marriage of her uncle and the consequent elevation of her father's status, she lived in a fine, rather than grand, house, the front door of which opened directly onto a peaceful Copenhagen street. She shared a bedroom with her sister, made many of her own clothes, was able to go into shops without restriction and travelled about the city unaccompanied – much as did Lady Diana Spencer before her marriage to

46

Prince Charles. Her education was not so much neglected as considered irrelevant. She had music lessons, learned to draw, acquired social graces and some French and English but little else. She could barely read. However, she grew up in an affectionate family home which gave her a strong sense of her own worth that later stood her in good stead.

Denmark had been financially impoverished by the Napoleonic wars, during which its Navy was all but destroyed. Alexandra grew up against a background of wounded national pride in which her country, now politically and economically weak, lived in constant fear of its neighbour, Prussia, which was anxious to annexe the Danish territory of Schleswig-Holstein. Although Alexandra came to suspect and abominate all things German, she married into the world's most powerful family, which was of German origin. Her marriage could not have been anticipated by her family. Years earlier, her father Prince Christian had hoped to marry Victoria (before she became Queen), but his suit had been dismissed. That Alexandra was able to marry Queen Victoria's heir in 1863 is an indication, perhaps, that Europe was running out of suitable princesses. Alexandra was by no means the first choice for Edward, but she had several advantages. She was willing, whereas others had turned him down, she was Protestant and the alliance with Denmark would create a useful political bridge. Alexandra's father must have seen a satisfying irony in his daughter being found so eminently suitable by the son of the woman who had rejected him some twenty-five years earlier. Alexandra herself, aged seventeen, was thrilled and excited at the prospect: she would never again have to sew on a button, let alone make her own clothes.

Her arrival in England in 1863 was celebrated by the Poet Laureate, Alfred Tennyson, in 'A Welcome to Alexandra' with verses which began:

> Sea King's daughter from over the sea,
> Alexandra!
> Saxon and Norman and Dane are we,
> But all of us Danes in our welcome of thee,
> Alexandra!

It was a true reflection both of Alexandra's immediate popularity and Britain's joy at the anticipated union with a Nordic country. Prussian territorial ambitions were well known, and an alliance between Britain and Denmark would enhance the latter's security. The proposed union, however, placed Victoria and her government in a somewhat delicate situation because of Vicky's position as Crown Princess of Prussia. Whether Victoria was motivated by a wish to see her eldest son married at any cost, or by the forlorn hope that perhaps at last the Boy could be happy, is still open to debate. Possibly she felt that the family links between Britain and Prussia were so strong that any serious political friction between the two countries could be avoided. Either way she seriously misjudged, or perhaps underestimated, her future daughter-in-law.

By the time of his marriage the Prince of Wales seemed to be genuinely in love. He wrote to his mother after his betrothal: 'I cannot tell you with what feelings my head is filled, and how happy I feel. I only hope it may be for her happiness and that I may do my duty towards her. Love her and cherish her you may be sure I will to the end of my life.'

Queen Victoria needed no convincing: after Alexandra's first visit to England she wrote, 'Can't say how I and we all love her! She is so good, so simple, unaffected, frank, bright and cheerful . . . This jewel! She is one of those sweet creatures who seem to come from the skies to help and bless poor mortals and lighten for a time their path!'

The honeymoon period of the marriage (not the pleasant days away that Edward and Alexandra enjoyed after their wedding or the London Season which followed) was short-lived. It was not long before the Queen was complaining to her son that he and Alix were tarnishing the dignity of the Crown by being seen publicly and socially too often. Edward's reply was that the Queen's seclusion gave him little choice – someone within the family had to be reassuringly visible – but this remained a source of tension between them until the Queen's Golden Jubilee in 1887.

Victoria even wrote to Vicky that Alix and Edward both looked ill and that her son and daughter-in-law were 'nothing but puppets, running about for show all day and night'. Once again she made an unfavourable comparison between her husband and her heir: 'Oh, how different poor foolish Bertie is to adored Papa, whose gentle, loving, wise motherly care of me when he was not yet twenty-one, exceeded everything!'

In the middle of the nineteenth century fashionable women were well built and statuesque. Alexandra, by contrast, was tall, slender, elegant, with a pale, grave beauty which did not conform to the fashionable stereotype. Her simplicity and good humour countered the smallness of her mouth and rather bulbous eyes. She had grace and style and, like the current Princess of Wales, became a leader of fashion. She wore pearl and diamond chokers – probably to hide a small scar on her neck – a style which immediately became popular. When rheumatic fever left her with a limp, limps were sometimes affected by her admirers as was her occasional use of a cane. She was undoubtedly cherished by the public and although this might have pleased her, it did not compensate for the deafness which affected her relationships with her husband and children.

A woman who must abandon her native tongue on her marriage is disadvantaged. Edward spoke German and French, as did Alexandra; she also had a little English, but they were able to communicate with each other only at the most superficial level. The subtleties and nuances of the English language – in which humour and cynicism as well as metaphors are expressed – were lost on Alexandra, and her hearing impairment would have exacerbated this. She was able to comprehend neither her husband's anxieties nor his needs, so he eventually ceased to burden her with them. Because of her deafness she was unable to hear her own voice clearly, which tended to become strident – tolerable in some situations, perhaps, but hardly conducive to private exchanges. Her husband had had a mother who did not listen to him, and now he had a wife who was unable to hear him. She was similarly unable to hear the voices of her children. Like many people with hearing difficulties, she was probably able to lip-read which would have alleviated the problem but not solved it.

Alix, like the current Princess of Wales, acquired the reputation of being a natural, free spirit. She enjoyed the popular music of her day, in so far as she was able, dancing, and parties. She supported children's charities and enjoyed mixing with people from the arts, finance, and business. Marlborough House, where she and Edward lived, came to be associated with wit, culture, wealth and glamour. It was not necessary to be titled, let alone royal, to be invited to a gathering there. In this milieu Alexandra shone: she was unconventional in that she was at ease with people from all walks of life, unlike other members of the Royal Family, and also in the house she kept and the clothes she wore, and was sufficiently decorative to compensate for her inability to engage in profound conversation. She was happy and relaxed, and her warm family background enabled her to socialize naturally. To Edward this was a revelation.

Alexandra was pregnant six times during the first eight years of her marriage. After her final pregnancy, during which she had been neglected by the local doctor who attended her during her confinement, she gave birth to a prince who died immediately, and was advised against having any more children. She was twenty-six, the succession was ensured, and now she had time to devote to her surviving children and the pursuits she had had to set aside on her marriage: dancing, skating, the theatre, and her clothes. Now that she was a mother and had been warned against further pregnancies, Edward seems to have turned for physical comfort to other women, invariably married and usually with children. Edward's affairs satisfied his sexual needs enabling him to 'find' the mother who had rejected him and at the same time punish the father whom he would inevitably have seen as his rival. His attempts at conquest were successful, but he could never make a true commitment because the original one with his mother was flawed. These patterns were compulsively repeated.

It was not until his last child was born that he became openly attracted to French night life and the company of the women whose expensive tastes drew them to heavy spenders like himself. Most were professional courtesans and at least one was a black-mailer from whom Edward had to buy back his indiscreet letters before she sold them to the highest bidder.

As time passed his sexual interests ran over into affairs with many of the married women in his circle of friends. They were usually sufficiently flattered by his attentions to pass the *cinq à sept* with him while their husbands were at their clubs. Out of all his many liaisons, only one illegitimate child has been acknowledged, although others were claimed, probably falsely in the hope of financial gain. Given the uncertainties of birth control in the nineteenth century, it would seem that Edward's preferred sexual techniques excluded penetrative sex. It was as if he had had enough of procreational sexual activity with his wife, both to secure the succession and also in his search for a 'mother'. Recreational sex was not only safer but more rewarding for a man who throughout his childhood had known very little of the give and take of love and affection.

Throughout this time the monarchy became increasingly threatened by almost daily disclosures of scandal. But as many of Edward's mistresses were popular public figures and Edward's lifestyle became entertainingly grand, the public ceased to condemn him. Towards the end of his life Edward became increasingly admired as a kindly and jovial man. Actresses featured among his partners. Lillie Langtry and Sarah Bernhardt, for example, were, like him, looking for approval and admiration. Another long-standing mistress, Alice Keppel, was so genuinely distraught by his last illness that Alexandra encouraged her to be at his bedside when he was dying in 1910. History has hallowed Alexandra as a forgiving wife and a selfless mother but she had little choice other than to tolerate her husband's indiscretions. She could hardly have packed her bags and gone home to Mother. But she behaved with dignity and appeared to see no evil – just as she heard none – in the circulating gossip. A woman with few inner resources, no intellectual interests, and an increasingly critical mother-in-law, she concentrated her energies on her children – and on unconsciously avenging herself on her husband. One of the ways in which she did this was with her notorious unpunctuality. She exasperated him by keeping him waiting for dinner or making him late for the opera, particularly cruel since his mother had never had 'time' for him. She would either ignore what he said to her, or would misunderstand because of her poor hearing. By such means she was able to exert a semblance of control within a marriage rooted in duty and compromise, as well as affection.

Alexandra's greatest area of influence was the nursery. Although her children came to see her as the personification of love and care, it was *they* who had to please their mother by obedience and good behaviour. Even when they were adults she liked them to address her as 'dearest little Motherdear' and was addicted to the love she had demanded from them when they were children. She could no longer command the unqualified love that Edward had offered her upon their marriage and as long as

Victoria lived he would look to his mother, rather than his wife, for approval. As a man of fifty he was still capable of needing to compose himself behind a pillar before confronting his mother's disapproval for lateness at dinner. Later, he named one of his racehorses Diamond Jubilee in an almost certainly unsuccessful attempt to please her.

The people of Britain, though, took Alexandra to their hearts. They applauded her frequent public appearances, in sharp contrast to the seclusion of the Queen, and seemed to feel that the splendid lifestyle of the Marlborough House set was proof that the state allowance of the royal couple was being well spent. Periodic complaints were made then, as now, about civil list payments, with the Queen sometimes accused of hoarding hers, but that Edward and Alexandra's extravagance was tolerantly regarded by so many was, in some measure, due to Alexandra's personal popularity as well as to the proverbial English willingness to 'love a lord'.

Princess Alexandra, isolated though she was by her deafness, suffering as she did from her husband's infidelities and never achieving the approval that she sought from her mother-in-law, retained a keen sense of humour coupled with a steely resolve. At the party held to celebrate her silver wedding anniversary, she pinned an orange in her hair (in parody of the orange blossom she had worn as a bride and symbolic of the ripe fruit that the fragile blossom had now become). Few other women of forty-two would have been able to carry off her gesture.

Her strengths were increasingly demonstrated after her husband's death. She was unwilling to accept that once her daughter-in-law had become queen, her own status had diminished, and expressed this reluctance by long refusing to move out of Buckingham Palace and back to Marlborough House. She would not return the small crown she had come to regard as her personal property, and finally upstaged Queen Mary at state occasions by demanding – and being granted – precedence over her. The pliable front presented by Alexandra was as artificial as the curls she wore on her forehead. On the face of it, 'Darling Motherdear' was warm and nurturing towards her children, but her smothering affection was demanded back with interest as she attempted to compensate for the love and attention she had been denied by her husband. The power play in keeping her husband waiting – even if she could not keep him faithful – was not enough for her. Nor was the popular adulation she received. With the passing of the years, she stayed with relatives outside Britain for increasingly long periods. It might have been assumed that she accepted her circumstances, made the best of them, and pleased herself, in so far as her position allowed, but 'Motherdear' was a frustrated, troubled, and embittered woman who had five cards in her hand and was determined to play them for all they were worth.

Her first son, the Duke of Clarence, was always called 'Eddy' even though, or probably because, he had been christened Albert Victor to please Queen Victoria. He was born prematurely, only hours after Alexandra had been skating at Sandringham. Eddy inherited his mother's large, bulbous eyes, narrow face and sloping chin and, although he never came to show promise of any kind, his mother was devoted to him. His younger brother, George, born a year later in 1865, was more fortunate. He was a better-looking version of his father, with a wide, open face, fair hair, and a strong jaw. The boys were treated as if they were twins in the nursery and the schoolroom and like little delinquents by their father, who seemed determined that his sons would not enjoy their childhoods any more than he had enjoyed his. They turned to their comparatively kind and affectionate mother for warmth and compensation. Although she was possessive of her sons, possibly contributing to Eddy's homosexuality and George's difficulty in relating intimately to his wife except through letters, their three sisters, Louise, Victoria and Maud (born between 1867 and 1869), seemed to be of less interest to her. Victoria, however, was not encouraged to marry because Alexandra was anxious to keep one child at home with her; 'Toria' was later described as 'little better than an unpaid companion' as she grew older, unmarriageable, spinsterly, embittered and therefore increasingly disliked by other members of the family. That Alexandra remained radiant and adored throughout her widowhood was, to a greater or lesser degree, at the expense of the happiness of her second daughter.

Alexandra's compulsion to make her children supply her emotional needs may be understood if not forgiven. Her husband had neglected her – never more so than during her final pregnancy when she contracted rheumatic fever and lost her third son. Edward was unsympathetic both about the child's death and the illness which from then on crippled Alexandra. He displayed a truculent jealousy, as if, even in her pain and grief, Alexandra should make *him* her priority at the expense of her feelings towards their children either dead or alive. Alexandra's concern for them was a constant, bitter reminder of his own mother's neglect. He envied them their mother's affection and, disregarding Alexandra's anguish – and being unnecessarily harsh – punished them accordingly. At the time of their son's death reproving remarks were heard that during her pregnancy Alexandra had spent too much time at her husband's side in society to limit temptations from other women. At Victoria's request he was chided about this by the Dean of Windsor but, with some indignation and possibly thinly veiled reproof for the professional widow, Edward wrote to his mother, '. . . I think it is in one's duty not to nurse one's sorrow . . . I shall also be glad when Alix resumes her social duties (with, of course, due care for her health). . .'

Alexandra also had to cope with Victoria's political truce with Prussia, whose territorial gaze was still fixed on the nearby Danish dependencies, Schleswig and Holstein. Victoria wrote of Alix to Vicky, 'good as she is – she is not worth the price we have paid for her – in having such a family connection'. In November 1863 Alix's father succeeded Frederick VII and became Christian IX, whereupon he was immediately threatened with invasion of the disputed territories by both Prussia and Austria. In Britain Parliament insisted that a neutral stance be adopted but Victoria assured her daughter Vicky that her sympathies were all with Prussia. She was not pleased when Edward openly supported his wife's differing point of view, and the wedge of friction between the queen and her daughter-in-law always remained, long after Schleswig was seized by Prussia and Holstein by Austria.

Victoria's behaviour towards Alexandra was unpredictable. Acid remarks in the Queen's diaries allude to late levées, irresponsible entertaining and evening gadding. Later, however, she would remark how dear Alix was and how fond Victoria was of this favourite daughter-in-law. When her Golden Jubilee was celebrated it was in the unenviable role of favourite that Alix was

An idealized representation of Queen Victoria and Prince Albert in 1846 with five of their children by the German portrait painter Franz Winterhalter. But the elegant façade hides many psychological problems. (Hulton–Deutsch Collection)

Above: Queen Victoria in deepest mourning for Prince Albert who had died fifteen months earlier. With her eyes on the bust of her beloved Albert she seems hardly aware that one hour earlier her heir Edward, Prince of Wales, had married nineteen-year-old Princess Alexandra of Denmark. (Hulton-Deutsch Collection)

Top Opposite: Edward, Prince of Wales, demonstrates his skill at his favourite outdoor sport. His victim is one of the famous wild white bulls at Chillingham Castle in Northumberland. Edward's son, George V, was also to displace his sense of victimization on to helpless wildlife. (Hulton-Deutsch Collection)

Bottom Opposite: King Edward VII with his son and grandchildren. They are all in Highland dress, the traditional Scots uniform of the British Kings. Conformity was highly regarded in their royal upbringing. (Hulton-Deutsch Collection)

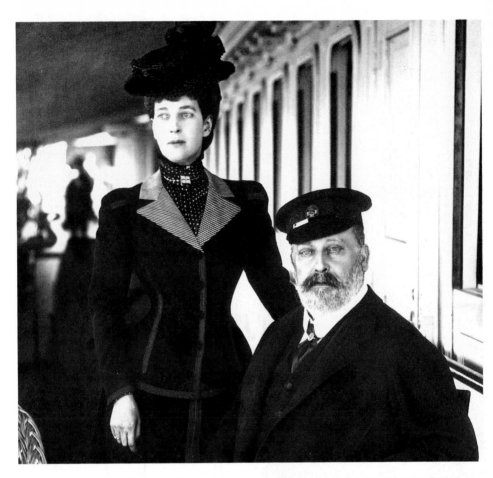

Above: King Edward VII on the royal yacht at Cowes about four months before his death. Queen Alexandra is at his side in spite of his well-publicized infidelities. (Hulton–Deutsch Collection)

Right: There is no doubting the look of determination on the face of Princess May of Teck at the age of three. Forty years later she became Queen. (Hulton–Deutsch Collection)

Above: Princess May was betrothed to Eddy, Duke of Clarence (*left*), heir to King Edward VII. Despite his premature death she fulfilled her destiny by marrying his brother, Prince George (*right*) one year later. (Hulton-Deutsch Collection)

Left: Queen Mary, resplendent at the wedding of her only daughter Princess Mary to Henry, Viscount Lascelles in 1922. Her obsessive love of jewellery and beautiful things provided some compensation for the lack of parental affection during her childhood. (Hulton-Deutsch Collection)

Top: The Duke of York with Lady Elizabeth Bowes-Lyon, shortly after she consented to marry him in January 1923, having turned him down on two previous occasions. (Hulton-Deutsch Collection)

Bottom: The Duke and Duchess of Windsor in Nazi Germany fascinated by Dr Robert Ley, leader of Hitler's Labour front in 1937. Dr Ley, indicted as a war criminal on 20 October 1945, hanged himself in his cell four days later. (Hulton-Deutsch Collection)

Princess Elizabeth, with her younger sister Princess Margaret Rose at Royal Lodge Windsor in 1940. Same hairstyle, same clothes – but different destiny. (Hulton-Deutsch Collection)

Top: Queen Elizabeth with her two children Princess Elizabeth and Princess Margaret Rose in a pantomime at Windsor Castle in 1941. Princess Margaret plays Cinderella. (Hulton-Deutsch Collection)

Bottom: An unusually relaxed and cheerful Prince Philip at his stag party in November 1947. He was to become more formal after his marriage. (Syndication International) deputed to persuade the Queen to appear in public in robes of state. She was not successful. Elizabeth Longford tells us that Alix said, 'I was never so snubbed,' when the Queen insisted on being driven to Westminster Abbey wearing not a crown but a mere bonnet.

Edward, meanwhile, continued to try to win his mother's approval, although Victoria's letters to Vicky suggested that he would never do so. When Edward attended a reception to honour Garibaldi in 1864 after his dashing and successful campaign to unify Italy she wrote to Vicky of '. . . the incredible folly and imprudence of your eldest brother going to see him without my knowledge!' His mother seemed quite unable to understand that for as long as she denied her son and heir access to state papers and red boxes, he would have difficulty in understanding the political minefields through which he obliviously trod. She thought him unworthy of such privileged information, yet was ready to criticize him when, as she saw it, he stumbled and blundered. The more she continued to deny him access and influence, the more he sought to compensate through eating, drinking, gambling, and sex. Some of his anger could have been sublimated in his favourite pastime, shooting game, at which he excelled, for the urge to take life in any form is essentially an attack on the ultimate source of life – the mother.

Victoria had turned her emotionally neglected child into an adult addicted to the very activities which reinforced her view that he was unready and unfit to assume regal responsibilities. The double-binding games, at which she was a skilled player, inevitably left Edward the loser. Nonetheless Victoria imagined that on her death Edward would be able to assume his duties effortlessly, while at the same time wanting him to fail, for his failure would underline her own considerable successes in diplomacy.

Once he became king, Edward had to overcome many obstacles, not the least of which was his mother's neglect, resentment, and, finally, revenge in handing over reins which she had not trained him to grasp. Edward, however, was brighter than his mother imagined. During his indolent travels as Prince of Wales he had come to know not only courtesans and actresses but heads of state, high-ranking army officials, and royal cousins. He realized, as astute businessmen do today, that as much could be achieved in a box at the opera, salmon-fishing in Scotland, or over a good lunch, as in formal circumstances, and that if his guests at the races, at Sandringham, or sailing off Cowes were indebted to him for their enjoyment, they were less likely to challenge British trade or imperial interests. His type of diplomacy was barely understood, though, and even less valued while his mother was alive, dismissed as further proof of his profligacy, rather than acknowledged as a political skill.

Edward spent several decades hoping for rather more than peripheral involvement in the stewardship of his country, but his hands were tied. He functioned as best he could, running between Paris, Baden-Baden, Biarritz and Cannes, from discussions with heads of state to choosing a favourite cloth for his suits (ever afterwards to be known as 'Prince of Wales check'), popularizing the Homburg hat, and training his little dog Caesar. By his common pursuits he reminded the people of Britain that their monarchy existed, and showed an endearing fallibility in his well-publicized, often successful, gambling at Ascot and on the tables at Monte Carlo. That his sensual appetites might be attributed to the emotional poverty of his childhood did not concern the British people, who saw an expansive man who appeared to share the same pleasures and vices as they did. They would have seen him, in the affectionately approving phrase of the time, as 'a bit of a dog'.

Despite the skill, tolerance, discretion, humour, patience and understanding Edward was able to display as a diplomat, he was not a good father to his children and inflicted considerable unhappiness upon his wife. While he did not subject his children to physical cruelty or deprivation beyond what was considered the norm at the time, he did neglect them, through his frequent absences, with his concern for his own pleasures and the freedom he now had to indulge in appetites which had until then been suppressed. While he worked intelligently to avoid political confrontations, his family life was a battleground in which the erstwhile victim became the persecutor. Inheriting a legacy of unhappiness and a miserable notion of what parenthood should be, his own childhood losses were set in a now familiar pattern, passed on largely unaltered to his children.

CHAPTER FOUR

Prince George and His Brother
The Duke of Clarence

'If it moves, shoot it . . .'

George V reigned over millions in territories which covered a
quarter of the world's surface. He was constitutional head of state
to dominions far too numerous and distant for him to visit. He
was blessed with better looks than many of his relatives, had a
large family, and a supportive wife. His wealth was prodigious
and – like his father King Edward VII – he was immensely
popular.

Although George was a man of limited intellectual powers,
Violet Markham's post-mortem opinion of him that 'In the end it
is character not cleverness that counts; goodness and simplicity,
not analytical subtlety and the power to spin verbal webs', might
well have been endorsed by his subjects. As far as his children
were concerned, however, Herman Hesse's comment in *A Child's
Heart* is probably nearer the mark: 'Would not God find a way
out, some superior deception such as the grown-ups and the
powerful always contrived, producing one more trump card at
the last moment, shaming me after all, not taking me seriously,
humiliating me under the damnable mask of kindness?' Both
George's sons were to suffer in the name of kindness just as
Edward VII had been made to suffer by Queen Victoria and
Prince Albert, 'for his own good'.

George was born in 1865, the second son of Edward and
Alexandra. He was not their favourite child. He became heir to
the throne following the untimely death of his elder brother
Albert Victor (Eddy), having married May of Teck to whom
Eddy had earlier been betrothed. As the younger brother he had

been groomed for naval command, to which he was both educationally and temperamentally suited, rather than for the responsibilities of the Crown.

When he succeeded, it was to wear the crown that had been destined for his brother, just as his bride had been. When he and Mary, as she was now known, moved into their first home, York Cottage in the grounds of Sandringham, George filled it with reproduction furniture from Maples, a seemingly bizarre choice for one who could have availed himself of the finest originals. By surrounding himself with fakes, as well as with copies of famous portraits, he lived with a constant reminder that he was himself not authentic or first choice either as husband or king.

There was little more than a year between the two brothers who were brought up and educated together – like so many other siblings in the British Royal Family – as if they were twins and they were very close. Eddy grew tall and lanky with elongated arms and neck (which he disguised off duty with high-collared, deep-cuffed shirts), almost entirely lacking face and body hair, and with a frailty suggestive of the genetic disorder Klinefelter's syndrome, often associated with impotence but always with infertility. He had inherited the haemophilia which ran through the female royal genes from Queen Victoria, was partially deaf from birth – which would have resulted in learning difficulties even had he been of normal intelligence – and his speech was affected by a lisp. Although his limited intellect offended Victoria and his father, his mother, who was herself far from bookish, loved him.

Unlike Eddy, George attained a height of only 5 feet 7 inches, but by contrast he was physically strong and athletic. He became a shy, diffident, and self-conscious man who hid himself behind a copious beard and moustache – the 'dark glasses' of the day. George was devastated when Eddy died. His grief was genuine although it is likely to have been accompanied by feelings of guilt: as the second son, with little chance of accession to the throne, George might have envied his elder brother and at times wished him out of the way.

As children, both Eddy and George (together with their sisters, Louise, Victoria and Maud) had had to cope with a remote father, who had been brought up to equate discipline with strength, and a mother who, with her stifling embraces and her possessiveness, was capable of inflicting a similar degree of psychological damage. In the days before effective hearing aids had been introduced a child who had to shout at his mother to make himself heard might conclude that she was not listening to him. When Alexandra talked to her children, it was in such a loud voice and with such a heavy Danish accent, that verbal communication between them was difficult. None of this, however, could shake George's devotion, akin to idolization, to his mother. 'I was brought up in an age of beautiful women and the two most beautiful of all were Empress Elisabeth of Austria and my own mother.' Like her mother-in-law and later her son, Alexandra found it easier to express herself on paper and her letters were full of references to 'her dearest, darling little Georgie'.

Neither Alexandra nor Edward VII had been well educated and their sons were to be brought up similarly impoverished. 'The melancholy thing is that neither he nor the darling Princess ever care to open a book,' wrote Lady Frederick Cavendish of her sovereign and his wife. Prince George, however, was open to instruction on more prosaic matters: his grandmother had given him a watch in 1873 and expressed the hope that it would remind him 'to be very punctual in everything and very exact in all your duties . . . I hope you will be a good, obedient, truthful boy, kind to all, humble-minded, dutiful and always trying to be of use to others!' Most of the Queen's exhortations were taken to heart. George's intellectual powers may have been limited, but they were greater than Eddy's, and both boys were educated at Eddy's slow pace, which undoubtedly held George back. Yet George looked up to his brother, both literally and figuratively, and turned to him for guidance when their father was absent on affairs of state, womanizing, gambling, or other self-gratificatory activity.

At the ages of fifteen and fourteen respectively, the boys were sent to spend three years in the Navy as cadets and were exposed to the traditions described later by Winston Churchill as principally 'rum, buggery and the lash'. While George enjoyed his duties as a sailor, their chaperone, the Reverend John Dalton, was 'sorry to report that Eddy had become increasingly dissolute, drinking and associating with ruffians in disreputable places'. Despite his best ministrations, the Queen was displeased by the boys' behaviour and wrote in 1872, 'They are such ill-bred, ill-trained children, I can't fancy them at all,' which might have been as much a veiled criticism of her eldest son and daughter-in-law as of the two young princes.

The efforts of Dalton, a classicist, to open the minds of his charges were largely unsuccessful. Loyally and optimistically, he reported scholarly progress, but Eddy was not interested in learning, and George showed enthusiasm only for the Navy which he had assumed to be his destiny. Even his duties as a seaman had their drawbacks: as an elderly man he told his librarian, Sir Owen Morshead, 'It never did me any good to be a Prince, I can tell you, and many was the time I wished I hadn't been . . . so far from making any allowances for our disadvantages, the other boys made a point of taking it out of us on the grounds that they'd never be able to do it later on . . .' Only a few years later, however, George sent his own unwilling sons to Osborne and Dartmouth for naval training in the belief that 'the Navy is all the education they will ever need', perpetuating his own unhappy experiences as a cadet.

Like their father, both Eddy and George acquired a number of tattoos commemorating their various ports of call. It was not customary for the aristocracy, and certainly not for royalty, to be tattooed during service in the Royal Navy; that both Eddy and George chose to identify with their shipmates in this respect says more for their need to be accepted by them than for a desire to have a permanent record of their travels engraved on their bodies. Dalton was only taken to task about their tattoos when it was reported back to London that they had had their noses tattooed in Barbados. He was able to reassure the Prince and Princess of Wales that the boys had been 'sniffing lilies in the botanical gardens there', and that they had neglected to wipe the pollen off their noses. (Some time later, when he had become King, George had his tattoos amended and improved by an eminent British tattooist at the suggestion of Queen Mary.)

Upon their return home from their tour of duty, the brothers were sent to Switzerland for six months in an unsuccessful attempt to improve their French and German. It was only after this that they were separated as George continued his naval career, and Eddy began his studies at Cambridge. 'My dear George. So we are at last to be separated for the first time and I can't tell you how strange it seems to be without you and how much I miss you in everything all day long,' he wrote. Although one of his tutors remarked that he did not think he derived 'much benefit from attending lectures. He hardly knows the meaning of the words to read', Eddy was awarded an honorary doctorate of law. Prime Minister William Gladstone asked permission to publish the Prince's reply to his subsequent letter of congratulation. He was forced to alter it himself to introduce structure and grammar and received permission from the Prince of Wales to publish it in its improved form. While at Cambridge, Eddy came to rely heavily upon his tutor, James Stephen, and they corresponded intimately after Eddy left to join the 10th Hussars (a regiment which at the time had a reputation for dissipation and excess and where Eddy's proclivities went largely unremarked). Stephen's attachment to his pupil became so intense that when they were parted he gave up academic life and was eventually admitted to a mental hospital. He went on hunger strike the day that Eddy's pneumonia was made public and died just before his prince.

Eddy had apparently been in love with at least two women before his engagement to Princess May of Teck. His behaviour, however, was so reprehensible, and the places he was rumoured to frequent – especially the Hundred Guineas in Cleveland Street, the most notorious homosexual club in London and a male brothel which became closely associated with the Whitechapel murders of Jack the Ripper – of such dubious repute, that doubts about the company he kept, and also his sexual orientation, became a matter not only for public concern but exercised both his family and Parliament. Doubts about his suitability for kingship were raised. So many scandalous stories about him were circulated (including the fanciful one that he was the 'Ripper') that it was agreed between the government and the King that Eddy must either marry or be sent away to govern one of the more distant colonies. Despite his probable homosexual tendencies, Eddy had expressed interest in marrying Hélène of Orléans, daughter of the president of the French Republic and a Roman Catholic. Since he was not regarded as being sufficiently able to govern even the smallest or farthest flung of colonies, suitable princesses were rare, and attractive ones rarer still, Queen Victoria had given her permission for this but the religious impediment was so great that the marriage was not approved in Parliament.

Eddy had been born prematurely before adequate preparations had been made for his birth. Alexandra fed him until a wet-nurse was found, at which point his mother's breast was denied him. Maternal comfort had been offered, then withdrawn, possibly sowing the seeds of ambivalence in Eddy's later attitudes to women.

He had been created Duke of Clarence and Avondale in 1890. The following year his father described his remaining in the army as a 'waste of time', and his future, Edward told the Queen, was 'a matter of some considerable anxiety to us . . .' Edward's concerns were soon resolved most dramatically: on 9 January 1892, the day after his twenty-eighth birthday, Eddy died from a lung infection. Had he lived and married, his likely genetic disorder would have precluded him from producing an heir. His potential for kingship had been often in doubt and many were relieved when his younger brother became Heir Apparent. After his death the Royal Family closed ranks, as if he had never existed, and the title Duke of Clarence was dropped from usage.

Prince George craved the attention he had lacked earlier, and perhaps reacted with resentment at the ambivalent way in which he had been treated by his mother: she had not only lavished mother-love upon him but had also used him to prop up her low self-esteem, reinforced by her husband's neglect. His seductive and flirtatious attitude towards her contrasts with the usual forms of address used to a parent: 'Dear, sweet, loving, beloved little Motherdear' might have been his attempt to comfort Alexandra for the neglect shown her by his father. He continued to depend on her heavily.

Alexandra, equally dependent upon her children, was a past mistress at making them feel guilty even about things beyond their control. On his fourteenth birthday, in a letter to George she chastized him about his stature: 'So old and so small!!! Oh my! You will have to make haste to grow, or I shall have the sad disgrace of being the mother of a dwarf!!!'

After his education – such as it was – had been completed, George spent the next few years as a serving naval officer, a life which he would have continued had circumstances permitted. Despite his apparent independence, however, he was capable of lamenting his inability to attend a family celebration by writing to his mother from HMS *Dreadnought* at the age of twenty-one, 'How I wish I was going to be there too, it almost makes me cry when I think of it. I wonder who will have that sweet little room of mine, you must go and see it sometimes and imagine that your little Georgie dear is living in it.' Still, at heart, a mother's boy.

Princess May of Teck, young, unmarried, educated, and living with her family in grace and favour accommodation in London, had become engaged to Eddy in late 1891. The betrothal was made with resignation rather than passion, although Princess May was not displeased at the prospect of improvement in her personal and family fortunes. By royal standards her family was impoverished, and she had not been the immediate choice of a suitable bride for Eddy. Queen Victoria deplored the extravagances of her mother, Princess Mary Adelaide,* and was irritated by her popularity. She was therefore surprised when she auditioned May, who was tall and handsome rather than beautiful, on Eddy's behalf at Balmoral. Victoria found a calm, intelligent, serious young woman with taste, quiet confidence, beautiful manners and exactly the kind of steadying presence it was believed that Eddy needed.

May had acquired an extraordinary respect for and knowledge of the British Royal Family and its constitution, and was proud to be part of it – if only, at that time, on the periphery. To be asked to marry the heir to the throne was an honour – to consent almost a duty – that far outweighed any reservations she may have harboured about her future husband. She accepted his proposal in December, and preparations began for a spring wedding in 1892. Early in the new year, when Eddy contracted his fatal illness and died, May made all the correct noises but possibly grieved more for the loss of the figurehead she revered than for the man she knew so little. 'It is so difficult to begin one's old life again after such a shock,' wrote May to a friend. 'Even reading, of which I am so fond, is a trouble to me & I

* Like Queen Victoria, Princess Mary Adelaide was a grandchild of George III so the two women were cousins. Mary Adelaide's father was Adolphus, Duke of Cambridge, who married Augusta, Princess of Hesse-Cassel. Mary Adelaide married Francis, Duke of Teck, and had three sons after her daughter May.

cannot settle down to anything . . .' After she recovered from the initial shock of Eddy's death, nothing suggests that she suffered further. She could not mourn a man she hardly knew. Her expectations, however, like those of her mother, had been raised. Who could blame her for dreading a return to 'poor relation' and to life dependent upon charity, when she had seen her future as Queen of England? In any event she was probably less distraught than her ambitious mother, who had gained considerable status as 'mother of the bride' and who saw Eddy's death as the disintegration of a dream and forerunner of financial ruin.

The two abortive love affairs which preceded George's 'second best' marriage to May are well documented. As a young man he was first in love with Julie Stonor, granddaughter of Sir Robert Peel, one of his mother's ladies-in-waiting – but a Roman Catholic as well as a commoner. Alexandra would have blessed the match had it been constitutionally possible: 'I only wish you could marry and be happy but, alas, I fear this cannot be,' she wrote. Later he became attached to and hoped to marry his cousin Princess Marie of Edinburgh, but she chose King Ferdinand of Romania instead. George's options were limited and, as his father's heir, he was now under pressure to marry, have children, and secure the succession.

When the time came, George, with his keen sense of duty, bowed to the inevitable. Weakened by a bout of typhoid fever from which he had only just recovered, and unable to marry the woman he loved, he was heart-broken when Eddy died. A few months later, when George and some of his family were staying on the French Riviera, Mary Adelaide took a house near by. George and May were thrown into each other's company. Mary Adelaide, not the most subtle of women, thought that a marriage between her daughter and the Prince would make perfect sense: May was no less suited to being a royal bride now than when she had been vetted by Victoria for Eddy the previous year. A decorous courtship ensued – both were still in mourning – and in May 1893 their engagement was announced. They were married in July.

Lady Geraldine Somerset, lady-in-waiting to Queen Alexandra, wrote acidly in her journal, 'It is clear there is not even a pretence at lovemaking. May is radiant at her *position* but placid and cold as always.' Lady Geraldine was not to know, however, that, stiff and formal as their public behaviour might be, May (now known as Mary) and George could show affection, indeed devotion, on paper. By expressing himself through *billets doux* – much as tongue-tied 'face-to-face' lovers of today are able to spend intimate hours on the telephone – George was repeating the distanced and non-verbal communication patterns of his child-hood. Although his bride had been handed down to him through the ghost of his beloved brother, and his prize gained by default, the popular press of the day hinted that it was George whom Mary had loved all along and that their marriage was made in heaven. Mary, anxious to deflect any suggestion that she was either a gold-digger or an afterthought, did not demur.

George's unhealthy childhood relationship with his mother affected his marriage. Mary liked her mother-in-law no better than Alexandra had liked hers. Alexandra's possessive attitude towards George was reflected in her wedding gift of York Cottage on the Sandringham estate. Its proximity enabled her to visit the newly-weds frequently and unannounced, making a tacit state-ment that she retained rights in the property and also in the man. York Cottage had originally been built to accommodate extra male guests shooting on the Sandringham estate. It was neither beautiful nor practical and certainly had not been designed for family life. It resembled a large suburban villa, ivy-clad and gabled, with a network of small dark rooms linked by draughty passages and inconvenient staircases. George decorated and fur-nished it according to his own taste, without reference to his bride. One of Mary's later idiosyncrasies, after she had become Queen, was the removal of the ivy which clung to the walls of her much grander houses. Was she, in retrospect, metaphorically stripping her mother-in-law of her stranglehold on George? Any woman would have quailed in the face of a woman who had the temerity to write about her son's marriage that 'There is a bond of love between us, that of mother and child, which nobody can ever diminish or render less binding – and nobody can, or ever shall, come between me and my darling Georgie boy.'

If Alexandra did not always give George and Mary as much privacy as they wished, it was perhaps because she was lonely for male company. Her husband had turned away from her, her first-born son had died, and she had lost her last child, John, shortly after his birth in 1871. The affection of her three daughters had never been important to her and she looked to her surviving son to compensate for her losses. He was the only man in her life, and she was reluctant to let him go. So possessive was she, so demanding, and so exploitative, that George never fully broke away from her to form a complete emotional bond with another woman. Alexandra, increasingly deaf and with her children growing up, now inhabited a contracting world in which her status would be usurped by her daughter-in-law. Eventually there were grandchildren to lighten and brighten her life, but at the time of her son's marriage (when she was forty-nine and probably going through the menopause) she could, understandably, have felt that her useful life was over.

Throughout his childhood, George would have had grounds to fear that his parents would reject him – unless he gave them the unqualified love, obedience, and compliance they demanded. His father had never had time for him and when he became king he tried to compensate for this (as well as for his fear of being kept waiting) by keeping the clocks at Sandringham five minutes fast. Like his father before him, George had a passion for punctuality.

George's legacy of low self-esteem was never to leave him, even after his marriage. He felt as inauthentic as his paintings, as much of a replica as the Maples' furniture. Only his solitary pastime, playing by himself and thus with himself, of his vast collection of every issue of British Empire stamps, each of which bore his own image, fulfilled his narcissistic needs and reassured him of his existence.

The 'Marlborough House Set' and the flamboyant circles in which his parents had moved did not appeal to George. His low self-esteem prevented him from feeling at home with 'smart' people, he had no wish to follow the pattern set down by the old king, and did not feel at home with the intelligentsia. Although Mary might have wished to socialize more, she deferred, as in everything, to her husband who was to exemplify family solidarity, a virtue received with as much enthusiasm in the 1920s and 1930s as his father's profligacy had been earlier.

The George who was typecast as a harmless and fundamentally decent man was, however, by no means the whole man. Shutting his eyes to the reality behind his assertion that 'it never did me any harm', and with the collusion of his wife, he humiliated and tortured, albeit 'for their own good', his children much as he had been humiliated and neglected, making them feel as fundamentally unworthy as he himself had been made to feel. Despite this punitive treatment, he expected to receive love from them (just as his mother had expected to receive love from him) and had no idea that loyalty, affection, and trust are the spontaneous response to a mutual loving interchange – which, in George's case, was never initiated – and that respect must be earned.

Birds, animals, and children – all defenceless victims – became targets for the anger George had never been able to express at the appropriate time or in the appropriate place. Gun in hand (like his father before him), he followed his socially acceptable and favourite outdoor pastime of what Tolstoy described as 'evil legitimized', the pursuit of game, in the domination over which George revelled and in the destruction of which he rejoiced. A passion for guns represents a desire for dominance. The language of shooting – a gun is cocked, raised and fired – is a metaphor for male sexuality. Although George had six children, five of whom survived, it is likely that his sex drive was low. Because of his attachment to his mother he was unable to relate satisfactorily to other women, and it is probable that to him sex was mainly procreational and that his partner, who rated duty above all else, would have been more concerned with his status than his virility. It is not uncommon for men to displace their sexuality on to aggressive and predominantly male sports, such as shooting, boxing and motor-racing.

At his coronation in 1911 George was faced with a dilemma: his mother demanded precedence in Westminster Abbey over his wife. George collapsed under his mother's pressure, yet again, just as he had allowed her to keep the little crown and to stay on at Buckingham Palace. By clinging to her former status Alexandra proved once again to her daughter-in-law that she was still able to manipulate her son.

George V's dullness and lack of intellect may have helped him to become a popular king. Britain's growing middle classes felt at home with a monarch who seemed comfortable in the field or on the quarterdeck and who instigated the tradition of the BBC Christmas broadcast to the Empire. Few people were privy to the darker side of his nature. Had they known more about his epileptic son John (seldom included in family portraits), who had

been banished to live with a nurse and to die unremarked, had
they known that his son, David, the immensely popular Prince of
Wales, was so frightened of his father that at the age of eighteen
he fainted in anticipation of a reprimand, they might have revised
their ideas about a gruff but kindly king whose heart was 'in the
right place'.

George's 'sense of humour' and his liking for practical jokes
was another manifestation of his aggression. He was renowned
for his habit in the Navy of making apple-pie beds for his fellow
cadets. His patent delight in the discomfort of others, remarked
upon by his tutor, John Dalton, reflected an unconscious desire to
hurt others as he himself had once been hurt.

As a consequence of his relationship with Alexandra, when
his own wife became a mother he saw to it that he was not
required to 'share' her. His sons in particular were not allowed to
take up any more of Mary's time than was essential. As always,
she colluded with his wishes – he thought this no more than his
due – and gave her children minimal attention. She knew to
whom she owed the status which gave her such pleasure and
which had restored her own sense of self-worth. George, with his
tattooed arms and his heavy smoking – Mary, too, enjoyed the
occasional Woodbine – was, in many respects, a contradiction to
the sedate persona perceived by his subjects. Society and the
intelligentsia rather despised the couple, as illustrated in Lady
Geraldine Somerset's diaries, and a few lines from a Max Beer-
bohm song:

> I found him with a rural dean
> Talking of District Visiting . . .
> The King is duller than the Queen
>
> At any rate he doesn't sew;
> You don't see him embellishing
> Yard after yard of calico . . .
> The Queen is duller than the King

. . . the truth is probably far more complicated than either of the
two imagined extremes. Their habit of committing their most
affectionate and intimate feelings to paper continued throughout
their married life, often prefaced by an apology about being
unable to express themselves face-to-face. Several years after their

wedding George wrote to Mary that he had not been much in love with her at the time of their engagement or marriage, but that he had come to love her very much. Her reply, typically, would have expressed agreement and relief.

They seem to have been a well-matched pair. Both were lonely, damaged, and insecure people who disguised their inadequacies – perhaps even to each other – with an outward display of hauteur and pride.

George was fond of and respected his father but deplored the way that his mother had been treated. Grief-stricken though he was when Edward died, he expressed oblique disapproval afterwards. 'We've seen enough of the intrigue and meddling of certain ladies. I'm not interested in any wife except my own.'

George was well served by his lack of imagination. This, probably more than anything else, enabled him apparently to overcome the difficulties experienced in his childhood. It did not, however, prevent him from inflicting similar pain upon his own children. Having witnessed few examples of constructive parental love and guidance, it was impossible for him to extend this to others. Narcissistic needs and child neglect were once again on the move.

CHAPTER FIVE

George, Mary
and Their Children

'Her price is far above rubies . . .'
PROVERBS

Princess May of Teck became a senior member of the British
Royal Family when, by default, she married Prince George, Duke
of York, the second son of Edward, Prince of Wales, in July 1892.

She was born at Kensington Palace in May 1867, the eldest of
four children. As the first-born, May received some early attention from her mother (herself a deprived child) but was quickly
displaced by the birth of her three brothers. Her father, the Duke
of Teck, had been prevented by his father's morganatic marriage
from inheriting family titles and money and had to manage on his
army pay. He came from Germany to England with his wife,
Princess Mary Adelaide, a first cousin of Queen Victoria, and
settled in a grace and favour apartment given to them by the
Queen, who took pity on the impoverished Tecks. Between 1883
and 1885, however, the Tecks' financial circumstances were so
straitened that they were obliged to live in Italy where the cost of
living was lower. May grew up, therefore, with both the expectation of luxury and a fear of the consequences of over-indulgence.
With relatively unimportant royal status and with little political
importance, she was not expected to make an especially brilliant
marriage, but she was, none the less, a royal princess and could
not entertain thoughts of marriage to anyone of lesser rank than
herself. This dilemma could well have made an old maid of her,
for, by her early twenties, she had developed a stiff, aloof, rather
spinsterly bearing. She also had a horror of 'vulgarity' and later

explained her disinclination to laugh by saying that she thought she sounded vulgar when she did so.

The Tecks' financial troubles had been caused partly by the profligacy of Princess Mary Adelaide. She weighed seventeen stone and became known affectionately as 'Fat Mary' by the British people. She was as flamboyant as Queen Victoria was reclusive, and had a passion for expensive jewellery and clothing, inherited by her daughter who, despite being left with only 'two little rings' after Eddy died, did not have long to wait for a more substantial collection. On her marriage Mary received personal gifts of jewellery then valued at over £1 million.

Princess Mary Adelaide's craving for food and possessions, as well as her denial of the family's financial situation, suggests that she had unfulfilled dependent needs. Having had very little love in her own childhood, she was unable to provide much for her daughter, who yearned for status and respect just as Mary Adelaide yearned for affection and food and who grew up with similar dependent needs. Although May was greedy for the trappings of wealth, she did not take kindly to later criticism by her mother for her enjoyment of them.

Mary Adelaide had enjoyed few luxuries when she was young and had not married until her early thirties, long after she was perceived as being marriageable. She later displayed an understandable enthusiasm to make up for lost time and to enjoy vicariously her daughter's prominence. It was her wish to see May placed as highly as possible, partly so that she herself might be able to afford her own indulgences. In this May colluded, and she accepted as her 'right' all the trappings of senior royalty.

Mary Adelaide, who was not only a voracious eater, but voraciously demanding in other respects, had never found it easy to be emotionally generous. Rather, it was May who was supposed to supply her mother, ultimately, with the means to support her lifestyle. When May was born Mary Adelaide saw an opportunity to gain the love that she herself had been denied. Her daughter was expected to be pleasing and dutiful, and May conformed to these expectations. In learning from that experience how to become a pleasing and dutiful wife, she learned also how to please herself. She developed an insatiable need to be valued (as a result of her low self-esteem), and found a way to compensate for her feelings of 'little worth' by adorning herself with the extravagant jewellery to which she was attracted. She saw these prized trinkets as representing love – her birthright and her entitlement – and, as Queen, she became well known as a country-house kleptomaniac. Either she simply pocketed valuables which took her fancy, or admired them so vociferously that her hostesses had little choice but to give them to her. They learnt quickly to put away their most cherished ornaments whenever Queen Mary, who simply did not understand that helping herself to 'symbols of love' from other people's homes was wrong, came to visit.

Her passion for adornment was legendary. Never since Elizabeth I was a queen so bejewelled: pearl and diamond chokers sometimes fifteen strands deep, ropes of pearls hanging to her waist, diamond stomachers, bracelets on both wrists, several brooches and orders pinned across her bodice, rings and a tiara would be worn at the same time. Jewels are often the symbol of a woman's captivity or possession by a man; in Mary's case, where many of the gems she wore were the property of the state, they proclaimed her primary allegiance to the Crown. Through self-adornment, and by dressing in magnificent robes, Mary glittered and dazzled as she thought befitted someone of her status. Pomp and ceremony outshone maternity as far as she was concerned, and led her to resent the pregnancies which precluded her from taking centre stage on state occasions. 'Of course it is a great bore for me & requires a great deal of patience to bear it, but this alas is the penalty of being a woman!' she wrote to her husband in 1905. She left her elder children as infants for lengthy tours as Princess of Wales and her entire family on other occasions as Queen. Although Princess May had been embarrassed by what she saw as attention-seeking behaviour in her mother, as Queen Mary she failed to recognize these same characteristics in herself.

The two little rings that May allowed the world to think were the only souvenirs of her first engagement were not long to be her only precious adornments. She and Prince George became engaged in May 1893 and married the following July. They saw little of each other during their engagement and were barely ever alone. It is clear from their letters that they were not yet at ease with each other: in June May wrote to her fiancé: 'I am very sorry that I am still so shy with you. I tried not to be the other day but alas failed, I was angry with myself! It is so stupid to be so stiff together and there is nothing I would not tell you except that I love you more than anyone else in the world . . .' George replied, 'Thank God we understand each other, and I think it really unnecessary for me to tell you how deep my love for you my darling is . . .'

It is likely that Mary, whose early life experiences had been cold and distant, would have also found difficulty in expressing sexual feelings and have sought gratification in the acquisition of possessions. Perhaps she regretted that she was not given the opportunity by her husband to furnish their first home, York Cottage, but she had her say in subsequent residences, and only her passion for clothes and jewellery exceeded her zeal for accumulating *objets* with which to adorn her homes. Impoverished and empty within, her narcissistic behaviour excluded those around her, except when they were called upon to satisfy her greed. It was hardly surprising that, surrounded by the glamour and fantasy of the world in which she lived, she appeared cold and selfish. A music-hall joke of the time had Mary asking George on the morning after their wedding night if the common people do 'that'. Her husband replied that yes, he believed they did. 'Well, it shouldn't be allowed. It's too good for them,' is Mary's apocryphal reply.

Within a year of marriage Mary had proved her worth by producing a male heir. Four more sons followed over the next eight years. David, the eldest, later became the maverick Edward VIII, Albert (later George VI) had greatness thrust upon him and died prematurely, Henry (later Duke of Gloucester) died in 1977, their fourth son, George (later Duke of Kent) was killed in an air crash in Scotland in 1942, and the youngest, John, died at the age of fourteen. Their only daughter, Mary, was born in 1897 and was married – not, it was thought, happily – to Henry, Viscount Lascelles.

The Princess of Wales saw her fecundity as serving her husband and future king, but took little interest or pleasure in her children, who were brought up by others and saw their parents as distant and cold. George and Mary may have brought up their family with all the love, interest, patience and understanding of which they were capable, but the results of their poor parenting were manifest in the psychologically disturbed lives of their children. Lord Derby reported that George said, 'My father was frightened of his mother: I was frightened of my father and I'm damn well going to see to it that my children are frightened of me.' One of his biographers, Kenneth Rose, disputes the authenticity of this.

George did, however, possess a measure of kindness and the ability to express pride in and affection for his children when they were very young. In 1894 he wrote to his wife of the pleasure he derived from looking at her photograph and that of 'darling Baby' when he was away from them: '. . . I like looking at my Tootsums little wife and my sweet child, it makes me happy when they are far away.' Mary, however, remained unemotional about motherhood. 'What a curious child he is,' she wrote wonderingly, after her baby son had been 'jumpy' in the morning but calmer after being taken out. Of her two-year-old son David, she wrote in 1896, 'I really believe he begins to like me at last. He is most civil to me.' It is significant that Mary equated civility and politeness with love and that the onus was on her son to love and be civil to his mother, rather than the other way round. 'The House of Hanover, like ducks, produce bad parents. They trample on their young,' Owen Morshead, the royal librarian, told Harold Nicolson, George V's official biographer. Another commentator, Alec Hardinge, a Private Secretary, remarked how strange it was that George V, who was 'such a kind man was such a brute to his children'.

Prince Edward Albert Christian George Andrew Patrick David was born to Princess May in June 1894 at White Lodge, Richmond. The seventy-five-year-old Queen Victoria was once again displeased that the new heir had not been given Albert as his first name. As a compromise (which at the same time honoured the people of Wales whose prince he was), the boy was always called David.

His mother was keen to resume public duties and had regained her regal (if corseted) figure within three months of his birth. His father left for Russia a few weeks later to attend the funeral of Tsar Alexander III, and – shortly afterwards – the marriage of the new Tsar, Nicholas II, to Alexandra of Hesse. Mary saw her baby briefly only once or twice a day and engaged a nurse, Mary Peters, to care for him. Less than eighteen months after his arrival,

Albert Frederick Arthur George made his appearance, and he, too, was handed over to the care of Mary Peters.

Although the psychological damage suffered by the boys was caused primarily by the neglect and cruelty of their parents, Mary Peters was also in part responsible. She was so besotted with Edward that she would pinch him until he cried before his evening rendezvous with his mother, so that Mary would demand he be taken away and returned to his nurse. When Albert was born, Peters resented having to look after him as well as Edward. She showed far less concern for him than for his older brother and has been accused of neglecting his diet (which may have contributed to his later stomach problems). Her ministrations might also have contributed to Edward VIII's association of love with pain, and some of the problems experienced by George VI in adulthood. Her influence in the nursery at York Cottage continued for three years.

Mary Peters was dismissed when her behaviour was brought to Princess Mary's attention indirectly by Charlotte 'Lala' Bill, the under-nanny. That she had got away with her curiously expressed and damaging affection for Edward and her indifference to Albert for so long, says much about the Princess's lack of interest in her children's welfare. It seems extraordinary that, in a smallish house, she, albeit uninterested or self-absorbed, was unaware of what was taking place in the nursery.

With the dismissal of Mary Peters, Lala Bill, who was later to care for Prince John after his banishment, took her place. Lala was a London woman to whom the children became attached. She was cheerful, kind and loving, as was their grandmother, Queen Alexandra, and the two women did their best to provide the children with what they lacked in maternal love. Grandparents often find it easier to express loving feelings to their grandchildren than to their own children, because they can leave discipline to parents and enjoy the pleasures of indulgence while obliquely demonstrating to their own children that *they* were good parents, especially when they knew they were not.

Princess Mary, George and Mary's only daughter, resembled her mother and was the child to whom the Duke of York was able to relate most easily. He felt a deep sense of loss when she married in 1921. 'I went up to Mary's room and took leave of her and quite broke down . . . Felt very low and depressed,' he wrote at the time. George and Mary both looked to their daughter for love to compensate for the absence of satisfactory loving from their own mothers.

Henry, their third son, was born in 1900 and was probably sufficiently insensitive to avoid some of the traumas experienced by his older brothers. He later became Duke of Gloucester, married late, and had two sons.

George, the youngest son to survive into adulthood, was born in 1902. He was the tallest and most personable of all the brothers, and theatrically handsome. When, as Duke of Kent, he married Marina of Greece they were known as 'that dazzling couple'. George was brighter than his brothers and being so far removed from the succession was probably brought up with less pressure. Like his mother, he was interested in books, history, architecture and pictures, and Mary gave him more affection and attention than she did her other sons. George, and also his older brother, the Prince of Wales, grew up to enjoy the company of commoners and of those working in the arts. He was just one of many royal males to have had only a questionable interest in women. Before his fatal flying accident in 1942, George was rumoured to have had homosexual relationships, as well as to have experimented with the then fashionable drugs. He was fortunate in that he chose as a partner a woman acknowledged to feel comfortable with homosexual males among whom were Danny Kaye (rumoured to have had a sexual relationship with Sir Laurence Olivier), Noël Coward and Sir Malcolm Sargent. It seems likely that she would not have made sexual demands on George to which he was unable to respond.

Prince John, George and Mary's last child, died in 1919. He had lived for years apart from the family in the care of Lala Bill. After his removal the Princess (possibly glad to be relieved of this reminder of failure and physical imperfection) wrote to her son but never visited him although he lived only a few miles from York Cottage. His brother Albert, playing a mother's role, had always shown him kindness and love, and was saddened by his absence, but gradually the memory of his youngest brother faded. Prince John did not see his mother again. When he died Mary wrote in her diaries of her grief, but there is nothing to suggest that she was truly distressed at his death. He had been his grandmother's favourite grandchild, however, and it was Queen Alexandra who lingered at his graveside and wept.

Pressure was placed early on George and Mary's two eldest sons. Their parents failed to recognize the boys' different abilities and were determined that they should conform to their expectations of them. Their father insisted that they should study hard – not to discover pleasure in learning and acquire breadth of thought but to enable them to pass their entrance examinations to Osborne where they were to become unwilling naval cadets.

Their mother was equally concerned that the boys should be cultured: in the few minutes that she spared them every evening, she read to them from the classics, not always in English, and set them long passages to learn and then recite on the following evening. Far from teaching them to enjoy and appreciate great writers, she made this a chore and in doing so probably ensured that neither would have the slightest adult interest in either literature or art. Many years later, Philip Ziegler tells us, Tommy Lascelles, then Edward, Prince of Wales's, private secretary, remembered him returning from a house party. 'Look at this extraordinary little book which Lady Desborough says I ought to read. Have you ever heard of it?' asked the Prince. The book was *Jane Eyre*. Another time he revealed in conversation to Thomas Hardy that he was sure some other fellow had written a book entitled *Tess of the D'Urbervilles*. While their mother read to them, the boys were encouraged to sew, embroider or crochet as she deplored idle hands. At that time boys were often taught needlework but seldom required to take their sewing kits (as Edward did) to the front during the First World War. It seems likely that Mary, famed for her tapestries, was once again displaying the egotism that enabled her to believe that if she, the future Queen, could see some noble point in the pastime, so should her sons.

George and Mary went on several tours abroad during the boys' early years. Two of these lasted eight months. During their absences the children were cared for by Edward VII and Alexandra. Albert developed a stutter, for which he was reprimanded, and was naturally left-handed which, in accordance with the thinking of the times, was frowned upon and 'corrected'. In the care of his grandparents, David was less often reminded of his future destiny, and the boys' lessons would finish early if either the King or Queen decided that it was time to play.

The two older boys had strict instructions to correspond with their parents while they were away: each was required to write a letter on alternate weeks. Not surprisingly the system failed occasionally and they were duly rebuked for the confusion. Neither George nor Mary understood the importance of spontaneous communication or that their children might wish to address their parents when they needed to do so. They appeared not to miss their children – and could not comprehend that they might miss and need them. But like battered wives who stand by their men, and tormented dogs who remain faithful to their masters, these 'abused' children retained a pathetic faith in the parents who had so neglected their duties towards them. Instead of affectionately responding to her children's dutiful letters, Princess Mary replied with only a few lines. Not even when children and parents were separated on birthdays or at Christmas did the boys receive loving messages. 'Darling Harry,' wrote Princess Mary, on a postcard from India in reply to one of her son's two Christmas letters, 'Papa and I thank you for your 2 long letters which were very nicely written, also for the little snowdrops you and Georgie sent. There are no flowers like this in this country. Love from Mama.'

Mama was too distracted by the durbars and ceremonies, the many opportunities to wear the Koh-i-Noor diamond, the adulation she was receiving in India, to listen to her children's cries for attention and reassurance. On one occasion, when his parents returned from a long tour, Henry failed to recognize his mother. As adults, both Edward and Albert said that they had never been alone with their mother: a servant or lady-in-waiting was always present when they had their meetings with her each evening. Any boy who has been deprived of a one-to-one relationship with his mother may find it difficult to establish intimacy with any woman when he is older.

Prince George was anxious to ensure that his two elder sons were intellectually equipped to join the Navy. Despite rigorous tutoring from Henry Hansell, however, Edward's marks were among the lowest in the Osborne exams and it seems likely that, had he not been the heir to the throne, he would not have been accepted. Small in stature, intellectually limited and teased by his contemporaries (who called him 'Sardine', a laboured diminutive of 'Whales'), he was unhappy there. He felt as lonely and inadequate as his great-nephew, Prince Edward, was to feel when in 1986 he was given no choice by his father, Prince Philip, other than to join the Marines.

Things improved a little for Edward when he was joined at Osborne a year later by Albert (who cried when he was separated from Lala Bill), who had fared even worse in the entrance exams. He looked forward to seeing his brother but the two were kept apart, and each was subjected to the strict regimes of the system. They saw each other when they could but opportunities were limited. Albert made some friends, and came to impress his teachers with his grit and persistence, but the princes were at the bottom of their year's intake and neither passed out of Osborne with any distinction. The cadet training, which their father had hoped would form their characters, was, academically, a dismal failure.

At the end of term, Albert, at least, was beside himself with excitement at the prospect of seeing his family, on whom he was still heavily dependent. (Paradoxically, the more time a child spends with his parents, the more independent and therefore self-assured he will become.) It says much about the Osborne regime and the dismal report that he would bring home, that even the semblance of family life was preferable to the disciplines of naval college. Both boys were pleased to leave, even if it was only to continue their naval education at Dartmouth.

Just when Edward and Albert reached an age where an adult relationship with their father might have been possible, however, their grandfather died and George became king. He was to remain an authority figure whose paternalism, ever tyrannical, restricted their hopes and dampened their aspirations.

CHAPTER SIX

Edward VIII

'. . . and thou beside me singing in the wilderness . . .'
OMAR KHAYYAM

Uncrowned, dishonoured, and scarcely mourned, Edward VIII has been the subject of more speculation, investigation, and discussion than any other recent monarch. From the moment of his birth on 23 June 1894, through his extraordinary adulthood, to his death in 1972, his story, from bright beginning to inglorious end, has attracted widespread comment.

When Edward Albert Christian George Andrew Patrick David was christened, one prophetic voice was heard in the wilderness of public acclamation. Keir Hardie, Britain's first socialist member of Parliament), announced in the House of Commons that 'From his childhood onward this boy will be surrounded by sycophants and flatterers by the score . . . A line will be drawn between him and the people he is to be called upon some day to reign over. In due course . . . he will be sent on a tour round the world, and probably rumours of a morganatic alliance will follow, and the end of it will be that the country will be called upon to pay the bill.'

When Edward was born, his great-grandmother Queen Victoria was still on the throne. Her son, Edward, an ageing Prince of Wales, waited to take the reins, and her grandson, Prince George, was expected to succeed his father. Although, as was triumphantly pointed out by *The Times*, there were already two heirs in direct line of inheritance, another prince had now been born to take the Royal Family far into the next century. It went on: 'The young prince is heir to a noble inheritance, not only to a station of unequalled dignity, but more than all to the affection of a loyal people, which it will be his office to keep and to make his own. Our heartfelt prayer is that he may prove worthy of so great a trust.' Most readers of *The Times* would have endorsed these sentiments, and it is ironic that Edward, welcomed as the future protector of the realm, was to be the cause of its greatest constitutional crisis.

Although Mary had not enjoyed her pregnancy, she was delighted to have set the seal on her illustrious marriage by producing the heir for which everyone had been waiting, but when her initial satisfaction in having done her duty palled her interest in her son faded. Her interest in the Empire, conversely, increased.

From the day of his birth, Edward was the Empire's favourite son. Unfortunately the same degree of wholehearted approbation was not forthcoming from his parents. His father was strict, inflexible, and quick to anger – although he was also capable of kindness – and his mother never had any doubts about where her first duty lay. According to Sir John Wheeler-Bennett she would 'seldom stand between them [her children] and the sudden gusts of their father's wrath'. Edward, then, could not rely on his mother to speak for him, he was forbidden to speak for himself, and in the face of his father's harsh discipline, he stood con-demned. Judged by his parents, with advocacy denied him, the foundations were laid for Edward's adult life which would be dogged by feelings of rejection and isolation. The repressed child was to grow into an adult who would, of necessity, remain secretive. Only through sexual activity with the woman who finally understood him, and to whom he clung through hell and high water, was he able to re-enact the pain, the humiliation, and the anger of his childhood. Edward grew up terrified of his father, betrayed by his mother, with an unfulfilled longing to experience the rightful privileges of childhood, and an inborn distaste for his destiny.

Early on, his progress was assiduously followed, while later, his every utterance was reported, and his social proclivities and idiosyncratic style of dress imitated and reproduced, in a way that was unprecedented, and which would not have been possible had it not been for the development of mass communication. As Edward grew up, Mary managed to summon up a grudging affection for him, as she came to acknowledge his status and prospects. Her aunt by marriage, Princess Vicky (Empress

Frederick of Prussia), who as the Prince Consort's favourite child had had some experience of tender parenting, said that Mary was 'very cold, stiff and unmaternal'. Years later, as Prince of Wales, Edward remonstrated tellingly with one of the daughters of his then mistress Freda Dudley Ward: 'You see, you are so much loved you are spoilt. You have no idea of the lives of many children.' He felt at ease with children and could identify with their needs. It brought him, once again, in touch with a mother whom he desperately needed but to whom he could not make a commitment, since no mother had made a commitment to him.

It was Mary Peters who provided Edward with the only structure and security that he knew as a young child. She came with the best of reputations and references from the Duke and Duchess of Newcastle: she was autocratic, stern, and even sadistic, but she was also devoted to Edward. The two Marys could not have been more different: his mother's remoteness and Mary Peters's warmth were poles apart, and the effects of this duality remained with him throughout his life, influencing his subsequent relationships with women. As far as Edward was concerned, his mother had rejected him and his nanny had loved him. His mother represented the glory and panoply of the Crown with its inherent metallic coldness; his nanny epitomized physical contact, love, support, and availability. Later, when he had to decide between the Crown and Wallis Simpson, his choice was determined by his indifferent mother having earlier directed him into the open arms of his nanny. That Wallis Simpson instinctively responded to the Prince of Wales's 'nursery' needs, and that he could compulsively act them out with her, ensured that his brother would come to the throne in his place. At the age of forty-four, Edward, asserting himself at last, insisted – in the face of opposition from Ministers of the Crown – that from now on he would accept responsibility for himself. In Mrs Simpson, who caused him to suffer and then consoled him, he rediscovered his first and only true love Mary Peters; it was inevitable that he would marry her.

Edward's ambivalence towards women stemmed possibly from the mixed messages he received from Mary Peters, her habit of making him cry before his nightly audience with his mother, then holding him to her to comfort him. Later, as a confused adult, he came to associate love with suffering, and sacrificed his royal future for a sado-masochistic one with his wife.

Lala Bill's kindness to Edward and his siblings is widely acknowledged. It was to her that Edward owed the faint Cockney accent that marked his speech. Her affection for him, however, emphasized the remoteness between the heir and his mother, and led him ever after, as an adult, to re-enact the happy, physical contacts of his childhood with women who were caring, authoritative, controlling, and never of his class. Even Lala Bill, though, who loved Edward unconditionally, let him down from time to time when her duties with his younger siblings, especially Albert, prevented her from giving him her sole attention. Mary was always formal with her son. Her letters are more suggestive of a pen-friend than a mother. When Edward was still a child of thirteen, she missed the first two weeks of his holidays from Osborne. 'I hope that we will have great fun together when we do meet' is an expression of neither warmth nor affection.

Although Edward's physical contact with his mother was restricted, the ongoing presence of his nannies predicated that in later life there would always be 'another' woman to care for him. He replicated this need for two carers by never terminating one relationship before he had set up the next. This pattern continued until he met Wallis Simpson who, fortunately for him, encapsulated all his needs.

Edward was an attractive child but in photographs his face is invariably sad. Although as an adult he retained his boyish good looks, the melancholy expression remained. He was unusually short, which was possibly genetic, but growth hormone could have been inhibited by stress in his childhood. In Edward's case, the neglect of one care-giver and the possessiveness of another could have been a contributory factor.

His mother worked for years on vast tapestries and taught Edward to sew, an activity he continued, unusually, in adulthood. His lack of height, and his accustomed inferior position – on a stool at his mother's knee – ensured that afterwards he was obliged to 'look up' to women, not necessarily with affection.

While Edward was neglected by his mother, his father involved himself with his son, but mainly as a disciplinarian whose demands were excessive and humiliating, crushing the boy's emotional growth and self-confidence. Prince George's certainty that where his sons were concerned he knew best led him even to ignore the well-meaning advice of Edward's tutor, Henry Hansell. An honourable man, Hansell had placed his own position in jeopardy by suggesting to Prince George that Edward and his younger brother would benefit from going to school with other boys. Hansell's concern for Edward could also have contributed to the boy's insecurity, as his recommendations might have sounded as if even his tutor wanted to be rid of him.

In deferring to her husband's notions of what would constitute the best education for her sons, Mary once again demonstrated her priorities. That neither Edward nor Albert cared much for the sports and games on which Mr Hansell placed great emphasis, concerned her very little. In 1907 she wrote to her aunt, Augusta of Mecklenburg-Strelitz: 'We have taken no end of trouble with their education . . . one feels all is being done to help them.' Perhaps she felt that her own efforts to interest her children in history, literature, and the arts were sufficient. Mary's own introduction to culture came late, and, according to James Pope-Hennessy, the Queen saw *Hamlet* performed for the first time when she was seventy-five, and discovered the great Russian novelists when she was in her eighties.

Any attempt to encourage Edward's intellectual development failed: years later, even when he spent some months at Oxford, he admitted that he preferred picture books to written texts despite – or because of – his mother's earlier insistence on his memorizing and reciting pieces from the classics. When he went to Osborne, and later Dartmouth as a naval cadet, greater emphasis was placed on mathematics and the sciences, but he had no great aptitude for either. The more general offerings of the schoolroom – the learning of a sense of fair play, self-confidence, tolerance, courage, generosity, and humility – were no easier for him to acquire. None of these attributes could be imbibed by rote.

As part of their normal development, all infants have negative behaviour patterns which demanding, controlling, disciplining parents will attempt to eradicate, by employing the weapon of 'parental disapproval', in the face of which a child is helpless. All children depend entirely on their parents for love and acceptance, withdrawal of which will ensure complete but temporary suppression of negative behaviour – including selfishness, rage, jealousy and greed, all the 'deadly sins' of adult life. Parents, naturally, wish their children to grow into fair-minded, generous, and well-adjusted adults, and this they will do *if* they are allowed to express themselves freely in the nursery. Greed in an infant is normal: he has no mechanism for controlling hunger. Tolerance and the ability to wait may be learned only with a mother whose availability is never in doubt. To 'love oneself' must precede the ability to love another. It is not possible to give love unless one has received it, either in tangible form as toys or food, or in the abstract, as a sense of security and self-confidence. No child can ever love anyone else until he or she has been loved. No child can be selfless until he or she has been selfish. Although Edward's parents must have been familiar with the Christian imperative, 'Love thy neighbour as thyself', he grew up with all his 'negatives' – which were to surface at a time when he and the nation least needed them – unsuccessfully suppressed.

By the time he was sixteen and his grandfather, Edward VII, died, Edward would have been aware of the friendship the King had maintained for twelve years with Alice Keppel, a frequent guest at Sandringham. This perplexing relationship must have had a profound effect on the sensitive boy. While he associated his grandparents with love and affection, he also observed that his grandmother tolerated the presence of his grandfather's mistress in the house; his parents, however, who had always seemed devoted to each other but were unable to express positive feelings for their children, disapproved of 'Mrs K', as they referred to her. Edward was to grow up with the idea that some happily married women (Mrs Keppel's family were devoted to her) could be sources of pleasure, while others (his mother) were not.

As Duke of Windsor, Edward wrote that he could remember only one parental embrace from his childhood, and that had been after they had been away for eight months, and as he never saw his mother without a servant or a lady-in-waiting in attendance, whatever anger and frustration he experienced could hardly have been expressed. He therefore carried these feelings with him into adulthood. His fear as a young man of his father, the tears and fainting, were the reactions of a helpless victim whose tears are of rage, rather than of sadness, and ensured that as an adult he would understand and empathize with persecutors. His brief flirtation with Nazi philosophy seems to confirm this. Edward's slight deafness in one ear caused George to shout at him and he associated even conversation with his father as discordant and harsh.

Unable to articulate his feelings, insecure – his childish fears of the dark persisted into adult life – and emotionally impoverished, Edward's few efforts at assertive behaviour were doomed to failure. He had been denied his essential needs and he felt cheated. His final rebellion brought him the love and affection he had craved all his life – but cost him his birthright.

During his brief kingship, Edward sought to compensate himself for earlier deprivations, by demanding almost divine rights. Crown property – from Balmoral to the jewellery he bestowed on Wallis Simpson – was treated as if it were his own. He underestimated his personal wealth by a factor of twelve so that he might receive a larger state allowance after he abdicated, and he fought to keep as much as possible of what he saw as his 'inheritance'. Having been given little but an uneasy sense of destiny, he was unwilling to forfeit its trappings. Although he abdicated kingship possibly as compensation for childhood losses and with what therefore seemed to him good reason, it was effected without grace, and with avarice, which was as understandable as it was inevitable.

Edward was supportive and protective to his brothers and sister, although he could not resist using them as scapegoats for his long-suppressed hostility to his parents. Like his father he was keen on practical jokes, which were invariably cutting and unkind: even as an adult he victimized house-guests by making them apple-pie beds, but he would not tolerate any retaliation. It amused him to see the discomfort of others but, aware of his status, he balked at being a target himself.

Because he was self-conscious, and unwilling to confront the responsibilities of his destiny, Edward was quick to turn the page of any magazine which carried a picture of him, or reference to him as future sovereign. He threw a tantrum prior to his investiture as Prince of Wales in Caernarvon in 1911 because he feared his fellow cadets at Dartmouth would mock him for the purple velvet robes and white satin breeches he had to wear. Edward was content to enjoy, however, the ease, privilege and wealth that came with his status.

George V, like his grandmother Queen Victoria, was suspicious of friendship, which possibly accounted for his refusal to allow his elder sons to go to public school, although he had been advised that this would benefit them. Edward's initial disadvantages were compounded: as the eldest child of six children, he had been the leader in nursery games; as heir to the throne, while he was constantly made aware of his destiny and importance, he was also constantly belittled by his father yet denied the rough-and-tumble of the classroom and playing field. Football with the deferential village lads near Sandringham was no substitute for the levelling of Eton or Harrow, and Edward grew up without the qualities – a sense of fair play, responsibility, confidence, courage, enterprise and enquiry – these schools aim to instil.

His parents were so concerned at his lack of the qualities which they believed an heir to the throne should possess that they called in a leading phrenologist to examine his cranium (just as Victoria and Albert had the heir's head examined). Many unqualified practitioners then worked as phrenologists, and their opinions were treated as seriously as those of a psychologist would be today. The findings were not revealing. They smacked of sycophancy and an eagerness to please: the shape of Edward's skull was declared to reveal only 'outstanding qualities'!

Further similarities existed between the young Prince of Wales and his grandfather. He should 'learn to govern', his mother decreed, yet, like his grandfather, Edward was not given access to the information, papers, and people that might have stimulated an interest in the affairs his parents wanted the heir to address. He was sent instead, as his father's representative, to ceremonies and memorials. Edward described these activities as 'princing'. Some men, he wrote in his memoirs, may be chained to their desks, 'I was chained to the banqueting table.'

The writer Compton Mackenzie noticed a strong physical resemblance between Edward and his grandfather, Edward VII. 'If there had been anyone left alive . . . with long enough memories of the likeness between the young Prince of Wales and his grandfather when he was a young Prince of Wales it could not have failed to strike them. They would have recognized the same shyness, the same hint of sadness . . .' In fact, as the Prince grew older, he came more to resemble the actor Buster Keaton, his near contemporary, having the same sad, intense gaze but lacking Keaton's grace.

Some time in his late adolescence it was decided that Edward should learn not about 'love', on which he had missed out in his childhood, but about 'sex'. *In loco parentis*, a Doctor of Divinity (the Reverend Mr Wright), proffered some instruction, which was more likely to have been biological rather than erotic in nature. Shortly afterwards, in a letter to a friend, Edward claimed that he had never been troubled by 'sexual hunger'.

During his time at the front in the First World War, Edward was taken by his equerries (who rotated their duties) to a brothel in Calais where he found the sight of the prostitutes there 'perfectly filthy and revolting'. Given the ambivalence towards women with which his upbringing had left him, this is not surprising. Also, Edward might not have seen a naked woman before and the sight of a working-class French prostitute could well have unnerved him. However, he had his first sexual experience in Amiens, and thereafter seemed to find such activity agreeable. Following a relationship with a courtesan in Paris, and probably unaware of his grandfather's similar experience, he was unwise enough to write compromising letters to her. A brief blackmail scare followed, when the woman threatened to make the letters public, but she was 'dissuaded' and the panic died down.

In London, once more, where he was already courting Lady Sybil Cadogan, Edward fell in love with the already married Lady Marian Coke, wife of the heir to the Earl of Leicester and twelve years older than the Prince. She might have realized that a man who is involved with two women at once is displaying hostility to both of them. Other dalliances followed, none serious, and Edward was advised by his mother not to rush into marriage. He remained a bachelor sufficiently long for her to worry that he had taken her remark too literally. He was content to have numerous 'encounters' with married women, to tour the Empire and to hold court at Fort Belvedere, the architectural eccentricity in Windsor Great Park which he had persuaded his father to give him and where he entertained his mistresses and friends. Satisfying his need to be seen as a man in his own right, he also bought a ranch in Canada, which he believed, wrongly, to lie on oil-rich land.

According to her maid, Else, Edward's sister Mary, who had a better relationship with their parents than he, found it difficult to understand why Edward did not love her parents as much as she did or why he had grown up to be so bitter and resentful. Mary was her father's favourite child: she was not exposed to the same verbal and written admonishments as Edward, and did not suffer the same confusion as the boys whose letters from their father were often couched in terms of affection before launching into criticism and threat. 'My Dearest Bertie', wrote the Prince, 'I'm sorry to have to say that the last reports from Mr Watt [at Osborne] are not at all satisfactory, he says you don't seem to take your work at all seriously, nor do you appear to be very keen about it. My dear boy, this will not do . . .' And later, when Edward was at the front and evidently oblivious to the potential dangers to life in France, his father wrote to him about a breach of diplomatic protocol. 'Ld Cavan has written to Digge about your wearing the ribbon of the Legion of Honour. It is very silly of you not doing what I told you at Easter time . . .' Queen Mary's lady-in-waiting, Mabell Airlie, was well placed to observe the tension between father and son. In her memoirs, *Thatched With Gold*, she wrote that 'The King was proud of his sons but he was often harsh with them simply because he could not bridge the gulf between their generation and his . . . As the heir to the throne grew older the stream of paternal criticism increased, but the Prince's behaviour, when his father hauled him over the coals for being "the worst dressed man in London" and laid traps for him with orders and decorations, showed the utmost forbearance.' George V was putting his son in a double-bind by honouring him and then complaining when the medals were not positioned exactly according to protocol. His criticisms might have been justified, but linking chastisement with endearment perhaps rendered loving expression meaningless to Edward, particularly since physical demonstrations of love were non-existent. Having not been given love, but only status – about which he seemed to display mixed feelings – Edward, as might have been expected, clung to its benefits when he released himself from its responsibilities.

Edward's indolence showed itself in 1928 when he was on safari in Kenya. He was handed a telegram with the news that the King was seriously ill. Edward had difficulty in confronting the possibility that the responsibilities of kingship were imminent, and complained at having to cut short his holiday. He managed to find time, however, before leaving for England, to comfort himself by seducing the wife of a government official.

On this occasion the King rallied but his health went into decline. When he died in 1936 Edward's overt grief is more likely to have been connected to the new realities of his situation than with the loss of his father. His bereavement was the end of his long 'reign' of privilege without responsibility and he could not identify with the grief of other members of his family. On his arrival at Sandringham he immediately readjusted the clocks and began to institute economies at Buckingham Palace in order to augment his own income. King George might have set the clocks fast to make up for the lack of time given to him as a child but his son's instinct was to minimize the time he would have to give to his duties. In dismantling so soon some of his late father's idiosyncrasies Edward was flexing his muscles and, at the same time, denying those who grieved some minor but potent memories of the dead King.

As Prince of Wales, Edward had been credited with being Britain's greatest salesman as he toured the world ostensibly promoting international friendship and British manufacture. Opinions as to his effectiveness, however, differed. In Argentina, in 1931, the American ambassador said that 'his cordial, carefree democratic manner wins even those who would go out of their way to criticize him . . .' The same year, though, the National Archives in Washington record that in Uruguay the Prince '. . . appeared to be deeply tired, rather uninterested, and to have unfortunately lost a great deal of the personal charm which was so long the most engaging of his many delightful qualities.'

He was unable to cope with public speaking, and apart from long tours of the Empire, which were virtually prolonged holidays, he fulfilled few public duties and did not associate himself with worthy causes or charities. Edward, whose remark about the plight of miners in South Wales that 'Something must be done' was long remembered, did little but enjoy himself to compensate for the carefree childhood which had been denied him.

It has been said of Edward VIII that he cared only about three things: golf, money, and his wife. A concern with finance is only to be expected in one whose sense of self-worth is so low. During the abdication crisis, having been told, to his surprise, that he did not own Balmoral and Sandringham, Edward was allowed to 'lease' a lifetime interest in both from the Crown. He had been left no share of his father's £3 million of personal wealth as George V had assumed that his eldest son would inherit a kingdom and a civil list allowance, and was aware that Edward had, in addition, a substantial income from the Duchy of Cornwall. (After the abdication, a generous financial arrangement was reached recognising his interest in Balmoral and Sandringham. By today's standards his annual income would have exceeded £1 million.) Edward's most serious grievance, however, was that although he would continue to be styled a Royal Highness, his wife's title was that of a non-royal duchess.

Before his liaison with Wallis Simpson, Edward had been heavily involved with Freda Dudley Ward. She was several years his senior, a popular society figure, divorced wife of an MP and mother of two daughters, but was regarded as 'very good for him' as she encouraged him to be more responsible. Her sexual interest in Edward diminished after a few years, but she remained his friend, confidante, companion, and smokescreen. Freda Dudley Ward was petite, sensible, generally well liked and bore a passing resemblance to the Duchess of York. She was well enough placed in London society to move in the same circles as the Prince of Wales, and to understand and observe the same rules of discretion that surrounded his grandfather's illicit affairs, but not so well placed – or sufficiently emotionally involved – to cause a scandal. In her, Edward found a loving 'mother', someone who could show and verbalize affection, and he remained devoted to her for fourteen years.

His well-known affair with Thelma, Lady Furness, might have come as a relief to Freda although she and her daughters continued to value Edward's friendship. It was Thelma, a ravishingly attractive American whose twin sister had married a Vanderbilt, who introduced Edward to Wallis Simpson early in 1931, unwittingly bringing to an end her own liaison with him.

The most eligible bachelor in the world showed no inclination whatever to marry any of the many suitable young women at his disposal. It was not as if he was required to restrict himself to royal princesses, since his father had made it clear that he could marry a commoner if he so wished. His younger brother, Albert, had already married Lady Elizabeth Bowes-Lyon, the daughter of the Scottish Earl of Strathmore and Kinghorne, but although King George and Queen Mary were delighted by this match, they were perhaps a little disappointed that Elizabeth had chosen to accept Albert's proposal after she had been approved as a potential bride for the Prince of Wales.

Edward enjoyed the company of his two nieces, Princesses Elizabeth and Margaret Rose, just as he liked to visit Freda Dudley Ward's daughters, even in the absence of their mother. Yet while he liked to be part of a close-knit group, he showed no inclination to create a family of his own. Edward discovered the childhood he had missed after his father became king, when he found other 'children' (bachelor friends) to play with, a series of married women to 'mother' him, and revelled in the attention of his public both on official business, at home or in the Dominions, and on holiday. The charismatic Prince was fêted in North America, where the song 'I've danced with a man who danced with a girl who danced with the Prince of Wales . . .', which he inspired, was pure popular hero-worship. He felt loved at last. Realizing that marriage to a 'suitable' bride would rob him of his independence and dilute the adulation his presence aroused, Edward would have liked to remain in this enchanted and enchanting state. Marriage would have rendered difficult the pattern described by Tommy Lascelles as 'one shattering and absorbing love affair after another', and forced him to consider – from time to time – someone other than himself. His delusions were maintained and supported by the popular press: Edward as the 'caring-sharing' Prince, the man of the people, was as illusory as the image of his great-nephew Prince Andrew, placed in the role of hero after his brief but much publicized participation in the Falklands conflict of 1982. In both instances the press acknowledged the longing of readers for a 'handsome prince'. Edward symbolized the charisma of monarchy, while Andrew's macho image showed today's Royal Family to be in tune with the times.

Edward showed no real concern, however, for people less fortunate than himself; given the lack of emotional input from his parents, it would have been virtually impossible for him to be either caring or sharing. Much of his time was spent indulging his own interests, on the beach, in nightclubs, at the casino, in the beds of married women, or discussing the cut of a suit with his tailor. His interest in his appearance reflected that of his grand-father, Edward VII, who gave his name to the 'Prince of Wales check', while his grandson popularized the 'Windsor knot' (wind-ing the tie twice round the knot at the throat), and the Argyle pattern for sweaters and socks. He wore plus-fours on the golf course, adopted the working-man's flat cap, and sunbathed with-out his shirt. His contributions to the history of fashion also satisfied his need for approval and admiration.

Whereas Edward's desire to appear attractive reflected his conviction that he was not, his sexual behaviour emphasized his belief that a 'mother' would never love him and that seductive behaviour was an essential prerequisite in making a conquest. An infant's need for a mother's love is so compulsive that if it is not satisfied in a one-to-one relationship during childhood, the urge to make up the deficiency will persist throughout life. To make a 'conquest', with its implications of battle and the overcoming of resistance, is in itself a hostile act.

Edward fought for love because he could not believe that it would otherwise be available to him. When he succeeded in acquiring it, he could not be convinced for long that he was worth loving, and the process had to be constantly repeated. The compulsion to repeat the patterns of early life led him to be attracted to married women with children since, like his grand-father Edward VII whose childhood was similar, it was a mother's love for which he searched. When the 'mother' was captivated, or rather 'captured' by him, he would also have vanquished a 'father' (her husband), his original rival in the Oedipal contest for his mother's love.

Edward first met Ernest and Wallis Simpson in 1931 at the home of Thelma, Lady Furness. Wallis had married her second husband in 1928. This elegantly dressed, but almost mannish woman seemed to make little impression on the Prince at the time, but a year later he was the Simpsons' dinner guest. Following that, he fell in love with Wallis. The relationship developed rapidly into the persecutor/victim pattern of Edward's childhood: Wallis humiliated him in front of his friends by nagging and rudeness and more than once reduced him to tears. John Aird, the Prince's equerry, wrote in 1934 that Edward had 'lost all confidence in himself and follows W around like a dog'. Most people at the time believed that she did not love him, yet

Edward was infatuated with her, and it was not long before he dropped Lady Furness and Freda Dudley Ward, much to their bafflement and dismay. By 1935 George V had accused his son of keeping Wallis as a mistress, which Edward indignantly denied, but it became clear that he had lied to his father when servants at Fort Belvedere claimed they had seen the couple in bed together. Edward's denial, however, could be interpreted as the truth if he did not have penetrative sex with Wallis. It might be that, in re-enacting the humiliations of his childhood with a woman who enjoyed hurting him, adult sexuality was set aside in favour of passive nursery gratification.

Nevertheless his family became increasingly disapproving, particularly since Edward was known to be giving Wallis not only large amounts of money but also jewellery left to him by his grandmother Queen Alexandra, in particular a collection of emeralds thought to have been entrusted to him for his own queen. It was at this point, too, that his brother the Duke of York began to lose patience with him. (This became even more apparent when he refused to co-operate with Edward's wishes after the abdication and during the weeks leading up to his exile. Later, as King, George VI's disapproval was reinforced by Edward's interest in the Nazis, which was shared by Wallis to the extent that it was rumoured she was a German spy whose task was to encourage Edward's infatuation with Hitler. The couple visited Hitler in October 1937 when Edward, as Duke of Windsor, expressed an admiration for the social reforms in Germany that was, in fact, shared by many of his former subjects. But the very idea that Edward could again plunge the nation into turmoil and division in being championed by Germany – with the support of like-minded Englishmen – as a puppet King-in-waiting was politically disastrous for him.

By 1936 it had become clear that Edward intended to marry Wallis Simpson and that 'the fabric [of the monarchy] . . . could crumble under the shock and strain of it all!' – a view expressed by the Duke of York to the King's assistant private secretary but shared by many.

When Edward fell in love with Wallis Simpson, he chose a woman a little older than he, who would, like her predecessors, replicate the love he had not received from his mother. If he married her, he would also receive the bonus of being relieved of the responsibilities of a crown of which he had been made to feel unworthy, and which he had never wished to wear. In Wallis he recognized what he had been seeking all his life: a dominant woman who, he believed, loved him for himself, and who would, in some way, force him towards the choice he was happy to make. He continued to make use of charm, manipulation, and seductiveness – the tools of the unloved child – in his behaviour towards her. During his pursuit of Wallis (especially when he was away from her and anxious lest her interest diminish in his absence), the Prince of Wales wrote letters to her couched in the language of the nursery. Long after they were married, and living in Paris, he would dutifully defer to her as to a much-loved nanny. Diana Hood, who worked for them in Paris, remembers, 'The Duke behaved on occasion with almost childlike impulsive-ness . . . One afternoon he called [out of the window] to his valet on the pavement outside. The Duchess, happening to come into the room, simply said, as to a wayward child, "David!" He turned quickly from the window to explain, "It's the dogs, darling. They might have been run over."'

The phenomenon of identification with a persecutor is a defence against the loneliness and isolation which are felt by a victim in a situation where helplessness is so frightening that the only escape from it is to become 'at one' with the persecutor. The persecutor in Edward's life was his autocratic father, who had denied both his elder sons their democratic rights. Edward was to unload his sense of victimization onto anyone who could even remotely be seen to accommodate it. Women, second class citizens in the 1920s and 1930s, were suitable candidates.

His brother George VI's feelings of persecution took a differ-ent route. Having acceded to the throne just before the Second World War, he saw himself as being at one with his people who found themselves the victims of another tyrant, Adolf Hitler. King George's children were fortunate in that they were both girls. Had he produced a son, the repetition compulsion, which exists in the unconscious and over which one has no control unless one is aware of it, would have caused him to use the boy as scapegoat, as he had been a scapegoat for his father's anger.

Alan 'Tommy' Lascelles joined the Prince of Wales's staff as assistant private secretary in 1920. At the time his mixed feelings about Edward were biased towards admiration, and he found him attractive and charming. When he resigned eight years later he said, 'For some hereditary or physiological reason his mental and spiritual growth stopped dead in his adolescence . . .' In this he was in agreement with Stanley Baldwin who was even more terse: 'He is an abnormal being, half child, half genius . . . it is almost as if two or three cells in his brain had remained entirely undeveloped . . .' Lascelles remained on the Prince's staff as long as he could stand the self-indulgence and mercurial moods of his employer. After the abdication he took some glee in analysing the Prince's character over lunch with Harold Nicolson who reported Lascelles as saying: 'He says the King was like the child in the fairy stories who has been given every gift except a soul. He said there was nothing in him which understood the intellectual or artistic sides of life and that all art, poetry, music, etc, were dead to him. Even nature meant nothing to him . . . and his gardening at the Fort meant nothing beyond a form of exercise . . . he had no friends in this country, nobody whom he would ever wish to see again . . . He hated his country since he had no soul and did not like being reminded of his duties.' Lascelles's description of his character suggests that he had a personality disorder. Edward's faults and prejudices, like those of any psychopath, can be explained but not condoned.

Edward did not support women's suffrage, and he was also racially prejudiced: in 1925 *en route* for South Africa he noted that it was 'too much' to expect him to dance with black women in Sierra Leone and that he had refused to. Years later, in 1940 during his governorship of the Bahamas, he was able to write of Étienne Dupuch, editor of the *Nassau Daily Tribune*, 'Dupuch is more than half Negro, and due to the peculiar mentality of this Race, they seem unable to rise to prominence without losing their equilibrium.' Such opinions may merely be seen to reflect the commonly held sentiments of the day about 'natives', but the Duke was not a common man: he was custodian of a part of an empire and Commonwealth that paid more than lip service to notions of democracy, equality and essential human rights. He needed to be reassured that there were other victims in the world, and he played 'role-reversal' games to the extent, as we have seen, that he showed admiration for Hitler. All victims, such as hostages, those who have been violently abused, or simply deprived, by their circumstances, tend to switch from victim to identification with the persecutor. Latter-day political hostages, when released have often been only too ready to express views which support those of their captors, on the basis that if you cannot beat them, you join them. Edward's deprivations caused him to empathize with persecutors. With hindsight many people came to feel that it was a blessing that such a man had not been entrusted with the guardianship of a kingdom and an empire let alone a family of his own. With Edward's abdication, as with the Duke of Clarence's death, the people were spared a man whose upbringing and subsequent behaviour had rerouted him into one of history's culs-de-sac.

CHAPTER SEVEN

George VI and
Elizabeth Bowes-Lyon

'. . . and some have greatness thrust upon them . . .'
WILLIAM SHAKESPEARE

George VI, the second son of George V and Queen Mary, was a modest, self-effacing man who, after his elder brother's abdication, had kingship thrust upon him. He rose to the challenge admirably, and although he was ill-equipped and untrained for the role he was obliged to play, he had a strong sense of duty and was later to impress the country with his leadership qualities. Although he had an anxious personality and was, in reality, an angry and frustrated man, his outer calm and concerned manner endeared him to his people during the stresses and hardship of the Second World War.

George VI was not an able public speaker (Winston Churchill's war-time demagoguery more than made up for this), but his quiet dignity, the example he set as paterfamilias, and his assiduous guardianship of the people and what was left of the empire, compounded his popularity. His renowned temper, like that of his father and grandfather, was a reaction to neglectful mothering and his nanny Mary Peters's preference for his elder brother. He was later robbed of Lala Bill's affection when she was taken away from him and placed in sole charge of the ailing Prince John.

'Now that you are five years old,' wrote George V to his second son in a birthday message, 'I hope you will always try and be obedient and do at once what you are told, as you will find it will come much easier to you the sooner you begin . . .' The threatening tone of this greeting illustrates the 'conditional' love to which George and Mary's children were exposed. Approval was forthcoming only if they were good, and complied with parental expectations.

Mabell, Lady Airlie, one of Princess Mary's ladies-in-waiting, wrote of the shy but affectionate Albert in 1902 '. . . he presented me with an Easter card. It was his own work and very well done for a child of six – a design of spring flowers and chicks . . . He was so anxious for me to receive it in time for Easter that he decided to deliver it in person. He waylaid me one morning when I came out of his mother's boudoir, but at the last moment his courage failed him, and thrusting the card into my hand without a word, he darted away . . .' The loving and generous instincts of the child were coupled with a fear of rejection, and it is significant that the card was made not for his mother, but for a woman who seemed, to Albert, to be warmer and more approachable. Albert suffered both from his parents' humiliating disregard for his feelings, and the mental and physical demands they made upon him, which he was incapable of fulfilling. He and his brother Edward, joint victims of persecutory parenting, accepted their parents' treatment of them as normal, but were later to develop behavioural problems which in Edward's case had national repercussions, and in Albert's personal ones. Family life was essentially an autocracy. Power was in the hands of George V and his wife, whose authority was absolute. Democratic values did not exist, issues were not debated, and no child had rights. Repressive orders from above were executed by minions on innocent victims with no right of appeal.

George and Mary, who spoke with one voice so that neither could act as an advocate for the accused, had no idea, in keeping with the times, of the damage they were inflicting on their children. They were simply carrying on a tradition which had been handed down to them by their own parents who had been similarly treated. This does not excuse their behaviour, nor did it provide any compensation for their children. If they thought about it at all, their actions were justified by the paternalistic belief, which was accepted by parents for at least another generation, that what they were doing was for the children's 'own good'. In reality, they were merely pleasing themselves.

Like many children, Bertie was untidy, which caused constant friction between him and his father, who was obsessionally concerned with order and neatness, an attribute seen by him as a *sine qua non* for a future naval cadet. Albert was not academic and, as his brother Edward, unlikely to have gained a place at Dartmouth, had it not been for his rank. Despite coaching and parental exhortation, he remained at the bottom of the class in all his assessments. At first the officers were concerned about his speech defect, with its inherent risk that as a naval officer he would be unable to issue a command during a crisis. Later, however, they became impressed by his firmness of purpose. His father, obviously, had not been. When Bertie was approaching his twelfth birthday, the King wrote to him, in his usual reproving terms, 'You must . . . remember now you are nearly 12 years old and ought no longer to behave like a little child of six.' He appeared to have no sense of a child's natural progress, and continually interfered in an effort to control his son's development.

Albert eventually did reasonably well at Dartmouth, winning the respect of his peers and tutors, both for his courage and his aptitude for games and sports. He played tennis, squash, football and cricket, and, unlike his elder brother, was accepted by his fellow cadets. As a result of this, he later promoted a national movement for the development of municipal playing fields, which would encourage the fraternization of boys from public schools with those from less advantaged backgrounds. In the society of young men Bertie had found a comfort and acceptance which he had not previously experienced. Although a few years later, he was to make a popular and nationally celebrated marriage and become the devoted father of two daughters, he was never more at ease than when he was addressing groups of young people from backgrounds generally less privileged than his own.

Although Bertie and Edward had always been close to, and supportive of, each other, Bertie's examination results at Dartmouth, his personal appearance, and his public utterances would never receive the same press coverage as those of his brother, and he would always, as he thought, be number two. This had its advantages in that it afforded him more freedom than his brother, and allowed him to express his anger more overtly than Edward who demonstrated his more indirectly. During the war, in 1916, as a senior midshipman on HMS *Collingwood* during naval manoeuvres, Bertie was usually far removed from the centre stage of the battle, but in May that year he saw action at the battle of Jutland. He was able to rid himself of some of the frustration which arose from years of having to play second fiddle to his brother, who was not allowed to be anywhere remotely danger- ous while he was in France.

'When I was on top of the turret,' Albert wrote to the Prince of Wales, 'I never felt any fear of shells or anything else. It seems curious but all sense of danger and everything else goes except the one longing of dealing death in every possible way to the enemy.' At last he had a real-life enemy and was able to act out all the suppressed rage generated by boyhood neglect, his resentment of his family, and even jealousy of his older brother, towards the person of the Kaiser (ironically his second cousin), for whom he could express legitimate hatred without fear of reprisal.

As a young adult Bertie began to show signs of addictive behaviour. The dangers of smoking had not yet been recognized, and the number of cigarettes he smoked each day was probably responsible for the arterial disease and the lung cancer which caused his death in 1952. Smoking was then considered a sign of sophistication and virility, a sad irony since it may also have caused George VI to become impotent. He suffered from Buer- ger's disease, in which circulatory obstruction occurs in the arterial supply to the legs and almost certainly results in reduction in the blood supply to the penis, leading to erectile impotence.

In 1916 his duodenal ulcer was diagnosed. His feelings of anger, resentment and jealousy, as well as the cruelty and pain to which he was subjected during his years of childhood neglect, were manifested in a physical illness which 'legitimized', by making publicly acceptable, his mental anguish. The legacy of Mary Peters who, as some historians suggest, provided an unsuit- able and damaging diet, was proving to be something of a time bomb, and the combination of his poor diet and the stressful atmosphere of Bertie's childhood made the development of his ulcer inevitable. (Later he became attracted to a young woman sympathetic to men who had 'suffered'.) Bertie also drank, and came to depend upon alcohol to some degree. He needed his whisky every day to relieve stress and reduce anxiety, although the appropriate time for his oral needs to have been gratified would have been in infancy, when the need for the breast is compulsive and cannot be delayed. It is hard to believe that

Queen Mary satisfied Albert in this respect, since she was more concerned with her own needs than with the comfort and security of her children.

Albert thrived during the First World War, first in the Royal Navy until his gastric problems necessitated his hospitalization, and later in the newly formed RAF until he was discharged from active service on grounds of ill-health. King George V was very conscious of the need to reduce criticism of the Royal Family's role during the war. He discouraged any quick return to civilian life for his two sons and insisted that they did not leave the services until the spring of 1919. There had been some rumblings in the trade union movement vaguely reminiscent, to the sensitive, of the violent anti-monarchism in Russia in 1917 (after which the fate of George's cousin, Tsar Nicholas II, his wife Alexandra and their children, had sent shock waves through the British Royal Family), and malicious rumours had been circulating concerning Albert's frequent and often prolonged periods of sick leave while on war service.

The 'losses' of Albert's childhood (his mother, his nurse, his parents' long and frequent absences, his 'banishment' to Dartmouth) did not augur well for adult life. He made a friend at Dartmouth, Surgeon Lt Louis Greig, who was his tennis and squash partner, and eventually became his equerry, but it was hard for Albert to establish strong bonds of friendship because of his shyness and the difficulties that he had in communicating with others due to his stammer.

When the time came for Bertie to marry, it was inevitable that he would gravitate towards a woman who had grown up with similar parental attitudes and had consequently similar views on performance-related approbation. The young girl who had learned much about cheering up, entertaining and nursing the wounded would not have found it difficult to adapt to caring for Bertie's psychological wounds. In tending these she was simultaneously rewarded by a husband's unflagging devotion, massive public attention and approval, and the wholehearted embrace of the Royal Family. Her childhood had not been marked by cruelty or significant unhappiness but it had been characterized by unintentional neglect. She and Albert saw much of themselves in each other.

He finally won his mother's approval – if not her love – when he became King and Queen Mary deferentially kissed his hand as her monarch. The experience of being second son and second best had been compounded in early adulthood, when Albert began to deputize for Edward at official engagements. With his brother's abdication, he achieved a status which it is possible he had unconsciously wanted since he first realized that he was less important than the heir. Although he may have resented the role that was forced upon him by events, he finally had his mother's approval, and no longer needed to 'please' his father.

Following Edward VIII's abdication, a coldness developed between the two brothers who had previously been so close. When Edward made requests for money and status in exile, George VI was much less obliging than might have been anticipated. He vehemently opposed his brother's petition for his wife to be known as Her Royal Highness, and turned down his application for property, and access to it, in England, as well as for the governorship of Australia. The most he was prepared to concede was governorship of the Bahamas, a sinecure that might have seemed appropriate for a man who liked to work on his tan, but one with which Edward soon became bored and frustrated and which he resented.

The First World War was a watershed for Prince Albert since it established him as an adult whose status was acknowledged for the first time, but the Second World War established his reputation as a wartime leader which may perhaps be explained partly as his identification with the free world in its battle against autocratic tyranny, of which he had had such bitter personal experience, but also by the success of his wife, who was the making of his ultimate popularity.

'A perfect little duck,' said Admiral Beatty.

'The perfect neighbour for a bungalow,' remarked Wallis Simpson.

'The most dangerous woman in Europe,' declared Adolf Hitler. Elizabeth Bowes-Lyon has been patronized and suburbanized, yet Adolf Hitler recognized her power although he might also have over-estimated it.

Elizabeth Bowes-Lyon, born in 1900, was the ninth and second youngest child of the Earl and Countess of Strathmore and Kinghorne. She was referred to as a commoner upon her marriage (as was Lady Diana Spencer), but although she was not royal she was well born. Her popularity with the press and the British people has been attributed to what was falsely regarded as her 'Cinderella' status.

Elizabeth spent an untroubled childhood in the family homes at Glamis in Scotland, Hertfordshire, and Mayfair. Glamis is a fine example of gothic Scottish baronial architecture, complete with turrets, high, narrow, stained-glass windows and fortified stonework. A story persists that at the end of some long, dank passage is a room in which lives the so-called Monster of Glamis, a hairy, egg-shaped creature with spindly legs which has survived, generation after generation, cared for but incarcerated, and from time to time clanking its chains. The legend has the same veracity as that of the Loch Ness monster, but although it was never discussed above stairs, it might have been the subject of staff gossip, rumour, and speculation, during Elizabeth's childhood.

Elizabeth and her younger brother, David, had a bolt-hole which they called the Flea House, in which they hid forbidden chocolate and Woodbines, addictive habits formed very early in their lives. Because of her childhood at Glamis, Elizabeth was to feel at home when she married into a family which harboured its own secrets. Most children enjoy the *frisson* of 'safe' fright – imagined ghosts and the fantasy demons of fairy-tale and theatre. Elizabeth was particularly attracted to the theatre and to dressing-up. She became a consummate role-player; the body language expressed in her gracious hand waves appearing to dismiss the flawed reality of her past.

Elizabeth, like Queen Victoria, and her own daughters, Elizabeth and Margaret Rose, participated in family charades and Christmas pantomimes. She was an extrovert child and enjoyed the limelight, which did not often come her way. By the 1920s it had become acceptable for well-bred young women to work in the theatre, and, had circumstances been different, she might have elected to go on the stage. As it was, she made an outstanding success of her central role in the Royal Family's public performances.

Elizabeth's parents, like those of her husband's grandmother, Alexandra, attached little importance to her education. She went to school for one brief period of a few months and was otherwise taught by governesses. She learned the social graces, a little French, but not much else, and attended lessons with her younger brother David, with whom she had a close, loving relationship. She rarely read a book, developing instead a liking for outdoor pursuits such as riding and walking.

Photographs taken when Elizabeth was young show her to have been a pretty child with thick dark hair, large eyes, and a sweet smile. She remained small, and prone to put on weight. From an early age, Elizabeth Bowes-Lyon used food to fulfil her needs. As a daughter, wife and mother, she craved attention. Her hats are chosen to display, rather than to shade, her face, which she explains by saying that people who make the effort to watch her public duties have a right to get a decent view. Despite her years, her shoes still almost always have high heels, no matter how inappropriate the occasion, nor how unfashionable they might be. High heels obviously make any woman appear taller. In Elizabeth's case they might also have helped encourage in her the stature and importance that she had earlier been denied. Her constant seeking of admiration – even in old age – may reflect her desire, as one of the youngest children in a large family, to be acknowledged.

Her parents were kindly but remote. As the second youngest child, Elizabeth was often solitary, lacking playmates, particularly after her brother David went away to school. The skeleton in *her* cupboard was not the legendary monster, but her lonely child-hood, and a mother who was probably depressed. One of Elizabeth's idolized elder brothers, Alexander, died when she was eleven and her mother forty-nine. A second brother, Fergus, was killed at the battle of Loos when Elizabeth was fourteen, her mother fifty-three, and possibly still suffering from the conse-quences of the menopause. Bereavement after the death of a child is probably more intensely felt than any other grief, so unnatural is it for a parent to survive a child.

During the First World War, when Glamis was converted to a nursing home for wounded officers, Elizabeth was little more than a child. With her limited education now abandoned and her mother in a melancholy decline (which lasted until 1938 when Lady Strathmore died aged seventy-six), she took upon her shoulders the responsibilities of the house. Over thirty wounded officers could convalesce at one time at Glamis. Like any young girl, Elizabeth enjoyed being given responsibility, and particularly welcomed the attention bestowed upon her by her 'heroic' and 'glamorous' young men. She was now able to express her talents and abilities to the full and, while identifying with the sufferers, proved herself to be kind and caring. She was able to absorb her grief at the death of her brothers by helping others to be restored to health.

According to Penelope Mortimer, Elizabeth once took twelve-year-old David, dressed as a girl, round the ward, and introduced him to the patients as her 'cousin'. Perhaps an unconscious wish to defend him from the fate of her elder brothers caused her to represent him as a girl. Using her brother as her alter ego, she was employing him to please grown-ups. Her fondness for dressing-up is a manifestation of dissatisfaction with her true self. Elizabeth is reported to have enjoyed her hospital duties and, with great charm, to have diverted the recuperating soldiers, who were grateful for her attention.

By her mid-teens, she was attracted to men, many of them dependent, like the wounded at Glamis. They brought out her sense of compassion, and furnished her with the attention she had sought, but which had not been forthcoming, in her childhood. Having a captive audience of bedridden and wounded men with whom physical contact was not merely legitimized but essential, she experienced a form of intimacy that was missing from her relationship with her father. It was also contact which placed her in a position of power and superiority. The end of hostilities was as much an anticlimax for Elizabeth as it was for Prince Albert and many others who had thrived on the stimulation and excitement of the war.

Although Elizabeth Bowes-Lyon had few material deprivations while she was growing up, she had been denied the full attention of her parents, the company of children her own age, an education, ongoing nursery care (maids and governesses were constantly changing), the company of her two deceased brothers, and her right to remain a child and to develop at her own pace. Most important of all, she was denied her mother, whom she 'lost' when her brothers died, which resulted in the 'charm' which she used with increasing frequency to gain the attention which, as a child, should have been hers as of right.

After the war she was involved in the traditional débutante

round of dances, balls, parties, and attendances at the Season's fixtures, such as Henley and Ascot. Although Elizabeth may not have been aware of it, Queen Mary was observing this attractive and confident young woman, and considering her as a potential candidate for marriage to Edward, her eldest son. Her approval was sealed when she invited Elizabeth to be a bridesmaid at the marriage of her daughter Mary, the Princess Royal, to Viscount Lascelles. (Elizabeth, however, might have been irked to find that when the official portrait of the wedding group was completed she had not been painted in.) Whether or not it concerned her that the Prince of Wales showed none of the interest in her for which his mother had hoped, is not known. What is known, however, is that during the abdication crisis (in the mid 1930s), the Duchess of York, as by then she had become, was hostile towards him in the manner of a 'woman scorned'.

By the early 1920s Elizabeth had become used to the attention of men, had experienced their gratitude (as she ministered to them in their sick beds), and had read enough newspaper accounts extolling her charm and beauty to turn any girl's head. During the war, Chips Channon had written, 'Everything at Glamis was beautiful, perfect. Being there was like living in a Van Dyck picture . . . I fell madly in love. They all did.' Except for the Prince of Wales.

Realizing that such a suitable bride was worth holding on to, just as she herself had been retained, Queen Mary made Elizabeth aware of her second son, Albert, and encouraged his courtship of her. Elizabeth was prepared to consider him, but she needed repeated proof of Bertie's love and did not make things easy for him. In making him work so hard to win her hand, she revealed her low self-esteem. Perhaps, too, she was unsure that she wanted to marry him. In any event, she needed to reassure herself that her future husband was committed to her and she made him jump through a series of hoops before she accepted him. Albert proposed to Elizabeth on three separate occasions. On the first two he was turned down. Although disappointed, he did not consider looking elsewhere and his persistence was ultimately rewarded – but only after Elizabeth had made absolutely sure of his devotion to her. Robert Lacey writes of Elizabeth's exacting standards: '. . . one immensely attractive man, the son of a neighbour, kept on trying. But he also had flirtations in between, and she wouldn't have that . . . More than any of her friends she knew what she wanted and that was absolute purity,' that is, absolute and unadulterated love.

What Elizabeth wanted was the unconditional love that a daughter has the right to expect from a father. She needed to be certain that she would receive this from her husband. No suitor who was the least bit 'shop-soiled' would do for her. Previous interest in a woman meant immediate disqualification. She had to be 'number one', to take top-billing, and to be totally accepted.

At the time of Albert's proposals, Elizabeth had a great many admirers, notably the Honourable James Stuart, a friend of Prince Albert, who was 'diplomatically' given an overseas posting when the Prince decided that he wanted to marry her. He needed all the persistence for which he had been praised at Dartmouth, before she accepted him, just over two years after their first meeting as adults. Elizabeth's distanced relationship with her father and the losses of her adolescence had led her to doubt the permanence of male affection. Originally, too, she had had doubts concerning the demands and pressures that being a member of the Royal Family might bring. However, eventually she told him, humorously, that if he was going to pursue her indefinitely, she might as well say yes. A delighted Albert, who had informed his parents of his intentions vis-à-vis Elizabeth, and who knew that for once his enterprise had their full support, sent them a tersely worded triumphant telegram: 'All right. Bertie.'

Elizabeth so charmed the frequently testy George V that he even looked tolerantly upon her habitual unpunctuality, and conceded to his son that he was lucky to have won her. She entered married life with the approval of her in-laws in addition to the devotion of her husband. Whatever reservations she may have had about her gauche, stammering, and emotionally disabled prince, Elizabeth was sure at least that she was treasured and cherished by him. She was also immediately embraced by the British people. They welcomed the panoply of her wedding in the post-war period of gloom and austerity, just as they were to welcome the marriage of her daughter, Elizabeth, to Prince Philip, shortly after the Second World War in 1947. Elizabeth's ongoing love affair with the public, who regarded her as 'one of them', contributed to the popularity that, as Queen Elizabeth the Queen Mother, she enjoys to this day.

In marrying Elizabeth, Bertie had at last done the 'right thing', and done it before his elder brother. When the wedding celebrations were over, however, Elizabeth might have felt that her life was undergoing another anticlimax. She had a series of 'minor illnesses', not the least of which was the pneumonia which blighted her honeymoon in Scotland, after which, it is said, on most mornings she stayed in bed until eleven. Her behaviour seems to have been that of a woman who was depressed, and although the birth of her two daughters increased her popularity, and that of her husband, her life seemed a see-saw of excitement and boredom during the early years of her marriage.

The popularity of the Duke and Duchess of York was enhanced by three seminal events. The births of Elizabeth and Margaret Rose, the abdication crisis – from which the Duke emerged as a reluctant but selfless hero – and the Second World War.

No one was more surprised than the plump little 'Queen' of Glamis – wife of the untrained tortoise who overtook the hare – when she became Queen of England. Like Lady Macbeth, however, she rose magnificently to the challenge. By her resolve she strengthened the purpose of her stuttering, self-conscious husband, and made of him an effective wartime leader and king.

When the Duke and Duchess of York were married, in 1923, neither had reason to suppose that Albert would accede to the throne. The Prince of Wales was still young and it was supposed that he would marry and have children. The Yorks' wedding – in the light of the Prince of Wales's seeming disinclination to find a bride – proved a popular and welcome diversion. When Princess Elizabeth was born, in 1926, and again when Princess Margaret Rose was born, in 1930, the Duke and his wife might have hoped for a son, but the 'happy family' that they and their daughters represented provided a reassuring example to the nation. Through the increasing number of illustrated periodicals and newsreels, their lives were followed with interest. The activities of the Yorks became an industry, and when their faces were reproduced on everything from mugs to the covers of magazines – sales soared.

At last Elizabeth was receiving the adulation she had always craved. Her husband doted on her, and her father-in-law – mellowing in late middle age – expressed affection for her which previously he had been able to give only to his daughter Mary.

The British people, enchanted by the Duchess and her daughters, provided her with even more fondness and trust.

Elizabeth, the actress, took to the limelight and public acclamation and revelled in it. She might have kept her husband waiting before she accepted his proposal – possibly in retaliation for having had to wait for love in her childhood – but by giving birth to their daughters, she enhanced his public image and his sense of self-esteem. Recognizing in Albert her source of love she grappled him to her soul with hoops of steel.

After their marriage and until the outbreak of the Second World War, the Yorks had few official duties and led undemanding lives. The Duchess followed the example of her mother-in-law and accompanied her husband on visits around the empire, leaving her daughters at home with their grandparents and nurses. This provided her with the necessary stimulation to counter any depression and simultaneously gave her opportunities to shine. Like Queen Mary, Elizabeth also needed the 'fix' of public approbation. She no longer needed to 'seduce' her husband, but, like all seductive people, her need for approval and reassurance might have been stronger than that for sexual satisfaction. In danger of slipping into an apathy after the early years of her marriage, Elizabeth elected to neglect her children in pursuit of the gratification of public esteem. It was perhaps as a result of this that after he became king, George VI formed an unusually close relationship with their elder daughter, Elizabeth.

Until the abdication of Edward VIII, the young Princess was not considered to have particular constitutional importance. Her father had, however, always lavished more affection and attention on her than had previous royal fathers on their children. King George V, when he was elderly and unwell, was similarly captivated by the Princess, and had requested her presence during the long period of recuperation after one of his last illnesses. Princess Elizabeth's significance for her father echoed that of Princess Mary to George V, and of 'Pussy' to Prince Albert. To a lesser extent it was the forerunner of Prince Philip's relationship with Princess Anne. The Duke of York's daughter, apparently with no future constitutional role to play, was able to be loved and indulged, rather than disciplined and trained, as she might have been had a crystal ball been available.

Later, the King showed his reluctance to accept that Elizabeth was independent of him. He resisted her wish to participate in the war effort as a uniformed member of ATS. He obstructed her engagement to Prince Philip, then insisted on a long and painful separation, while she accompanied the family to South Africa for several months following the Second World War. On her marriage he wrote a touching letter which exposes a father's sorrow at losing his much-loved daughter to another man. '. . . I have watched you grow up all these years with pride under the skilful direction of Mummy, who as you know is the most marvellous person in the world in my eyes, & I can, I know, always count on you and now Philip, to help us in our work . . . I can see that you are sublimely happy with Philip which is right but don't forget us is the wish of your ever loving and devoted Papa.'

Queen Elizabeth II had every reason to be confident in her father's love.

CHAPTER EIGHT

Queen Elizabeth II
and Prince Philip

Forty glorious years.

Queen Elizabeth II had a stable childhood and enjoyed a warm, loving relationship with at least one of her parents. The chain of psychological damage inherited from her ancestors, however, appears to remain unbroken and is reflected in the breakdown of her children's marriages and the apparent inability of her youngest son to form any relationship at all.

Although neither blame nor responsibility for the current crisis in the Royal Family can be laid directly at her door, it seems remarkable that not one of her sons, nor her daughter, has yet been able to leave behind their dysfunctional legacies to produce integrated families of their own.

When Elizabeth Alexandra Mary was born on 21 April 1926, at the home of her parents, the Duke and Duchess of York, in Bruton Street, off Piccadilly in London, she was third in line to the throne. Both her parents and her grandparents were delighted, Queen Mary overcoming her displeasure that the baby had not been born in Buckingham Palace. The British people took Princess Elizabeth to their hearts, and they have, for the most part, continued to admire and remain loyal to her ever since.

When Sarah Ferguson, also a Duchess of York, had *her* first daughter in 1988, the birth of Princess Beatrice did not arouse the same level of interest as that of her grandmother, whose day-to-day progress was, from the first, keenly followed in many parts of the world.

The excitement generated by Elizabeth's birth continued throughout her childhood as the public clamoured for news and photographs of her. She was pretty and photogenic. Her style of dress was widely copied as were many of her activities, in particular her much publicized membership of the Girl Guides. She led a healthy outdoor existence and her family life seemed happy. This 'family image' assumed great public importance during the late 1920s and 1930s when the life of the Royal Family provided a welcome antidote to the social and economic problems of the time.

The First World War had left Britain exhausted and drab. Although it had been instrumental in raising the status of women, resulting eventually in an emancipation from which they have never looked back, the population was both depressed and resentful that victory had not provided the improvement in their lives which they had been led to believe would take place – life was, if anything, harder. The 'all pull together' spirit had evaporated, there was no longer a legitimate enemy for the expression of negative feelings, and war-time excuses for severe shortages and hardship no longer applied. The continued existence of a wealthy and privileged nucleus of socialites did little to comfort the embittered majority.

The Royal Family, however, the embodiment of both the glorious past and the recent victory, escaped this contumely, and remained popular. The hunger, unemployment, and poverty of Britons who waited patiently for a sight of the green and pleasant land seemed more endurable in the dazzling light of the monarch. But with millions out of work, inadequate social services, and very little to lighten the gloom, the Royal Family could provide only a modicum of relief.

The birth of Princess Elizabeth was seen as a symbol of a bright future, a promise of better times, the hope that the post-war period was drawing to a close and prosperity was on the horizon. Yet with the 1926 general strike and the Jarrow hunger march still to come, the bleak years were far from over. Public attention was temporarily diverted by interest in the little Princess. The charming self-assurance with which she came to deal with their adulation was to ensure the enduring devotion of her subjects.

Princess Elizabeth, however, with her gravitas and dignity, was more than an attractive royal 'starlet'. (Both she and her near contemporary Shirley Temple captivated their audiences in child-hood and were later to become 'ambassadors' of their people.) Winston Churchill met the Princess at Balmoral and wrote to his wife: 'There is no one here at all except the family, the household and P. Elizabeth age 2. The latter is a character. She has an air of authority and reflectiveness astonishing in an infant.'

Elizabeth had the attention of her parents when time permitted, and the unqualified affection of her paternal grandparents – by whom she was referred to as 'the bambino [*sic*]'. Her grandfather, George V, asked for her to be with him while he was recovering from his penultimate illness at Bognor and he said that the child was a tonic for him. He would allow her to tug his beard and would go down on all fours so that Elizabeth could pretend that he was her pony while she 'rode' on his back. No adult had played like this with him when he was a child, and neither had he frolicked so with his own children. Now, however, skipping a generation, he found himself able to take an interest in his grandchildren, and that he *was* able to give love and affection to a child, just as Edward and Alexandra had with their grandchildren. Princess Elizabeth appreciated this attention from a father figure who was both available and loving. Her own father was loving, but was only intermittently available.

During the 1930s the monarchy was fortunate – or astute – in the timing of its pageants. In 1934 the stage-managed marriage of George, Duke of Kent to Princess Marina of Greece had been warmly received. In 1935, with the economy still depressed, the Silver Jubilee of King George V provided a welcome distraction from the struggle for survival. Both events were outdone by the coronation of King George VI and Queen Elizabeth in 1937.

For Princess Elizabeth, sadness at the death of the old King in 1936 and the trauma of his funeral procession (with the lying-in-state at Westminster Abbey), was shortly followed by the abdication crisis. Now, briefly transcending fears of another war in Europe, came the ultimate in spectacle in Westminster Abbey which was broadcast: a new, respected young king, his popular wife, and their two pretty daughters reflected once again hope for stability and security.

Princess Elizabeth held centre stage for four years before her sister Margaret Rose was born in 1930. Charles Higham, one of her biographers, suggests that Elizabeth was in danger of being slightly spoilt and had a tendency towards imperiousness. Bored, as her mother chatted to a female visitor, the three-year-old Princess rang for a footman and said, 'Kindly ring for a taxi. Our guest is leaving!' Charles Higham asserts that this imperiousness prevailed after Elizabeth succeeded to the throne, enquiring of slouching courtiers if they were unwell and, upon being reassured that they were not, reproving them for failing to maintain the bearing expected by a Sovereign.

As a child, Princess Elizabeth preferred to play with soldiers rather than dolls, which might have reflected her parents' disappointment that she had not turned out to be a son. Although she enjoyed outdoor pursuits, Elizabeth was by no means a tomboy, and was – possibly influenced by her mother – both feminine and fashion conscious. She even became – far more than any subsequent royal child – a trendsetter. For decades after her own early girlhood generations of children of both sexes were dressed in fitted, double-breasted overcoats, often made of bluish-grey herringbone tweed and almost always featuring velvet revers. Her full-skirted dresses with puffed sleeves, little lace collars and a sash at the waist remained the basic model for little girls' frocks until well into the 1960s when fashions for children began subtly to change in parallel with a burgeoning youth cult. The Queen Mother has seldom been associated with 'fashion', but, like Queen Mary, she enjoyed wearing ceremonial robes, had a taste for 'Winterhalter-style' ball-gowns and a passion for jewellery. On a brief visit to Paris in 1938, she took with her fifty trunks of clothes and £7 million worth of jewels. Her daughter Elizabeth was subsequently to establish a close connection with her mother's favourite dressmaker, Norman Hartnell.

When Princess Elizabeth was eight months old, she was left in the care of her nurse for five months while her parents visited Australia. Such neglect would justifiably attract criticism today, but in the 1920s it was unremarkable among the higher echelons of society, as it is to a lesser extent now.

Elizabeth's parental care may indeed have been intermittent, but it was genuinely affectionate, and she had, too, the constant support and devotion of surrogates. Her nurse, Alla, Clara Knights, cared for her throughout her babyhood and was assisted by 'Bobo', Margaret MacDonald, the nurserymaid, who today is the Queen's dresser. Both women overlapped with Marion Crawford – 'Crawfie' – who came into the household when Elizabeth was five and her sister still a baby.

Miss Crawford's first encounter with the Princess was in the night nursery. The child had tied her dressing gown cord to her bedposts and was holding the ends as if they were the reins of a carriage-horse. She solemnly informed her future governess that she usually took her horses for a drive round the garden before going to sleep. Crawfie stayed with the family, as teacher, friend, and adviser, until Margaret was eighteen. In 1950 she published *The Little Princesses*, which, unlike *Diana: Her True Story* published forty-two years later, was regarded as little less than treason, breaching as it did the Palace's code of 'discretion', then more moral than official, and resulted in her disgrace.

When Crawfie first met Elizabeth, she immediately assumed responsibility for her. Margaret Rose was still a baby in the care of Alla and Crawfie was able to establish a strong bond with Elizabeth before her sister joined them in the schoolroom. Marion Crawford always showed a preference for the elder sister. She states that 'Elizabeth was the better scholar, the sweeter-natured, the more natural swimmer and rider, had a better figure.' Margaret Rose, she concedes, could be bright, charming, disarming and quick-witted, but in her book all the more dignified virtues are ascribed to Elizabeth. Her account of life in the royal household has the Princesses invariably laughing and playing in their parents' rooms for an hour or so each morning, before lessons began. As we have already seen, some historians have noted that Queen Elizabeth seldom rose before eleven: it seems possible that the girls received less attention from their mother than was suggested by Crawfie, who also maintains that, on the rare occasions when both parents were at home, the family had lunch and tea together. The Princesses certainly saw a great deal more of their parents than was customary in the Royal Family, but the portrait which Miss Crawford painted was the one she thought the public wanted, rather than a true account of what took place. Such wholesome depictions were commonly used in the advertising of the time to promote family products such as Ovaltine and Hovis: a cosy hearth before which Father reads and Mother sews, while at their feet the children complete jigsaw puzzles and listen to the wireless. The Royal Family and their life at home seem to have inspired such images.

The Duke and Duchess of York had decided that their daughters were to be brought up and educated in an ordinary way. The Princesses' childhood, though, was only ordinary in so far as it was devoid of the abuse suffered by their father, and included only those aspects of their mother's childhood which she considered sound and healthy. Lessons usually finished at lunchtime, and outdoor activities were encouraged as well as work in the schoolroom.

As an adult, Elizabeth felt happiest with her dogs and her horses. Dorothy Laird wrote in 1959 that Elizabeth had once said that when she grew up, she would like to be 'a lady living in the country with lots of horses and dogs'. Her sister was different. Margaret Rose's enthusiasms then as now – ballet, opera, theatre – took place indoors and in the dark. The only outdoor pursuit which she is known to enjoy today is sunbathing (in the West Indies). As many biographers have noted, Elizabeth was always neat and tidy, apparently conforming to the structured upbringing in which she felt secure. Since the Duke and Duchess of York did not accede to the throne until she was ten years old, Elizabeth had their love and much of their attention at the most critical times in her development. She was adored by her grandparents and her nannies, but George VI and his queen were themselves the victims of loveless childhoods and repercussions were inevitably felt by their daughters.

'No one ever had employers who interfered so little,' wrote Marion Crawford. 'I had the feeling that the Duke and Duchess, most happy in their own married life, were not over-concerned with the higher education of their daughters.' Crawfie was writing with gratitude for the free hand which she was given in matters of the girls' education, but what seemed to her to be a commendable lack of 'interference' could be interpreted as a lack of interest, especially in the case of Margaret Rose who was not, unlike her sister, required to take lessons in constitutional history with the Vice-provost of Eton, Sir Henry Marton. Elizabeth's strong sense of duty and destiny was instilled in her by her father and her grandmother. It was Queen Mary who saw to it that she learnt to appreciate art and culture. Margaret Rose did not receive the same intensive tuition.

As they grew up, Elizabeth wore stockings, while Margaret was still in socks, and in the more formal portraits Elizabeth had two rows of pearls to Margaret's one. Princess Elizabeth not only had new clothes, while her sister often wore her cast-offs, but was treated preferentially in every way. She grew up with greater self-confidence, greater self-esteem, and more assurance than her sister. Even Betty Vacani, their dancing teacher, reported that while Margaret was 'quicksilver', Elizabeth was 'pure gold', and she was always to outshine her sister.

Of course vigorous sibling rivalry will exist in any healthy family and it was only normal and logical that a four-year age difference between sisters would lead to different routines, bed-times, clothes, lessons and privileges. Realistically the six-year-old Margaret Rose could not have been treated in exactly the same way as the ten-year-old Elizabeth. However, when it suited their parents – for the purposes of portraiture or public appearance – the sisters were presented as if they were twins. This habit of treating the two eldest siblings near-identically had been perpetuated within the Royal Family since Victoria and Albert robbed their heir and Prince Alfred of separate identities by ensuring that their upbringings were parallel for many years. In retrospect Margaret would doubtless agree that her elder sister should have received small recognitions of her superior age – wearing stockings instead of socks, two strings of pearls instead of one – but at the time (and having often been presented as half of a pair), the younger Princess would probably have felt puzzled and deprived while Elizabeth's confidence and sense of self-importance would have become firmly established.

Queen Elizabeth II's manner of dress has remained more or less static since her coronation in 1953. Her hairstyle, clothes, and general appearance, adopted in early adult life when she believed she was loved for herself, have altered little. After the upheavals of marriage and motherhood, the loss of her father and grandparents, and the stress of the coronation itself, she seems to have put change behind her.

Margaret's fashion-conscious appearance, by contrast, reflects both the times and the expectations of others, and she relies on external factors to compensate for the imbalance of childhood which resulted in her sister's self-confidence and her own lack of self-esteem. Both girls enjoyed dressing-up and Margaret's interest in theatre has persisted into adulthood. The Queen, however, while dutifully attending premières and galas, has never seemed seriously interested in the performing arts;

Princess Margaret looks admiringly at an umbrella at the British Industries Fair in London in 1953. But the true object of her affection, Group Captain Peter Townsend, the man she was forbidden to marry, remains in the background. (Hulton-Deutsch Collection)

Top: In 1954 Prince Charles, prematurely self-sufficient at the age of six, acknowledges his status from the back seat of his personal chauffeur-driven limousine. (Hulton–Deutsch Collection)

Bottom: Prince Charles does not live up to his father's expectations on the polo field at Windsor Great Park in 1965. (Syndication International)

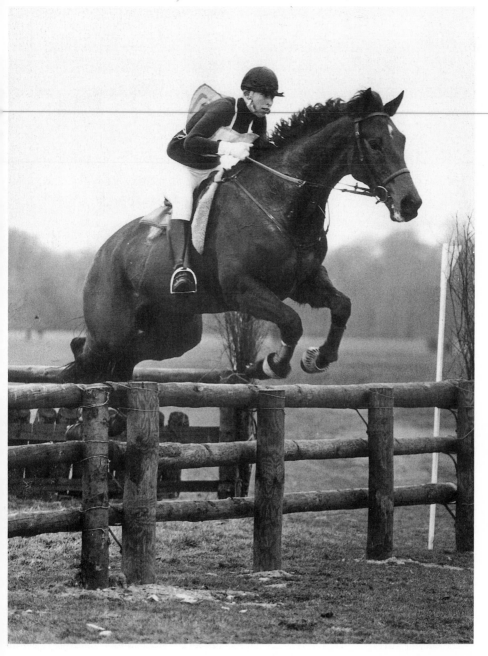

In 1975 Princess Anne is completely at one with her horse (and probably by extension with her father) at Windsor Horse Trials. (Hulton-Deutsch Collection)

Elizabeth II poses for her official portrait to commemorate her Silver Jubilee in 1977. She carries her ubiquitous handbag, a universal symbol of security. (Hulton-Deutsch Collection)

Left: An acceptable face of public grief. The Queen's horse loses in the 1985 Epsom Derby. (Syndication International)

Right: Princess Margaret seems indifferent to her fate as she smokes a forbidden cigarette shortly after major lung surgery in 1985. (Syndication International)

Left: A happy but apprehensive Diana 'under arrest' on her engagement to Charles in 1981. (Hulton-Deutsch Collection)

Right: A less than wholehearted embrace as Prince Charles leaves his fiancée for the first time for a five-week tour abroad in 1981. (Syndication International)

Left: An early revelation by Diana in 1981. More devastating ones came later. (Rex Features)

Right: Diana has sat on the bonnet of Charles's sports car, severely denting his ego, at Smith's Lawn, Windsor, in June 1987. (Syndication International)

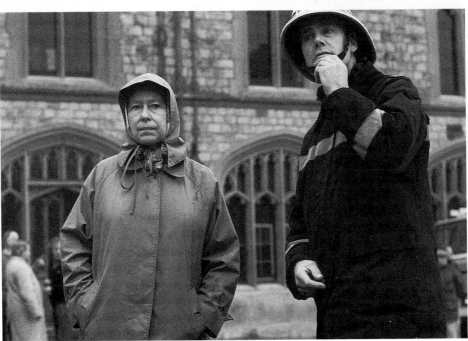

Top: Princess Beatrice is born to the Duke and Duchess of York in 1988. Sarah only has eyes for her new baby. (Syndication International)

Bottom: A sad Queen Elizabeth the day after Windsor Castle was severely damaged by fire in November 1992. A few weeks later the House of Windsor was shaken by the breakdown of her son's marriage to the Princess of Wales. (Press Association Photo Library) she is, however, the custodian of a magnificent private art collection.

At the time of the abdication crisis Elizabeth was still a child. Her secure upbringing had prepared her, psychologically, for her forthcoming role. She was by nature a serious, rather shy girl, who had, none the less, acquired a strong sense of her own importance: she had been allowed at the age of nine to say goodbye to the dying George V. She was about to move from a childhood which had been dominated by adult companionship into an adolescence and early adulthood which spanned both the abdication crisis and the Second World War.

Elizabeth emerged as a young woman primed for her destiny. The circumstances of this, extraordinary by any standards, meant that her mothering of her four children has not been entirely successful. Like her forebears, Elizabeth II has put duty to her country before continuing attention to her children. Queen Mary was probably right when she said of her granddaughter, 'There's something very steadfast and determined in her.' These qualities, however, reflect inflexibility, not a trait likely to enhance the nurturing of one's children.

Between 1937 and 1940, Elizabeth's life underwent rapid change. Apart from the onset of her own adolescence, her uncle David had been exiled, her father was now king, and she was expected to curtsy to him whenever he entered the room. King George VI was as fond of his elder daughter as he ever had been, but he now had other things to think about. The family moved into Buckingham Palace (where it took five minutes to walk from the nursery quarters to the garden) from their comfortable home at 145 Piccadilly. The King began to educate Elizabeth in affairs of state and instruct her in her future responsibilities. For the first months of the Second World War in later 1939 the Princesses were separated from their parents. They stayed in Scotland with Crawfie, then moved to Windsor where they were visited by the King and Queen whenever possible at weekends. Despite this splitting up of the Royal Family, its public image – guarding hearth and home and refusing to compromise the values for which the nation was fighting – was a powerful and inspiring one. If the popularity of the monarchy had been dealt a blow by the abdication crisis, it recovered public esteem during the war.

Elizabeth blossomed under her father's care and tuition, which increased throughout the war years. Having been taught to drive when she was seventeen, she joined the ATS, taking a driving and vehicle maintenance training course at Aldershot. She qualified as a driver in April 1945 and was promoted to junior commander in July. She visited factories, broadcast to the children of Britain, and was colonel-in-chief of the Grenadier Guards. Margaret, once again, was relegated to second place.

At the end of the war George VI commented that the 'poor darlings' had not had any fun yet. While it is true that the excitement of a Season, parties, balls and frivolities were denied to Elizabeth during the war, she had had the heady substitute of involvement in the national drama. Margaret, accustomed to sharing activities with her sister, had not. And by the time the war was over Elizabeth had fallen in love.

Aged thirteen, she had first met Prince Philip in 1939, when he was eighteen and a cadet at Dartmouth. Marion Crawford records that she was immediately impressed by this handsome, fair-haired distant cousin. When the Royal Yacht sailed away from Dartmouth, accompanied by a flotilla of small boats, one cadet followed its progress far out into the open sea. The oarsman was said to have been Philip of Greece, and the Princess is reported to have stood at the stern of the yacht with her binoculars trained upon him. Prince Philip has said that the story is exaggerated, but that this was the occasion on which the couple first met is not disputed.

Despite his nickname 'Phil the Greek', Philip's ancestors are Danish and German, and he has no Greek blood. His family survived the turmoil of nineteenth- and early twentieth-century Greece when, having rid themselves of their own monarchy, the Greeks offered the throne to princes from elsewhere in Europe. Their first choice was Alfred, Queen Victoria's second son, but he declined. Eventually Prince William of Denmark, encouraged by his parents, accepted the throne, and became King George of the Hellenes. He and his Russian wife Olga had seven children; their second youngest son, Andrew, was Philip's father.

Prince Andrew had been imprisoned and then exiled when his brother, the King, was deposed in 1922. He was told that he was lucky his life had been spared and that only the intervention of his cousin King George V had saved him. The Greek dictator,

General Pangalos, had personally driven him to the quayside where he embarked on the naval cruiser, HMS *Calypso*, which had been sent by Britain's foreign secretary, Lord Curzon, to rescue him and his family. They sailed to Corfu (then a British protectorate), where the year-old Philip, his mother, born Princess Alice of Battenberg, four elder sisters and their entirely female staff lived in a small house named Mon Repos. Philip is said to have been carried on to the ship in an orange-box and, leaving most of their possessions behind, the family went to Brindisi, in Italy. They took the train to Paris where Prince Andrew, tiring now of his increasingly deaf wife, with whom he was unable to share much conversation, rapidly found distracting companionship. He spent much of his time on the French Riviera, in particular in Monaco where he was usually to be found in the casino.

Like George V and his siblings, Philip suffered the disadvantage of his mother being unable to hear him. He learned to communicate with her in sign language which was less likely to encourage intimacy. Since his father was both feckless and largely absent, parental input was minimal. All of Philip's sisters were much older than he, the youngest was seven years his senior, and all eventually married German princelings. When the possibility of his marriage to Princess Elizabeth was under discussion, soon after the end of the Second World War, this caused some embarrassment. Stateless exiles, Philip and his family had 'settled' in Paris, with other wealthy, dispossessed relatives from the fragmented royal families of Europe, although they also spent long periods in Switzerland, Bucharest, Bavaria, and on the French Riviera. After a brief stay near the Bois de Boulogne, they went to live at St Cloud, outside Paris, in the lodge of a mansion owned by Prince Andrew's brother, George, married to Princess Marie Bonaparte. This aunt-by-marriage, a disciple of Sigmund Freud, was both glamorous and rich; she was kind and generous, too, to Philip and his family, but could, however, have passed confusing messages to the child: she represented stability, security, and comfort at the same time as an alluring Bohemianism.

Nurse Roose, Philip's nanny, was English but had none the less been baptized in the Greek Orthodox Church. It was she who made sure that he could communicate with his mother. He could speak English, German and French but no Greek. Nurse Roose as much as anyone wanted to ensure that he grew up to understand the ways of an English gentleman, and the support of the Milford Haven family, the English branch of the Mountbattens, ensured that this would take place. Roose had prepared Philip for integration with his relatives and for probable education in Britain. Philip's family depended heavily on the goodwill of relatives, including the Milford Havens, who passed their clothes down to Philip's sisters. The family was also supported by royal relatives in Romania. Philip formed friendships with his uncle George's two daughters; the company he kept was almost exclusively female. The Milford Havens were, by most standards, an unconventional aristocratic family. Uncle George, the Marquis of Milford Haven, was married to an exotic beauty, Nada, who was widely believed to be a lesbian and the lover of her sister-in-law Lady Louis Mountbatten, and he was a collector of erotica, kept in the library at Lynden Manor.

By normal standards Philip's extended family was far from poor and the children were educated privately. Philip attended the Elms, an infant school mainly for American children in St Cloud. It cannot have been pleasant, however, for the family to live on charity, and this must have been a confusing time for Philip. He had a mother who was unable to listen to him, displaced (if dazzling) princesses around him, and a father who was increasingly absent. According to Tim Heald's recent biography, however, Philip denied that he felt disorientated, and he dismissed any idea that the upheavals of his childhood could possibly have affected him.

By the time Philip was eight, it was decided – partly because of the absence of male role models in his life – that he should be sent to school in England. He went to Cheam and during the holidays he often stayed at the home of George Milford Haven. When Philip was ten, the family home at St Cloud broke up. His sisters had all married within a year, between 1931 and 1932, his mother entered a sanatorium and then returned to Athens to do charitable work.

Philip's 'homes' became the German castles of his married sisters. His sister Theodora, the wife of Berthold, Margrave of Baden, made him especially welcome and it seemed natural that Philip should continue his education in Salem, close to Baden.

The school had been founded by the revolutionary educational-ist–philosopher Kurt Hahn, and aimed to bring out the best in boys by inspiring self-confidence and moral strength through physical training. A strong body would, in theory, generate a healthy mental attitude to life, *mens sana in corpore sano*. Physical fearlessness would lead to intellectual bravery. Hahn was a Jew, and vehemently opposed to Nazism, although his German upbringing encouraged parallels between his own aims and the Nazi motto 'Strength through Joy'. He was forced to leave Salem and, in 1934, founded a similar school, Gordonstoun, in Moray-shire, Scotland, where Philip was one of its first pupils.

He thrived at Gordonstoun, excelling in sailing, climbing, cricket, and athletics, and took part in school dramas. By the time he left at the age of eighteen, he was Guardian, or head boy. Throughout these years, George Milford Haven and other rela-tives ensured that Philip was cared for during the school holidays when he was unable to get back to Germany. Whether he became acquainted with Milford Haven's collection of pornographic books – *Raped on the Railway*, *A Tale of the Birch*, and *Lady Gay: Sparkling Tales of Fun and Flagellation* – is not known.

Lord Louis Mountbatten was to influence his nephew's life profoundly. As Philip entered his late teens Mountbatten seemed to assume the role of *in loco parentis* from his brother George. Both Philip's childhood and early adulthood were shaped by brothers who had no sons of their own and who might have seen him as representative of the continuation of their dynasty and have planned accordingly. Mountbatten had supported Edward VIII during the abdication crisis but with his charm and extra-ordinary good looks, he and his wife, Edwina, had retained their popularity with the rest of the Royal Family. A distinguished naval career before and during the Second World War also helped. George VI, however, was reluctant to support Mountbatten's plans for a match between Princess Elizabeth and his nephew, first put forward in 1944 but possibly conceived some years earlier. Certainly it was Mountbatten who enabled Philip to enter Dartmouth Naval College at the age of eighteen, although few pupils were admitted if they had not begun their training at Osborne at the age of eleven, and Philip's German connections were not in his favour. Later, when the war was over, and Philip had relinquished any claim to the throne of Greece, and adopted the anglicized version of his mother's name – Mountbatten – his engagement to Elizabeth was announced. It was remarkable that this was achieved in spite of the existence of his close German relatives.*

In any case, it had been Mountbatten who arranged that Philip, the eighteen-year-old cadet, should entertain the Princesses Elizabeth and Margaret on the occasion that their parents visited Dartmouth in 1939. From that day her future with Philip was sealed.

Princess Elizabeth and Prince Philip met again at a Christmas party in 1943. Afterwards, the seventeen-year-old Princess kept a photograph of the dazzlingly handsome Prince – with full naval beard and moustache – in her room. The two corresponded and, after the war, Philip began to visit Elizabeth at Buckingham Palace. He came frequently to have supper with her, invariably joined by Margaret. Occasionally the three of them would go out together.

In autumn 1946, King George and Queen Elizabeth invited Philip to join their party at Balmoral. The visit lasted about a month, but no engagement announcement was forthcoming. The King, in particular, was anxious that because of the sheltered life Elizabeth had led, she should make the right choice of marriage partner. Both parents were concerned lest she fall too hastily for the first young man to court her.

Elizabeth and Philip were, in fact, allowed to become *unofficially* engaged, but it was announced, almost at once, that both Princesses were to accompany their parents on a cruise to South Africa early in 1947. This four-month absence would provide the 'cooling off' period it was felt that Elizabeth needed. Her parents did not want her to marry before her twenty-first birthday. Elizabeth remained firm in her determination to marry Philip, and their engagement was formally announced in July 1947. They were married on 19 November, and a year later their first son, Charles, was born, followed, less than two years afterwards in August 1950, by Princess Anne.

* Mountbatten was elated to see his family name enter Britain's constitutional records, albeit briefly, when his nephew married Princess Elizabeth. Shortly after the marriage it was decided that the family name would be simply Windsor but for a brief period it was, in fact, Mountbatten-Windsor. Years later he hoped for a marriage between his grand-daughter, Amanda Knatchbull, and Prince Charles but this was not to be.

A newspaper poll, taken at the time of their engagement, showed that 40 per cent of the population was opposed to the match: Philip was foreign, he had German relatives (his sisters were not allowed to attend the wedding), and Britain was involved in acrimonious negotiations with a new government in Greece. Despite his distinguished war record – at twenty-three Philip had been the youngest first lieutenant in the Royal Navy and had his own command – he was not seen as a suitable partner for the Princess. Perhaps it was his negative image, together with a need to prove that he was a man to be taken on his own terms, which decided Philip, once his wife was crowned, to become anything but a deferential consort.

Until the Queen's coronation Philip pursued his career in the Navy with notable success. He was promoted to Lieutenant Commander at the age of twenty-nine, and in 1953 was appointed an Admiral of the Fleet. Having been so much more than husband and father, the role of consort was not one which could have appealed to him. Although he was soon retired from naval duties he continued to be involved in activities which allowed him to be out of the country for long periods. His opening of the Melbourne Olympic Games in 1956, for instance, incorporated a four-month-long detour to study the wildlife in remote islands, which were by no means on a direct sea route from Britain. It was at around this time that rumours began to circulate about Philip's interest in women other than the Queen. A well-known French cabaret singer was said to be his most regular companion. She named her daughter Charlotte. Later there were suggestions that he was involved with a distinguished actress. However, in 1992, when asked about the rumours of his infidelity by Fiammetta Rocca in the *Independent on Sunday*, he said, 'Have you ever stopped to think that for the last 40 years, I have never moved anywhere without a policeman accompanying me? So how the *hell* could I get away with anything like that?'

The Duke of Edinburgh, as he had been known since shortly before his marriage, had been able to restore his sense of self-esteem by being in command of a ship. He had become used to travelling – if not drifting – throughout his childhood and adolescence, and felt at home on the sea. His private rooms now are as sparsely, neatly, and plainly furnished as a ship's cabin, echoing the cold formality of his childhood – in marked contrast to the swags, drapes, pastel colours, and clutter preferred by his wife.

His prolonged absences, however, were not compatible with attentive fatherhood: he was absent for six of Prince Charles's first eight birthdays, and for several of Princess Anne's earliest ones. Having had little experience of conventional family life himself, and having suppressed the memory of his own traumatic childhood, he was not really in touch with the needs of children.

The Queen, re-enacting *her* childhood, spent long periods away from her children, although she made a point of telephoning them every day. Even so, first as a princess and later as queen, she showed little hesitation in leaving her children in the charge of others. Apart from the long and, arguably, 'essential' tours throughout the Commonwealth, Princess Elizabeth toured Northern Ireland when her son was only a few months old, remained in Malta (with her husband) when Charles had tonsillitis in 1950 (before the availability of broad-spectrum antibiotics this was considered quite a serious condition), and later that year left her two-day-old daughter Anne in London while she attended Princess Margaret's birthday celebrations at Balmoral. She left both children, and her sick father, the following year, when she and Philip took Canada by storm on a highly successful visit. After her coronation, the new Queen embarked upon yet another tour, this time of six months' duration, when as 'mother' of the peoples of the Commonwealth, she was obliged to show herself. Her biological children were the victims of her long absences and, like her great-great-grandmother Queen Victoria, Queen Elizabeth II was demonstrating that she was a better 'mother' to her subjects than to her own flesh and blood. Prince Philip had had a poor role model on which to base his paternal instincts, and had been given, in his childhood, what was thought to have been good for him, which included Gordonstoun. Later he asserted his limited authority by sending his three sons there, against the wishes of the Queen, who had preferred the idea of Eton – sometimes referred to as her 'local comprehensive'. Philip applauded physical activity, but had little understanding of, or interest in, the emotional or intellectual aspects of child-rearing. His daughter, Anne, happened to get on with him better than anyone because she seemed intuitively to understand this and took up many of his outdoor interests.

Having been brought up surrounded by exotic royal relatives, and unsettled by his earlier experiences, he tends, in adulthood, to turn towards the conventional, and is suspicious of anyone who strays outside the norm. Prince Philip, hands clasped firmly behind his back, indicates a desire to keep his past behind him as, with his jaw thrust aggressively forward, he faces the future.

Philip's frustration at the disruptions, upheavals, and separations of his childhood could account for some of the tactless and irritable comments for which he is renowned. In 1987 he gave offence to the Chinese, by warning a group of British students in Peking that if they stayed much longer they would come back with 'slitty eyes'. He enraged working people in Britain by telling them to 'get their finger out'.

Philip is a man of many parts. He lends his patronage to macho youth schemes, such as the Duke of Edinburgh Award Scheme and Outward Bound, runs a team of polo ponies and keeps carriage horses, activities which are competitive and performance-related. He is President of the Worldwide Fund for Nature yet, paradoxically, he shoots. He is an accomplished photographer, and a passable painter of wild-life and landscapes. He is said to deride Prince Charles's interest in philosophical and intellectual matters, yet admits to reading poetry and sermons. He has been a strict father, possibly as a reaction to his own father's inability to be any sort of father at all. He has shown little interest in life beyond the superficial, as if by digging deeper he might discover things which are best left undisturbed. When his youngest son, Edward, decided to abandon his training with the Royal Marines in 1987, expressing a wish to work in the theatre instead of the armed forces, Philip was angry. He felt compelled to encourage his son in conventional macho activity and insist upon a lifestyle that Edward is clearly not suited to. The pressure of tradition dies hard in him. Dispossessed and displaced as a child, he has made it his business to make a place for himself in Britain. He may yet learn tolerance, but he had not acquired it when his children – in particular his sons – most needed it. His attitude to his sons is paradoxical. His own background was insecure and he could well have been unloading his early conflicts on to them. He has an urge towards creativity acquired with his sisters but male-like defences against it.

Philip displays opposing attitudes towards his three sons and his daughter: it is as if he is in competition with his sons. With Charles he has shown disappointment mixed with jealousy (Charles will probably be king and Philip never will); from Andrew, who has been able to pursue his naval career, unlike Philip who had to give it up, he withholds approval; and he denigrates Edward's artistic aspirations.

Only towards his daughter does Prince Philip show affection. From the day of Anne's birth her father saw her (as Prince Albert did Vicky, and George V his daughter Princess Mary) as a source of love, compensating for the distanced love of his mother. The Princess Royal, who has had her own problems, has, none the less, been spared the ordeal of having to live up to her father. There is between them something which approximates to a 'normal' relationship, underpinned, now that they are both adults, by mutual admiration, affection and approval. It is not unusual for a specific bond to develop between a father and his only daughter, particularly if she aspires to be the 'chip off the old block' which her brothers have no ambition to become, realizing from early childhood that this would please him and provoke loving responses that he was only too happy to exchange with her.

Perhaps because he was aware that his own marriage was to a certain extent 'arranged', and therefore his choice limited, he refused to support Margaret in her desire to marry Peter Townsend, the man she loved. Philip may have seen Townsend as a member of a privileged clique who had enjoyed the approval of King George VI and who had done everything in his power to blunt Elizabeth's affection for himself.

Philip has expressed his 'otherness' from the royal clan by wearing flannels, rather than the kilt, when he was being 'auditioned' by George VI at Balmoral, and by being seen openly drinking, dancing, and smoking at nightclubs, after he had taken Princess Elizabeth home at the required hour of 10.30 p.m. Before his marriage, he displayed a provocative desire to irritate the powers-that-be, and after it had taken place he strove to retain a separate identity.

King George VI died on 6 February 1952. The following year Elizabeth lost as her adviser the prime minister, Winston Churchill, who had a stroke and upon whom she had relied (in much the same way as the young Victoria had relied upon Lord Melbourne). In March 1953, three months before Elizabeth's coronation, her grandmother, Queen Mary, also died.

At the coronation the world's attention was focused upon Elizabeth as never before. A series of highly stressful events had marked her life in the previous five or six years and she appeared tense, gaunt, and frightened, as she was clothed in her coronation robes by the Archbishop of Canterbury. By the time she walked down the great nave of Westminster Abbey however, anointed and crowned, she radiated dignity, confidence, and optimism, and displayed a power which was reported by *Time* magazine to represent, express and effect the aspirations of her subjects throughout the world. In demonstrating to the Commonwealth her ability to bear her responsibilities, the Queen found the strength to wear the three-and-a-half-pound symbol of state on her head, the substantial weight of the velvet train behind her, and the sceptre and orb in her hands, for the long walk down the aisle of Westminster Abbey. Rejoicing in the guardianship of her crown, the new Queen did not immediately remove it upon returning to Buckingham Palace.

Sadly for her children – two infants and two as yet unborn – the main thrust of Elizabeth's power and the principal disposition of her strength were to go towards maintenance of the remnants of Victoria's Empire and the Commonwealth. 'Thank God I was wrong,' wrote Winston Churchill to R. A. Butler in 1953, reflecting upon his support of Edward VIII at the time of the Abdication, 'We could not possibly have got a better King.' Churchill was referring to George VI and, by implication, his daughter. But the great surge of royalist euphoria that attended the Queen's coronation lasted only four years, during which Churchill retired, John Osborne wrote in *Look Back in Anger* that the monarchy was 'a gold filling in a mouth full of decay,' and those rumours of the Duke of Edinburgh's infidelities and Princess Margaret's unseemly passion for a divorcé were circulating.

The Queen was under enormous pressure. In commendable efforts to be progressive, she abolished the presentation of débutantes at court, supported the introduction of life peerages, appeared on television for Christmas broadcasts, travelled widely throughout the Commonwealth, and endured the criticisms of Lord Altrincham who described her as sounding like a 'priggish schoolgirl' for whom 'it will not be enough to go through the motions: she will have to say things that people will remember and do things on her own initiative which will make people sit up and take notice. As yet there is little sign that such a personality is emerging.'

In the face of such criticism it is little wonder that the Queen has at times erred on the side of caution, has made mistakes, and – although she had good reason to suppose that she would be able to muddle through like any other young mother – been able to spend less time than she should have done with her children.

It has been rumoured that, before the coronation, Elizabeth suffered from stress-related symptoms. Given the adverse life events which she had to confront, this would have been understandable. Her children must have suffered from her preoccupation with her duties: their mother was not only bereaved, but had to cope with the excruciating pressures of her new role. She spent her energy on self-preservation rather than on her children, and left them to join their father – still a serving naval officer – as often as she could.

While she had been brought up to believe that nothing was beyond her, and had already proved herself capable, having assumed the Crown at a time when she might reasonably have expected to enjoy several years of relatively normal married life before her accession, nothing in her training had prepared her for her dual role.

A few years into Elizabeth's reign, when some stability might have been anticipated within the family, a new crisis shook the constitution. The Queen was faced with the uncomfortable duty of discouraging Princess Margaret's relationship with Group Captain Peter Townsend whom she wished to marry.

This public and domestic drama was played out against a backdrop of speculation that problems existed within the Queen's own marriage as her husband's name was linked with those of other women. His long friendship with the French cabaret star was once again scrutinized and it was suggested that he had a sexual relationship with the actress Pat Kirkwood. (In 1988 Miss Kirkwood told the journalist Terry O'Hanlon that 'I might have developed a crush on him . . . but despite all those rumours, we did not have an affair.') The Queen's dignity allowed her to rise above such gossip, however, and by the end of the 1950s harmony seemed to have been restored with the announcement of the Queen's third pregnancy and Princess Margaret's engagement to Antony Armstrong-Jones. Prince Andrew was born in February 1960, three months before Margaret's wedding.

The Queen, despite her unimaginative image, has, quietly, been much more than the statutory figure-head proclaimed by her detractors. She is said to have opposed Margaret Thatcher over the issue of sanctions against South Africa in 1986. Rather less significantly, she publicly greeted her daughter-in-law's father, Major Ronald Ferguson, after his well-publicized visit to a massage parlour. Later, she showed a sensitive understanding of the problems that were occurring in her children's marriages. This displays a tolerance and an independence of spirit which says much for the tolerance and love she experienced as a child. Also, however, it shows that like many other high-principled people, she is understanding and forgiving of others' peccadilloes.

The Queen carries her handbag wherever she goes. There is barely a photograph of her where it is not looped over her arm. In a recent television documentary she even took the bag into breakfast in her own homes. The contents of a woman's handbag (a symbolic extension of the self) – keys, passport, money, driving licence, cheque book – represent both security and independence. A handbag can also be identified with the womb, within which can be found those aspects of the self which are highly valued, namely integrity, both personal and sexual. The constant presence of the handbag indicates that the Queen will never relinquish its symbolic contents. Those unsure of themselves will cling to their handbag through thick and thin and will often feel lost and abandoned without it. The Queen's handbags, moreover, are usually very large, considering that they may only contain a handkerchief and a lipstick. Compared with the diminutive clutch purses held by Madame Delors or Nancy Reagan at photocalls before state dinners, the Queen's bag seems clumsy. Perhaps its size indicates the extent of her need for a prop. The Queen's ubiquitous handbag gives the lie to all that we have come to believe about aspects of her security and independence. Of all the royals since Victoria, she alone has received appropriate, and at least adequate, parental attention. While acknowledging her undoubted strength of purpose and leadership, however, and until recently her command of her mount when she took the salute as

Colonel-in-Chief of the Regiment at the Trooping the Colour ceremony every year, we see that she carries her survival kit with her almost everywhere. Only at Balmoral where she feels most secure, and at sporting events where she is in touch with her true self, has she been seen to abandon it. Even at the races, however, the Queen has a prop – her binoculars. These have a more practical purpose than the almost empty handbag but they are, none the less, a comforting weight at her side and something with which she can screen her face and mask her true emotions when she is free to enjoy herself.

It is from Balmoral that Queen Victoria's 'I will be good' echoes down the generations. Queen Elizabeth has displayed the same sense of duty, at the expense of her children, as Victoria, but has been only as good a mother to them as her commitments have allowed. In a speech in the City of London to mark the fortieth anniversary of her accession to the throne, Queen Elizabeth admitted that members of her family, by implication like any other family, were not immune to the consequences of human frailty. She pleaded for more understanding and expressed the hope that history would take a more compassionate view than those of contemporary commentators. The year 1992 had certainly not been a happy one. First Andrew's and then Charles's marriage finally came to an end, and the fire which threatened the destruction of Windsor Castle, if not the House of Windsor itself, seemed an omen from the ashes of which the phoenix of a 'new' monarchy might arise. There is no doubt of the 'quality' love that Queen Elizabeth II has bestowed on Charles, Anne, Andrew, and Edward, but 'quantity' love – the presence of continuing availability by one care-giver, so long as it is needed – has not, of necessity, been available to them.

Paradoxically she has also been a good 'father' to her children, just as George VI was a good father to her, since Philip was often emotionally distanced from them. A father serves no *biological* need in being present during his children's upbringing. By nature he is the provider, the hunter, the protector. In that all the family's wealth is invested in her, Queen Elizabeth (like Queen Victoria), has been 'father' and 'mother' to both her people and her children. Sadly, in the case of both these monarchs, it is the children who, in having to share her so extensively, have lost out.

CHAPTER NINE

Princess Margaret

'Now that Papa is King, I am nothing.'
HRH PRINCESS MARGARET

For Princess Margaret Rose, born to parents who were hoping for a boy, life has not been easy. She was the first female member of the Royal Family in recent times to test the boundaries of the rigid formality into which she was born, and to blaze a trail which has been enthusiastically followed by the present generation. So convinced were the Duke and Duchess of York that their second child would be a boy that girl's names had not even been considered for the new baby. 'Margaret' and 'Rose' were names quickly chosen to pre-empt her grandmother, Queen Mary, insisting on her preferences.

Margaret Rose, as she was then known, was destined to be neither a favourite child nor a favourite grandchild. Queen Mary, who described Elizabeth as 'enchanting', considered her younger sister 'very ugly'. Physically, Margaret Rose was different from her sister. She was small and dark, and in appearance unlike other members of the House of Windsor. From the beginning she was compared unfavourably with her sister, which might have made her feel unwanted, unloved and excluded, and have left her with the impression that she was always to be the odd one out. Queen Mary's tactless remark to her second granddaughter, 'Why are you so small? Why don't you grow up?' would have done nothing for Margaret's already low self-esteem.

'Let Margo burn,' Princess Elizabeth is reported to have said when her sister chose to stay in bed during morning fire drills at Sandringham. This may have been intended to be humorous but, according to Freud, there is no such thing as a joke, and the remark might have reflected barely concealed animosity.

Although Elizabeth would seem to have been the favoured one, nevertheless it was she who was displaced when Margaret Rose was born and it is quite possible that she felt some hostility towards her sister. Given the circumstances of their respective childhoods and the separations from their parents, each might have assumed that the other was receiving the most parental attention.

The two sisters were, for the most part, close to and fond of each other, but this would not preclude Elizabeth's taking advantage of her seniority leaving Margaret Rose angry and frustrated. However devoted two sisters may be, jealousy will inevitably be felt at times. 'Look after your Empire and I'll look after my life,' is said to have been Margaret's sharp retort, as an adult, to the Queen, after being reprimanded by her sister for her flirtatious behaviour. This remark must surely reflect feelings which were suppressed in the nursery. Both sisters, however, have done exactly that, and each, in her own way, has been moderately successful.

Young Margaret Rose's feelings of jealousy and her own unimportance are reflected in her childhood complaint to her parents: 'You gave Lilibet three names. Why didn't you give me three instead of only two?' and later, as a girl of sixteen, she is recorded as sulking if she was not allowed the same degree of freedom that Lilibet was gradually acquiring.

Her feeling of inferiority, reinforced by her diminutive stature – she is barely five feet two inches tall – was later echoed when she continued to wear platform-soled shoes and bouffant hairstyles, long after both had gone out of fashion, in an attempt to elevate both her presence and her stature.

Princess Margaret is left-handed, like her father, which may have added to her sense of apartness. She takes after her mother in height and a tendency to put on weight. Again mirroring both her parents she suffered from unintentional neglect and discrimination in childhood which have had their effect upon her compulsive needs.

Margaret Rose was born in 1930 at Glamis, her mother's family home. Here, at least, there was rejoicing at the arrival of the first royal princess to be born in Scotland, and the announcement of her birth was celebrated by the lighting of beacons across the country. At the time, there was no reason to suppose that the

Duke and Duchess of York would not eventually produce a male heir; there was therefore no pressure on Margaret Rose to be anything other than a welcome addition to the York family.

Unfortunately, however, she was considered unattractive not only by her grandmother, but later by her governess, Marion Crawford, who openly favoured Elizabeth. In her book *The Little Princesses*, she described the two sisters in their bathing costumes before their first swimming lessons. 'Lilibet looked so pretty in hers. She was a long, slender child with beautiful legs. Margaret, everyone owned, looked like a plump navy-blue fish.'

An antipathy existed between Marion Crawford and Clara Knight (Alla), who was in charge of the nursery and who cared for Margaret Rose in the years after Elizabeth had begun lessons.

It is likely that Marion Crawford's greater attachment to Princess Elizabeth came about because when she first came to teach the girls, Margaret was still a baby. Crawfie had several years of a one-to-one relationship with Elizabeth before Margaret was old enough to join them for lessons.

Margaret Rose's smallness and her boisterousness contributed to her being thought of as the baby of the family, long after she was emotionally mature. Just as Clara Knight was reluctant to see Margaret join Elizabeth in the schoolroom, her father later refused to acknowledge that she was a woman with womanly emotions, which might be associated with her need for 'fatherly' attention. George VI died unaware that Margaret had been in love with a married man since she was sixteen. Perhaps the King, having been obliged to instruct Elizabeth in her future responsibilities as queen, had wanted to keep Margaret a child as long as he could.

Margaret was not only dressed identically to her sister, but often had to wear Elizabeth's hand-me-downs, which gave her what Cecil Beaton described as a 'home-made' look. Their identical frocks may have been a source of irritation to Margaret – who felt unable to express her own personality – but her mother, keen to set an example of domestic thrift, and incidentally penalizing only Margaret, let it be known that Elizabeth's clothes, sometimes identical to garments Margaret had outgrown, were always saved until the younger sister had grown into them. At their parents' coronation in 1937, Margaret was dismayed to find that her train was shorter than her sister's. Elizabeth was given regular pocket money, while Margaret received the occasional shilling. The bias went deeper than pocket money: Margaret was not allowed to attend the gillies' ball at Balmoral at the same age as Elizabeth first went; she was not encouraged to drive until some time after she was legally allowed to; when the two girls toured South Africa with their parents after the Second World War, and were each given a collection of diamonds, Margaret's were inferior. It is hardly surprising that, having been brought up to think small, when she chose a car for herself in the early 1960s, she selected a Mini.

Princess Margaret was clever, had a love of mimicry (like the Prince Consort and her mother), was cheeky, charming, and manipulative. Queen Mary described her as 'so outrageously amusing that one can't help but encourage her'. That from an early age Margaret had to develop a seductive charm and manipulative behaviour to provoke loving responses from indifferent adults is a sad reflection on her parents and governess. Throughout her adult life she has had to look for an alternative to the nurturing which she failed to receive in her childhood. The apotheosis of this lay in her doomed relationship with Group Captain Townsend.

Margaret sensed that the role in which she would be most acceptable within the family was that of 'tearaway'. Elizabeth Longford recounts how Margaret was dressed as an angel for a children's fancy-dress party. Her mother remarked, with amusement, that she did not look very angelic. 'That's all right,' replied Margaret. 'I'll be a Holy Terror.'

Royal children are taught to ride as a matter of course but, unlike her sister, Margaret never developed a love of horses, dogs, or any outdoor activity although she was encouraged to do so by her parents and governess. She is certainly not in favour of any blood sports. Margaret's interests have, by and large, removed her from the mainstream of Royal Family life but since that in itself seems not to have been particularly agreeable to her, it is understandable that she should have turned her back on it. Her apparent wish to make night into day, often frequenting night-spots and dark theatres, contrasts sharply with Elizabeth's love of fresh-air pursuits. (During the painful years between her decision not to marry Peter Townsend and her eventual marriage to Antony Armstrong-Jones, she and her friends staged a revue to raise money for a children's charity, for which Margaret not only understudied but played the part of a night-club hostess!) In *The Picnic Papers* (published in 1983) in which social luminaries were asked to describe their favourite picnics, Margaret's was indoors, at the Banqueting House of Hampton Court. 'Night' and 'darkness' are reminders of childhood separation from care-givers: a neglected child may never learn to cope with being alone at night. Many children avoid going to bed for as long as possible each evening, because they are afraid that their parents may die while they are asleep, leaving them to fend for themselves. Margaret's need to turn night into day is a defence against her separation fears.

As a child Margaret came into her own in family charades and pantomimes. Dressing-up and appearing before an appreciative audience provided her with welcome attention. On reaching adulthood she turned to the fantasy world of the theatre, and later to the sunshine and warmth of the West Indies, to bask in its 'nurturing' sun, a belated attempt to enjoy a life-enhancer freely available to all. It is the sun that provides life for all vegetation on the earth: without it, crops will die and bread, the staff of life, will be unavailable. Princess Margaret lives in Kensington Palace, but owns no property in Britain. The only place she can call her own is a house in the Caribbean, on the island of Mustique. Living on an island satisfies her expectations of being cut off from mainland and mainstream activity.

Like many lonely children, Margaret had imaginary friends. She shifted the blame on to 'Cousin Halifax', 'Pinkle Ponkle', and 'Bombax', for her own alleged misdemeanours. She learned to gain attention by being disobedient and excused her behaviour by absolving herself of responsibility and displacing it on to her 'friends'. In the garden of the replica house at Frogmore, Y Bythwyn Bach, given to the girls by the people of Wales, Princess Margaret chose to grow potatoes (buried in Mother Earth and, like her, seldom to see the light of day) rather than the flowers, more typical of the fragrant blossoming Elizabeth, chosen and grown by her. As a young woman, when Margaret sat for one of her first official portraits without her sister in a Hartnell ballgown, she remarked to Cecil Beaton that the elegant embroidery on the dress reminded her of potato peel.

The differences between the two Princesses became even more apparent as Margaret grew older. She smoked, against medical advice even following lung surgery, in 1985, and drank, while

Elizabeth either as Princess or Queen did neither (although in 1982, Michael Fagan, an unreliable witness, the intruder who scaled the walls of Buckingham Palace and found his way into the Queen's bedroom, claimed that Her Majesty had a packet of cigarettes on her bedside table, and that he asked if he could have one). Margaret's addictive habits compensate her for lack of maternal attention in childhood: substitutes for the breast are inevitably oral. Her father, whose childhood was also deprived, drank and smoked to excess, while her mother, who was more or less abandoned by *her* mother (who was increasingly unavailable after her two sons died) is also known to drink small but regular amounts of alcohol.

Unlike Elizabeth, in adulthood Margaret has always chosen her own friends – uncommon in the Royal Family. While Elizabeth is said to avoid evening engagements whenever possible and when she is at home enjoys a simple meal on a tray, Princess Margaret gives dinner parties for her friends at Kensington Palace or goes with them to the opera or restaurants.

Elizabeth grew up a conformist and Margaret a rebel. In her wish to please both parents the elder daughter followed many of the Queen's, mainly outdoor, interests but Margaret, finding it difficult to gain the approval she needed, however pleasing she was, gave up trying and opted instead for opposition. According to Lady Airlie her father referred to her as an *'enfant terrible'*.

Only when her parents were crowned, in 1937, could the six-year-old Margaret have begun to realize the way in which her life might develop. Disruption following the abdication, the family move, first to Buckingham Palace and then to Windsor after the outbreak of war in 1939, must have been both baffling and exciting for her. This 'second-fiddle' princess must have noticed that her father spent more and more time with her sister than with her, and she was probably envious that Elizabeth was able to join the ATS while she was still at lessons with Crawfie. Her high spirits, at the same time indulged and deplored, were the only way she knew of asserting herself.

In 1947, when Princess Margaret was sixteen, she accompanied her parents and sister on an extended post-war tour of South Africa. It was during this trip that she fell in love with the man she would not be allowed to marry. It was the first time that she had been allowed to wear clothes of her own choosing, which were neither cast-offs nor copies of her sister's, and that she was treated as an adult, particularly during her official engagements. Her father's equerry, Group Captain Peter Townsend, was deputed to be a companion for the two young Princesses, and four months later, by the time the tour ended, a strong affection had developed between him and Margaret.

The romance was decorous, conducted properly and privately, and the bond between them became stronger over the next few years. Margaret continued to go to parties, the theatre, and night-clubs with her friends, while Townsend quietly divorced his wife, citing her adultery. The furore when the relationship became public did not surface until 1953, after the Queen's coronation.

The likelihood of Margaret's acceding to the throne became more remote with the birth of each of her sister's children. When the Duke of Edinburgh was created regent upon his wife's coronation, Margaret lost her right of regency, and was no longer a Privy Counsellor. While never having voiced a wish to be queen, as far as we know, Margaret must have been aware of her diminishing constitutional importance and, as a consequence, displayed ever less reverence for duty than her sister. Her strongest suit was her personal charisma and popularity, which was followed with interest by the media and which brought about the cataclysm in her life. By the time she was crowned, Elizabeth was a young matron with domestic as well as constitutional responsibilities and Margaret was required to stand in for her sister on many public occasions; her expertise as a deputy, her charm and good looks attracted attention wherever she went. She even inadvertently upstaged her sister at the coronation – with disastrous personal results.

When Margaret casually removed a speck of fluff from Peter Townsend's jacket before the world's cameramen, their secret was out. In an unguarded moment, with her unambiguous, proprietorial gesture – more shocking at the time than Sarah Ferguson's South of France exposure forty years later – Margaret had as good as announced publicly that Peter Townsend was the man she cared for. When she confirmed to her sister that she wanted to marry Townsend, both a family and a constitutional crisis erupted. The abdication of Edward VIII was too fresh in the public mind and family memory for there to be any question of a member of the Royal Family marrying a divorcé. Margaret's relationship with Group Captain Peter Townsend was discouraged, and a judicious separation arranged.

Townsend was posted to Belgium and Margaret was given to understand that, if she waited until she was twenty-five and still wished to marry Townsend, she would be permitted to do so on condition that she renounced her right of succession, and forfeited all royal privileges including her Civil List income. These sanctions, coupled with pressure from her family and from the Church, led her to make a poignant public statement in which she said she had agreed to give up Group Captain Peter Townsend. In the vanguard of those who pressed hardest for her rebuttal of him, was her brother-in-law, Prince Philip.

It was at about this time that Margaret bought herself a tiara. In the Royal Family, by tradition, it is only married women who wear tiaras; these are family heirlooms usually bestowed at the time of the wedding. Believing that she was never to receive one through marriage, Margaret – like any unhappy woman who consoles herself with a new hair-style or outfit – went shopping for a tiara. Denied her wish to marry the man who loved her, Margaret suffered a blow not only to her self-esteem but to her femininity. Hair symbolizes sexuality and is a woman's 'crowning glory'. Margaret made a statement about her sexuality, her femininity, and attractiveness by emphasizing hers with her tiara.

In 1956 Margaret accepted a proposal of marriage from an old flame, Billy Wallace, but the engagement, on her side, was as short-lived as it was half-hearted. The Princess was unwilling to compromise and not yet ready to enter into a serious new relationship. It was another three years – probably spent in loneliness and resentment – before she announced her engagement to Antony Armstrong-Jones, whom she married in 1960. Noël Coward wrote that some members of the family disapproved of the match: Marina, Duchess of Kent, and Princess Alexandra 'were not pleased . . . there was a distinct *froideur* when I mentioned it'. Her immediate family, however, was relieved.

For a while Princess Margaret appeared to be happy with her husband, but in 1977, after they had been living amicably apart for some time, they agreed to divorce. In the light of this divorce, and those of other close family members more recently, the

Princess has every right to feel bitter that she was prevented by royal protocol from marrying the man she loved.

The aftermath of the break-up of her marriage, civilized as this was, and the media attention that was focused upon her a year later during her friendship with Roddy Llewellyn, took its toll. She was believed to have overdosed on sleeping tablets, but she denied this: 'I was so exhausted because of everything that all I wanted to do was sleep . . . and I did, right through to the following afternoon.'

When she was asked whether she would ever marry again, the Princess's reply was, 'Remarriage would be a devil of a trouble. And one would not want to be a bind . . . But if one did find someone nice . . .' Through this wistful, yet candid and defiant statement Margaret reveals her sense of humility – coupled, in her use of RAF slang, with an unconscious reminder of Group Captain Townsend.

Princess Margaret now lives in a large grace-and-favour apartment in Kensington Palace. Since her divorce she has had that one, much-publicized romantic involvement with a younger man, but there has been no suggestion of remarriage. Her children and friends – clever, amusing, artistic, and discreet – seem to sustain her, as does her passion for opera, ballet, and the theatre.

Given her sad history and the social expectations of her day, it is not hard to see how Princess Margaret came to be perceived by some as hedonistic and irresponsible. She has, in fact, fulfilled more than her share of royal duties and has graciously bestowed her patronage on numerous worthy causes. The Royal Family give their support to the charities of their own choice and Margaret has involved herself with the Migraine Trust, perhaps understandably since her life has been such a headache; she is Patron of the National Society for the Prevention of Cruelty to Children, identifying with disadvantaged children – as later the Princess of Wales has done with Aids victims – having been disadvantaged in childhood by always seeing herself as the 'number two' princess. The way in which she has brought up her own son and daughter reflects her awareness of the need in all children for loving attention.

As a young mother, however, she left her son shortly after his birth, when she went on holiday to the West Indies. In the unenlightened climate of the day, as far as child-rearing was concerned, she was spared the public outcry that ensued when Sarah, Duchess of York, left *her* baby to join her husband in Australia. Margaret's two children appear to be well adjusted and successful. While it is true that her son, Viscount Linley, has collected a string of speeding convictions and demonstrated a degree of public arrogance, the custom-built furniture business, which he established, has thrived. Her daughter, Lady Sarah Armstrong-Jones, lives quietly and is equally independent.

Self-expression is difficult for members of the Royal Family. Princess Margaret has never sought to make her views public, but has managed to achieve a degree of self-fulfilment and to gain self-esteem through her many artistic interests and involvement with selected charities. In her hey-day, she was the 'Princess Diana' of her devoted public and, like the Princess of Wales, her every move was followed, photographed, and commented upon.

Now aged sixty-two, she lives quietly. She is a devout Christian, and the faith which has helped her through major surgery has emphasized her moral strength. She has acquired a serenity and dignity more often associated with her sister, and although it is claimed that she is a difficult woman, she has often been misunderstood and underestimated. The stories of the 'fairy-tale' childhood, which has always been ascribed to her, have not taken account of the less favourable aspects of her upbringing.

The Princess has described herself as being no angel. When she says she has no ambition, or that only her startlingly blue eyes are worth looking at, she displays the same false modesty as that with which the Princess of Wales announces publicly that she has a brain 'the size of a pea'. Both princesses are 'fishing': they long to be contradicted and thereby reassured of their value. Many paradoxes surround Margaret: having been at the epicentre of a major constitutional crisis, she is yet able to say, 'In our family, we do not have rifts. A very occasional row, but never a rift'; having associated herself with the unconventional and theatrical, she has refused to be photographed with Boy George because of his appearance; having courted the attention of the media with her eyebrow raising activities, she is able to announce, 'I have been misreported and misrepresented since the age of seventeen.' Although somehow she has managed to weather her storms, the price has been high. Her friend Jocelyn Stevens said, 'I have always regarded her as a bird in a gilded cage. She would have loved to break free, but was never able to.'

Were a film to be made of the life of Princess Margaret, the obvious choice for the role would be Elizabeth Taylor. The two women are the same age, share similar physical characteristics, and have endured and overcome many of the same problems. They have glamour, courage, and spirit, and have surmounted the disadvantage of having been in the public eye since childhood. Both are survivors. The long shadow of her great-great-grand-mother has fallen upon Princess Margaret. All her life she has tried to be 'good' and 'dutiful' but she had neither Queen Victoria's position nor her power.

Princess Margaret is known to have a large collection of seashells, which she keeps in Kensington Palace and which she looks after herself. This collection symbolizes the inner vulner-ability and softness which lie beneath the carapace under which she has concealed her vicissitudes. With her ear to an empty shell, if she listens carefully, she can hear the sea on the shore of a tropical island, the distant sounds of a paradise she once glimpsed but lost, never to regain.

CHAPTER TEN

Prince Charles

'. . . when the husband walks back from the altar, he has
already swallowed the choicest dainties of his banquet. The
beef and pudding of married life are then in store for him –
or perhaps only the bread and cheese.'
ANTHONY TROLLOPE
Framley Parsonage

By the summer of 1992 the unhappy relationship between the
Prince and Princess of Wales had reached crisis point. Widespread
sympathy for Diana was due, in part, to Andrew Morton's *Diana:
Her True Story*, published apparently with the Princess's approval,
which revealed her version of what the marriage had been. When
a tape-recording of what purported to be a conversation between
the Princess and a male friend was made public, many people
wanted to believe that it had been faked, while others thought
that it was indeed the voice of the Princess complaining about her
treatment by her husband. It was generally felt that the media had
overstepped the mark in sensationalism and gone beyond the
bounds of decency in their invasion of privacy.

The 'Diana tape', available for a while to telephone callers,
and its contents transcribed and printed in the *Sun*, followed the
newspaper publication of photographs of the topless Duchess of
York on holiday in the South of France, embracing her 'financial
adviser' beside a swimming-pool, taken immediately before the
Duchess was said to be returning to Balmoral to patch up her
marriage. That the Duchess's two small daughters, Princesses
Beatrice and Eugenie, and her detectives were witness to the
impropriety seemed inexcusable. The reputation of the House
of Windsor was being destabilized as much by its members as by

the media, and the continuing existence of the monarchy, in its present form at any rate, seemed seriously in question.

In the light of these revelations, and playing devil's advocate, the newspapers howled not for the blood of the Royal Family (whose activities, after all, sold a great many newspapers), but for a curb to their privileges and – in keeping with the recessionary times – a tax on the Queen's fabled income. Throughout all the mud-slinging, rivers of condemnatory newsprint – from salacious tabloids *and* respected broadsheets – and the full-frontal attacks that the sexual revelations made on her family, the Queen maintained a dignified silence.

What, if any, conclusions can be drawn from the fact that it is the marriages contracted *outside* the royal circle – Princess Margaret and the Earl of Snowdon, the Princess Royal and Captain Mark Phillips, the Duke and Duchess of York, and now the Prince and Princess of Wales – that seem to have come to grief? Did the old dictum, that royalty must marry royalty (however minor) account for the previous apparent stability of the reigning family? Would Charles's union have had a greater chance of success had he married Marie-Astrid of Luxembourg, with whom his name had been linked before his marriage to Diana Spencer?

The Royal Family is in danger of disintegrating, not through marital crises with their ensuing scandals, or because the prejudiced have become more prejudiced and the judgemental more condemning, but because 'Buckingham Palace' has become a soap opera brought into our homes by television cameras. A hitherto 'closed' or 'secret' society, the immediate Royal Family, has been infiltrated by commoners lacking an overriding sense of duty, who have not been trained by years of conditioning, as they would have been had they been royal, to maintain 'in-house' confidentiality. Demystification, leading us to see the Royal Family much as we see ourselves, may gradually rebound upon itself, making our need for them redundant. As a nation we are collectively unhappy with behaviour which we feel is conspicuous and ostentatious; as individuals we value self-effacement and modesty. Splitting off the extravagant in ourselves, and displacing it on to the Royal Family, enables us conveniently to disown that aspect of our psyches upon which our culture frowns.

★

The Prince of Wales regards himself as being the end product of centuries of carefully planned breeding. He acknowledges that in his blood and bones reside the aspirations of nations. With his separation from Diana the future of the Royal Family is seriously threatened. How much of the responsibility for the present situation can be laid at Charles's door? He has been trained all his life for kingship and, having played fast and loose with his marriage treating his carefully selected partner with contempt, appears to have shot himself in the foot. Also, if the so-called Camillagate tapes are ever shown to be genuine, there would be the major constitutional problems of a self-confessed adulterer assuming the role of Defender of the Faith and Head of the Church of England when such activity is proscribed by that Church – and virtually every other major religion in the Commonwealth?

Like his great-uncle, Edward VIII (a former Prince of Wales), Charles demands all the deference and privilege of his rank, but simultaneously wants to be seen as a 'man of the people'. Needing the security of limits and boundaries, Charles is a stickler for protocol – any informality seems forced and artificial and appears to have been stage-managed. His immediate family only may call him by his first name and even his former girl-friends were required to address him as 'sir'. His well-publicized interest in social problems, the environment, architecture and competitive sport reflects a need for structure and acceptance by his peers, since the 'architecture' of his inner world seems uncertain and in peril. His concern with the problems of farmers in the Duchy of Cornwall echoes his great-uncle's hollow remark in the face of the sufferings of miners in South Wales that 'something must be done'. Both Charles and his predecessor might have been asking for something to be done for *them*, to redress unrecognized wrongs within their respective psyches.

Princess Elizabeth and the Duke of Edinburgh might have supposed when Charles was born, in November 1948 (his father was playing squash at the time), that since his grandfather, King George VI, was still only fifty-three, and seemed likely to reign for many more years, their son's early childhood could safely resemble as far as possible that of any other of their aristocratic contemporaries. They proclaimed that they hoped to create an 'ordinary' environment for him at their homes in Clarence House and at Windsor, although since Charles was second in the line of succession this idea seemed far-fetched. The premature death of George VI in 1952 threw Charles's immediate family into a state of turmoil and put paid to any hopes of 'normality' as far as his upbringing was concerned.

In any event, he was unlikely to have experienced anything other than minimal parental involvement during his infancy. His father was a serving naval officer and his mother joined her husband abroad whenever she could. Elizabeth was also expected to resume her royal duties towards the end of Charles's first year. Charles spent a great deal of time with his grandparents, and a special bond of affection grew between him and Queen Elizabeth, the Queen Mother, echoing the bonds that had existed between Queen Alexandra and her grandsons, George V and Princess Elizabeth. He remained her favourite grandchild and this could be seen to have compensated her for never having had a son herself.

His sister Anne was born twenty-one months after Charles. When she was only four months old at Christmas in 1950, her parents spent several weeks together in Malta leaving the two children at home with the King and Queen. In 1951 they were again left behind, when Elizabeth and the Duke of Edinburgh embarked on the tour of Africa which was cut short, in February 1952, by the death of George VI. Although the Princess did her best to communicate with her children on the telephone every day when she was away, it was of necessity a 'long-distance' affection or 'love at arm's length' which she was expressing, such as Charles would come to believe was acceptable in his later commitments, as opposed to his adventures outside marriage, as an adult.

Three women were influential in Charles's early life: his mother, whom he respected but to whom he was not close, and two nannies, Mabel Anderson and Helen Lightbody, with whom he was more intimate and who provided him with constant and ongoing affection. This pattern, of a loving 'hands-on' relationship with his nannies and a more formal one with his mother, led to a need for two simultaneous partners throughout his life. His wife, Diana – at first the untouchable Madonna on a pedestal, looked-up to, but out of reach – had always to compete with other women, notably Camilla Parker-Bowles, who reflected the warmth and love of his erstwhile nannies.

Charles was put in the care of several other surrogates during his childhood leading him to believe that others, usually women, would always be available to him. He was never short either of paid attendants (nannies and teachers), unpaid ones (his grand-parents), or other admirers (his watchful and appreciative public). His routine at Buckingham Palace was strict and his time with his mother, when she was at home, was limited. He would be dressed by 7 a.m., spend two hours in the nursery, then visit the Queen at 9 if her schedules permitted. He saw his mother again at tea-time, and she would occasionally bath him, after which he was sometimes dressed again to be presented to distinguished visitors. By the time he was three Charles had learned to bow to his grandmother and to stand in his grandfather's presence unless given permission to sit down. These rituals are perpetuated in his adult life and he is said to insist that those leaving his presence do so backwards. It is obvious that he does not feel happy or comfortable when people have their backs to him and that he sees this as a rejection, having been sensitized to being 'turned away from' by frequently absent parents so often as a child. In his expectations of deference from all with whom he associates, he is re-enacting, through role-reversal, what was expected of him as a child. Self-aggrandizing rituals may also be seen as a defence against feelings of inadequacy: it is hard for a child to convince himself that there is a valid reason for his parents' absence, without his suspecting that he is to blame and that he is unworthy of their love. Anthony Holden has described Charles's father as being little more than a 'stranger', who described his first-born son dismissively as a 'plum-pudding', to him during his child-hood. The Duke of Edinburgh was probably unaware of the importance of his presence on the occasions of his elder children's rites of passage, since he was absent for six out of Charles's first eight birthdays.

When George VI died, at the age of fifty-eight, and Charles became heir-apparent, his mother had to cope simultaneously with her grief at the death of her beloved father and the awesome burden of her new responsibilities. She became preoccupied with the preparations for, and the consequences of, her coronation. Family concern with her sister's romance with Group Captain Peter Townsend, and the move to Buckingham Palace from Clarence House caused further tensions. Charles's status within the royal household was immediately changed, and at the age of four he was assigned his own car and driver. Far from being bewildered by this treatment, Charles grew up to accept distant parenting and special privileges as the norm.

By the time he became heir to the throne the paradoxes that were to characterize his life were increasing: he was being encouraged to be independent long before he was ready for it, and therefore his dependent needs were ignored. No child at such an age should be asked to play a role he is not ready for, while simultaneously having withheld from him the love, support and attention that only a mother can provide. Jealous of the duties and obligations that took his mother away from him, and envious of his siblings whom he would have felt had the love he was missing, Charles grew up to be fiercely competitive with all males. In describing his brother Andrew as 'the one with the Robert Redford looks' he was expressing both insecurity about his own appearance (reinforced as a child by being nicknamed 'Fatty' at school and teased about the size and shape of his ears) and his feelings of being short-changed by his parents. His sister Anne established a bond of affection with their father, which Charles never achieved. His younger brothers enjoyed childhoods in which their parents were around much more, and had possibly ingested some of the wisdom of child-rearing, disseminated by, among others who climbed on the bandwagon, Dr Benjamin Spock, whose book on childcare had rapidly become a household bible.

Charles's resentment of his siblings carried into his relationship with his wife and he is sometimes as dismissive of his children's needs as he feels his parents were of his. He is on record as saying, 'Girls are so much nicer than boys, don't you think?' (a comment he perhaps heard in the nursery) and 'I would love to have a daughter', perhaps reflecting his hope that a loving daughter, like Prince Albert's Vicky or George VI's Lilibet, would make up to him for the disappointments he experienced as a child. By identifying with a girl baby, he would be fulfilling the role of preferred child, which he believed Anne had been.

Charles was old enough at the time of his grandfather's death to be aware of his mother's distress and of her increased public obligations, but he learned by imitation that emotions must be controlled, and that the self-sufficiency demanded by parental unavailability was essential. Many parents value and reward 'pseudo-independence' with the result that their children grow up in isolation with an arrogant disregard of a fundamental need to relate to others – which, indeed, we noticed in Queen Victoria as a girl. In adult life Charles's 'privileges' led him to become solitary, over-solemn, to approach friendship with caution, and experience difficulties in integrating with his peers. Charles's behaviour was fashioned by the formality of the Palace, by the constant presence of the adults by whom he was surrounded, and by their high expectations of him. He was required to be tidy and neatly groomed at all times since he was frequently 'on show' and his over-concern with appearance has persisted. A preoccupation with the outward façade is often a defence against inner decay, which may be neither recognized nor acknowledged. He is criticized for emphasizing how buildings look rather than how they function, which might well have been the case in his own home with Diana, which was definitely not in good order.

Many had refused to believe the problems that were leaked almost daily to the press: a public denial was taking place by those who needed the panoply associated with royalty. Royalty has a human face, but no one wanted to see it. The Royal Family has a cancer called public disclosure, which is eating away at its fabric and which, if not effectively treated, could lead to its death. Millions throughout the world who 'depend' on the existence of royalty refused to accept the diagnosis. The Royal Family acts as blotting paper for our envy and jealousy, pride and inability to express love and devotion. As in the icons of the Russian Orthodox Church, we see a two-dimensional image which allows us to focus on a 'Holy Family' with whom we can transact hope and aspiration, rage and violence, love and compassion. The secularization of this fantasy family leaves us having to deal with our emotions within ourselves and with our peers.

When Charles was five his formal education began under the tutelage of a young Scottish woman, Catherine Peebles. The change in his routine coincided with his parents' absence on a six-month tour abroad. He was no longer seeing as much of his nannies as he had previously, and an exaggerated sense of self-sufficiency was forced upon him too early. His need for love was so intense that his anger at having it withheld in early infancy has led him to seek scapegoats in adult life. Although it was his mother who was responsible for the absences that led to Charles's early 'independence', it was another 'mother' – Diana – who bore the brunt of his suppressed hostility. This was well illustrated when, shortly after their engagement, she caused a sensation by appearing at a charity gala wearing a strapless, black taffeta dress. Charles disguised his disapproval by declaring that black was an unsuitable colour for her, but in reality his discomfort was related to the public glimpse of her breasts, caught as she was getting out of her limousine, the ultimate source of nurture and, in his case, a disappointing one.

As a child, Charles did not demonstrate outstanding intellectual ability. He found it difficult to learn because of the absence of other children in the school. As an adult however, he likes to mix with academics – architects, writers, historians and philosophers.

When he was eight Charles was sent to Hill House school in Knightsbridge, at which point Catherine Peebles, to whom he had become accustomed, left the family's employ – another change associated with the absence of a care-giver. Charles was the first heir to the British throne to go to school: to begin with he attended only in the afternoon, whereas the other children were there full-time and were integrated with one another, leaving him isolated and lonely. Some months later another change took place when he was sent to his father's former prep school, Cheam, by now located in Hampshire. The Queen asked the headmaster if he would kindly explain to the parents, and also to the other boys, that Charles must be treated as any other pupil. Inevitably he was not. He found it hard to make friends, and, like many children sent to boarding school, had difficulty in adjusting to sleeping in a dormitory after having his own rooms in Buckingham Palace, and remembers his early days there as being disagreeable and unhappy.

Eventually he learnt to mix but, being aware of his position and suspicious of other boys' motives, he was wary of overtures of friendship. When teased, he learnt to retaliate with his fists. His reports were quite promising, but the only subject for which he had any noticeable gift was music. Sport was encouraged and, doubtless to his father's satisfaction, Charles became captain of both cricket and rugby, but apart from polo, on which his father was keen, Charles displayed no interest in team games after he left Cheam.

Gordonstoun, where his father had been Guardian, or head boy, followed. The Queen had wanted Charles to go to Eton, which was close to Windsor and his family, but Philip was adamant that the rigours of Gordonstoun were what was needed to toughen up his son. He also mistakenly believed that its remote location would spare Charles from public gaze. Charles was less keen than his father on the pursuit of 'rugged individualism', but he lost weight, fished, and enjoyed seeing his grandmother whose private home, the Castle of Mey, was nearby. He made respectable, but not spectacular, academic progress.

By the time he was ready to go up to Cambridge in 1967, Britain was undergoing social changes that threatened to make the Prince of Wales an anachronism. A socialist government was in power and the monarchy was openly criticized. The mid to late 1960s saw the continuing rise of a 'youth cult' and it is hard to imagine a more mature teenager than Prince Charles. His short, neat hair was as unfashionable as his formal clothes and the upper-class vowels of his speech.

At Trinity College he studied history and archaeology, a choice which he happily accepted, unconsciously driven by an internal, unresolved, and almost certainly unrecognized concern with his personal past. The mistakes of the past will be repeated by all those who forget it: although 'lest we forget' memorials were erected everywhere after the First World War, twenty-one years later another generation had clearly forgotten what had gone before and therefore repeated the vicious persecutor-victim cycle. An individual understanding of history cannot affect the course of events, and the archaeologist who digs up our collective past learns nothing about his own, but the urge to uncover what has gone before is present in all those whose early life remains a mystery to them. The thinking-out of personal problems to avoid repeating them can be obscured by defences such as acting-out (rituals such as Trooping the Colour, dressing in uniforms), scapegoating (Charles has used his wife in this), role reversal, the unloading of feelings of victimization onto others (his unintentional indifference to his children's needs), or camouflaged by an interest in the wider issues of history and archaeology. Charles's concern with these subjects reflects an urge to return to a past whose secrets he had suppressed.

Charles's work with the Prince's Trust, the charity he set up to enable disadvantaged young people to fulfil their personal and professional potential, suggests that he felt robbed of opportunities for personal growth in his own adolescence. Because he feels disadvantaged he is able to experience a vicarious satisfaction in encouraging others to make the best of themselves. He identifies with young people, supporting rock concerts and raising money for his Trust. (It was said, however, in a recent television documentary about Britain's monarchy that Charles's attention span in these projects is limited and that he soon loses interest in individual enterprises.) Wearing a double-breasted suit, and seldom smiling, he appears to endure rather than enjoy the music of those who may one day be his subjects. Over the years, it has been the lot of journalists to create an image of Charles to suit the times. During the late 1960s when he made a couple of weak jokes in public and appeared in a Cambridge revue, he was attributed with a 'wacky sense of humour'; his friendship with the comedian Spike Milligan has reinforced the idea that Charles is a 'frustrated comic'; during a safe and sanitized period in the forces – he spent some time in the RAF and the Navy – he was depicted as 'Action Man'; following his enthusiasm for organic vegetables and plants and having formed a friendship with Sir Laurens van der Post, he was lampooned by *Private Eye* as an 'eccentric'. Since childhood, when he found it hard to please his father, through early adulthood – when his attempts to seem 'with it' were unnatural and forced – to recent middle age, when the job for which he has been trained may still elude him, Charles has seldom been allowed to be himself.

Prince Charles's marriage to Lady Diana Spencer (in 1981), could have been devised by Central Casting: the bride was young, beautiful and virginal, and it was she who would rescue the Prince from sadness and isolation. Before his marriage, Charles had a number of aristocratic girlfriends, many of whom were blonde and often a little older than he. They tended to be sporty, outdoor types, unsullied by scandal. One of them, with whom Charles was said to be smitten, was quickly dropped when it was belatedly learned that she had once lived with another man. By the time he was thirty, Charles was under public and family pressure to marry. It has been assumed that any one of the heir's *inamorata* would have been willing to accept a proposal from him, although he had made it clear on several occasions that he could not afford to make a mistake and had to be extremely careful in his choice of future queen and consort. Few women surely, however, would relish being required to address a boyfriend as 'sir' (even, it has been said, in bed), and another – with whom the Prince is said to have been in love – ended her relationship with Charles after a ball at Windsor at which he had completely ignored her.

Charles's brief was to find a girl who was well born, though not necessarily English, and untainted by scandal. By the early 1980s this was by no means easy. Diana Spencer had had a distant schoolgirl crush on the Prince when he was dating her sister Sarah. When he and Diana started to see each other she had grown into an attractive, charming nineteen-year-old. She was taller than Charles and, although he might have resented 'looking up to her', she seemed, in a limited field, to have most of the necessary qualifications for the job. Her background was impeccable, she was congenial company, no skeletons lay in her cupboard, and she was touchingly devoted. She had no interest in horses, was fond of neither sailing, classical music nor Scotland, but at the time of their courtship this seemed not to matter. The Prince of Wales was not free to follow his own heart and Lady Diana Spencer was a highly acceptable compromise.

When the couple were asked if they were in love, Diana's reply was an unhesitating 'yes', while Charles mumbled – significantly – that he supposed so 'whatever being in love means'. From the moment of their engagement in February 1981 Diana became the object of the world's adulation and Charles was judged a lucky man.

The Princess of Wales was allowed to upstage her husband on the memorable day of their wedding. When she continued to do so he was less happy about it. Marriage to Diana heightened, at the time, Charles's own popularity: she was delightfully open, friendly and like a breath of fresh air in royal circles. Later his 'jokes', 'I'm sorry I've only got one wife and she's over there on the other side of the street. You'll have to make do with me instead', betrayed his envy and bitterness.

To establish his precedence over his wife, after his marriage Charles embraced causes which excluded her. It was not that Diana had no interest in intellectual pursuits, but that Charles had wanted it presumed that concerns such as the environment or philosophy were his alone. The resentment that he displayed towards his wife underlined his inability to take pride in her successes. When these reflected well upon him, and she appeared to flatter his self-image, he could afford to be generous towards her. Once it became clear that she had made a niche for herself in the public estimation and that she was not merely her husband's satellite, he sulked.

His jealousy of what the public thought of as his 'glittering prize' was reinforced during the Gulf War in 1991 when Diana had hoped to visit the troops, but was relegated to meeting only the wives by her husband who wanted all the credit for himself. Charles has also, allegedly, been known to delete Diana's name from thank-you notes, preferring such gestures to seem to come only from him.

As well as providing him with homes of his own, Charles's marriage to Diana gave him a clearer identity as the husband of a beautiful and esteemed wife, and the father of two handsome sons, William and Harry. As Diana's children, confidence, and independence grew, however, and she became to him the 'mother' with whom sex was taboo, Charles turned once again for support from the 'nannies' of his childhood, in the persons of old friends such as Camilla Parker-Bowles. As far as Diana was concerned, Charles expected unreasonably that her needs would be satisfied by the adoration of the public and the affection of her children. It had become increasingly apparent that the rifts in their marriage, known to their friends to be serious and deep, had been growing wider for some time. The 'authorized' revelations in Andrew Morton's book published in June 1992 of that year seemed publicly to confirm what many others had suspected. As Diana and Charles went their separate ways, the marriage became increasingly threatened and, in December, they officially agreed to lead separate private and professional lives.

As early as the first Christmas of their marriage, Diana, according to Morton, had attempted suicide by throwing herself down the stairs at Sandringham. If this was a cry for help, Charles did not heed it: insufficient attention having been paid to him as a child, he found it hard to show concern for others, especially his wife. His 'coldness' is reflected in his concern for the preservation of stones in old buildings rather than for the protection of humans, and even his paintings seldom, if ever, include people.

It has been suggested that the Waleses' happiest period was

when Diana was pregnant with Harry. Although Charles's friendship with Camilla Parker-Bowles had continued, some of the pressures upon the Prince and Princess to be the ideal couple had been removed as the succession was assured. This could have been a time to establish the companionship side of the marriage. The Princess has said, however, that the spiritual side, such as it was, of her marriage died on the day that Prince Harry was born, when her husband, having remarked dismissively upon his new son's reddish colouring, left for a polo match, just as his father had opted for squash when Charles was born. Shortly afterwards, at the christening, he insulted Diana's entire family by complaining once more, this time to his mother-in-law, about her grandson's appearance. Although he was a middle-aged man, he still experienced the baffled hurt of a neglected small child, and so fierce was his resentment that he felt the need to belittle his baby son during the ceremony which marked his baptism into the Church.

While Diana continued to devote her energies to her sons and to the welfare of the socially disadvantaged, Charles concentrated on his own 'good causes' – although the royal commentator James Whitaker made a cogent point about the Prince's dedication to public service when he said that Charles's summer engagements were worked around his polo programme. Fifty matches in the season meant that he played nearly every day – while distracting himself with women friends who bolstered his ego. That Diana was so easily able to find out that he was still friendly with Camilla Parker-Bowles by checking the redial button on his telephone indicates Charles's indifference to her feelings.

Charles's silence following the publication of Andrew Morton's book might have indicated his contempt for it. It might, on the other hand, have suggested a desire to see his wife fall flat on her face after the years of public adulation. However, it was not until January 1993 that the real reason for his low-key response became apparent. A tape-recording made in 1989 of a telephone conversation allegedly between Charles and Camilla Parker-Bowles, published in full in an Australian newspaper and subsequently in the UK, suggests, if genuine, not only that an ongoing sexual relationship existed between them but that they had been in love for many years. Few questioned Diana's motives in allegedly endorsing a book in which Charles came out so badly, and most readers sympathized with her.

Self-aggrandizement characterizes Charles's behaviour, but, then, a small child who is given a car, staff, and a personal suite as well as a sense of destiny is likely to develop a strong belief in his own importance. His elder son is already demonstrating his father's tendency to hide behind his rank. He once told a fellow pupil at school, 'My daddy is the Prince of Wales and he can beat up your daddy.'

Although Charles has been surrounded by sycophants all his life, he was deprived of crucial early nurturing by the one person who really mattered: his mother. Had he received this, his adult life might have been happier and he would certainly have made a better father. When Prince Philip told his son, shortly after his marriage, that if it was not working well after five years he should look elsewhere, he was simultaneously revealing his own contempt for women, and offering his son a chance, at last, of forming a man-to-man bond with him. Charles was virtually given *carte blanche* to allow his marriage to fail, and had he not acted upon this advice he would, once again, have been disappointing the father whose approval had always eluded him. It is interesting to note that Camilla Parker-Bowles is a descendant of Alice Keppel, the last and most beloved of Charles's great-great-grandfather's mistresses.

Throughout his adult life, Charles has had a series of male mentors who have supported and advised him in a way that his father failed to do. At Cambridge he relied upon the kindly care of R. A. Butler, Master of his college. Later his equerry, Sir John Millar, fulfilled this role. Sir Edward Adeane, the Prince's private secretary, was similarly privileged until he resigned. His two best-known counsellors, however, were his uncle Lord Louis Mountbatten, to whom Charles referred as his 'honorary grandfather', and the South African philosopher and writer, Sir Laurens van der Post. Mountbatten was as keen to see Charles married to his granddaughter, Amanda Knatchbull, as he had been to see his nephew married to Princess Elizabeth, but Charles showed no interest. He continued, however, to confide in his uncle, and to rely upon his worldly experience. With van der Post, Charles is able to express the metaphysical side of his nature as he never could with his father.

Like his grandfather, George VI, Charles is intolerant. He is not only impatient with those who fail to offer him what he perceives to be proper respect, but also with servants who are in no position to answer back. He has said with some candour, referring to his sons, that he does not like four-year-olds, which reflects his own unhappy memories of being that age. It seems likely that he will be no better a father to his sons than Philip was to him. His wife's devoted mothering of their children compensates her for the absent mothering of her own childhood, and supplies Princes William and Harry with unconditional love.

As Charles continues to demand respect and approval, he also insists upon petty economies in the running of his household echoing his feelings of 'inner poverty'. He finds great difficulty in giving to others something which he never had: a sense of worth acquired from loving, freely available parents.

When he is at leisure he fishes, gardens, and, like his father, depicts in landscape paintings an idealized unpeopled world, in which he perhaps would like to live. His concern with ecology suggests that the real world is not to his liking, and that possibly by making a belated attempt to protect the interests of 'Mother' Earth, he hopes that she might bestow upon him that which has always been denied to him. He plays the cello, an instrument whose shape has been compared to that of a woman's body, and which responds to his caresses by passively echoing his tune. On the polo field, where he is at one with his pony, he is able to demonstrate to his father (another polo enthusiast and also a rival for his mother's love) that he too is dominant and powerful. Through risk-taking activities, such as parachute jumping, in which he was involved in early manhood, and, allegedly, an illicit love affair, he was able to obtain the arousal and stimulation which were lacking in his infancy. For him, variety is the spice of life, but the life source, namely the mother, should have been able to provide him with the contentment and satisfaction that would have fulfilled all his needs. Spice, therefore, in the form of variety, should not have been necessary. All activities which are compulsively carried out, in particular hobbies, may often be coded representations of earlier life patterns: those who are addicted to performance games, such as tennis or squash, for example, play to win and are heavily dependent on the satisfaction gained from their achievements and from spectator approval. A bad loser cannot cope with absence of admiration and feels rejected. A loser invariably feels depressed, often guilty and sometimes unlovable, yet is compelled continually to try to succeed. Collecting small fragile pots, or antique (breast-shaped) wine-glasses, is a reminder of the meagre and unsatisfying feeds of infancy. An inevitable compensatory obesity is often to be found in those who have an urge to acquire small containers. The mountaineer is compelled to climb the icy slopes of breast-like peaks, constant reminders to him of the cold disappointment that he once had in his struggle to feed. Other hobbies such as the collecting of old clocks and watches are reminders of a wish for the time which was not available in one's own remote past. A knitter of baby clothes may be simultaneously repeating her own insufficiently fulfilled procreative needs and also, by identifying with the baby, a need to return to the warm enclosing arms of a loving care-giver, more so when those loving arms have been insufficiently available.

Prince Charles has one particularly significant hobby: collecting lavatory seats. To use a lavatory seat it is necessary to turn one's back to it. When Charles adds to his collection he acts out his own sense of rejection. The lavatory seat becomes a metaphor for his wish to retaliate against all those who, at one time or another, have turned their backs on him – his parents, and now, finally his wife.

Charles had always learned to anticipate rejection. He made it impossible for his wife to love him. It could be that he will only feel comfortable and at ease with himself if and when he is seated on what will be the jewel in his bizarre collection: the throne of England.

CHAPTER ELEVEN

Princess Diana

'. . . a girl who danced with the Prince of Wales'.

Lady Diana Spencer was a commoner when she married Prince Charles but, like her grandmother-in-law Elizabeth Bowes-Lyon, came from among the highest echelons of society.

Her immediate family background was troubled. Her father, Earl Spencer who died in 1992, was a genial, friendly man and fond of his children. He had three daughters, of whom Diana, born in 1961, is the youngest, and a son, Charles, born in 1964. Despite her material advantages, Diana was not happy. Shortly after Charles's birth Diana's mother, the former Frances Roche, fell in love with Peter Shand Kydd, and when Diana was six the Spencers divorced. Frances sought to keep her children but their father was awarded custody amid considerable publicity. It was he who brought up Diana, although she continued to see her mother during school holidays.

Children often blame themselves for the break-up of their parents' marriage and Diana was clearly disturbed by the divorce and the divided life she led afterwards. Until she went to boarding school aged eight, she at least experienced the constant care of her governess, Gertrude Allen, and also had an affectionate relationship with her sisters and brother, for whom she developed a protective concern. When Charles outgrew his baby clothes Diana dressed her teddy-bear in them. Usually, a cuddly toy, a transitional object, acts as a comforting reminder of the child's former attachment to his or her mother; unusually Diana's teddy became an extension of her brother, since it seems that Charles became an alternative love object because of her mother's absences. Fortunately for Diana she, like Prince Charles, had a loving grandmother in Ruth, Lady Fermoy, who showed kindness and compassion to the sick and socially disadvantaged, and must have recognized intuitively that the emotionally bruised Diana came into the second category.

At this early age Diana dealt with her feelings of being one of society's victims by identifying with the helpless and the trapped – role reversal – caring for a series of small caged animals, guinea pigs, hamsters, and other household pets. She was helpful and seldom naughty, which is typical of a child who feels abandoned growing up heavily dependent on approval that was conditional but should have been available to her freely and by right. She was also neat and tidy, perhaps trying to compensate for the chaos and disorder in her life. The unhappy child who made up for the absence of her mother by raiding the Althorp larder and compulsively consuming all the left-overs seemed already set on the course which led to her later eating problems. No matter how loving Diana's grandparents and other care-givers may have been, however, they would have been unable to compensate her for the feelings of emptiness caused by her mother's unavailability.

Further painful separations took place when Diana was sent away to school. She lost Gertrude Allen, who left the family, and her cat died. These events would have reinforced the grief first experienced when she 'lost' her mother two years earlier. It seems that Diana tended to fantasize at about this time: in fact, finding reality intolerable, she had invented a fantasy world in which she could live more happily. In addition she lost regular contact with her father and brother, and when she visited her mother in school holidays, she had to adapt to seeing her with a man who was not her father. It was probably from around this time that Diana would have first become aware of depression. Although the losses she was experiencing had not resulted from the death of a loved one, nevertheless the more subtle losses of being left, of change and of moving on were occurring too early for her to be able to cope with them and would lead, later in life, to inappropriate compensations such as food and hopeless attachments. All of life's losses are rites of passage and are inevitable, necessary and have to be confronted, but most of them usually occur later, when the realization that letting go is essential for growth and development.

For years Diana was ferried between her mother and father. She acknowledged Althorp as her home but even that secure base was disturbed when her father remarried. Diana did not form a close relationship with her step-mother, Raine, the daughter of the novelist Barbara Cartland. Her older sisters 'mothered' her, however, and the girls were supportive of each other. Diana, as the youngest girl, could not easily articulate her frustration and anger, and therefore experienced her father's transference of affection to another woman more acutely than her sisters and brother. She later expressed her feelings through food, seeing it at first as compensation for a caring mother, but then rejecting it. This unsatisfactory situation was replicated in her marriage: at first she binged on the adulation provided by an adoring public, the glamour of the Crown, and Charles's acceptance of her as a royal princess, until circumstances obliged her to re-evaluate her role and regurgitate a significant part of it. Although there is a well-documented connection between eating disorder in adults and childhood sexual abuse, in Diana's case there is no evidence whatsoever of this other than her current feeling that Charles, in turning away from her sexually after the birth of their children, abused the position of trust that he occupied within their marriage, thus compromising his role as husband and father. Childhood abuse does not necessarily have to be sexual and its echo in adult life may take place with another 'father'.

Diana's compulsive urge to eat sweets and nursery food persisted: she looked for other compensations as she grew up, such as admiration, but would inevitably have been disappointed as early patterns tend to repeat themselves. The seeds of her need for approval and love were sown in early childhood. After her mother left, it seems unlikely that she would have been allowed to verbalize her anger and anyway would have found it difficult to do so for fear of alienating her still available parent on whom she had become heavily dependent. During this unhappy time she fell off her pony and broke her arm. This could have been an accident which was 'waiting to happen' since anger turned in on itself may be destructive.

A teacher at Diana's first boarding school says that Diana was known as 'the Duchess' because she was neat, composed and serious. Her feelings remained over-controlled, unless she broke down, when she became unreachable; on one occasion Diana burst into tears without explanation during an art class. Her pictures were usually dedicated to 'Mummy and Daddy' reflecting a non-verbal wish to see her parents together.

The role of the teacher is that of surrogate mother: they care for their charges throughout the day until the children are returned to their real mothers. The teachers *in loco parentis* to Diana could never hand her over to her mother at the end of the day, nor, even, at the end of term, since Diana's mother, having remarried, spent much of her time in Australia. If Diana believed it was her fault that her mother left her, two courses of action were available to her, both of which she exercised. The first was to be as pleasing as possible to authority figures, so that they would love her and stay with her rather than abandoning her. The second was to attempt to relieve her guilt through self-inflicted suffering. Diana was pleasant and agreeable throughout her childhood but after marriage and motherhood, she came to realize that the approval of others was poor compensation for self-esteem. She could hardly have been expected to like herself, though, if at some level she thought that she had been abandoned because she was unworthy or not valued, or that it was her bad behaviour which had driven her mother away.

As Diana grew into an adolescent she became increasingly self-conscious. Most adolescents have image problems, are easily embarrassed and sensitive to criticism, but Diana would have had a real struggle with her appearance since she saw herself as both overweight and unattractive. Like many of her peers in the late 1970s, Diana's role-models were tall and slim. She was tall, but in her compulsive need for food she had not only found momentary comfort but also gained weight. She knew that, among her circle of friends, slimness was valued and preferred, but because she believed herself unlovable she set out to prove it. The chocolate and puddings of her nursery days still represented the love that she had missed, but her compulsive need to binge could only be managed if weight-gain was controlled by inducing vomiting.

At school Diana never spoke of her parents' messy divorce. Even later, at West Heath School where she is remembered as being good company and gregarious, she never discussed her feelings. She continued to satisfy the expectations of teachers, was a good team player at games, a particularly keen swimmer and kind to younger pupils. She read the romantic, asexual novels of her step-grandmother, Barbara Cartland, yearning for maternal affection that would never be hers. She dressed as flamboyantly as possible when not required to be in uniform, and took more baths each week – like many other girls concerned with their appearance – than the regulation three that the school required. 'I knew I was in the wrong shell,' she has said of herself at that period. She was unhappy with her body, but the frequent baths could not wash away her unhappiness.

Later on at school, some of Diana's true feelings began to surface: she was not only miserable but became rebellious. Unlike her older sisters, she failed to distinguish herself academically and, because of her fear of failure and the disapproval that this would provoke, she decided not to retake her O levels. It is possible that she was 'exam-phobic', believing that there was no test that she would ever pass sufficiently well to please others. Instead, she insisted on being sent to finishing school in Switzerland, but returned home after only six weeks. 'Home', however, was no longer home. Since the advent of Raine, in common with her sisters and brother, Diana no longer felt comfortable there.

Diana gravitated towards menial work, reinforcing her view that she was a person of no importance, and her compulsion to care for and serve those who were disadvantaged and helpless (like herself) persisted. At school she had been commended for her work, which she had enjoyed, with sick and handicapped people in the area; she was as much of a success in these activities outside the classroom, as she had felt a failure within it. She gained reassurance from work which proved to her that she could be useful to others.

Like many other well-connected young women who mark time before marriage by working as waitresses, cleaners, nannies or bar-maids, Diana took a succession of short-lived jobs in London. Comforted by a need to create order out of chaos and by caring for others, Diana, her flat-mates say, enjoyed vacuuming and washing-up. At Highgrove, the Waleses' house in Gloucestershire, until recently Diana was said to do her own ironing to the accompaniment of soap operas such as *Neighbours* or *EastEnders*, which enabled her to identify, in fantasy at least, with the good-neighbourliness and family life of the television characters which she had never enjoyed.

Money inherited from her American great-grandmother enabled Diana to buy a flat in 1979 in an exclusive block in Kensington, which she shared with three friends – and a now famous, and then prophetic, collection of frogs, including a cushion on which was inscribed 'You have to kiss a lot of frogs before you find your Prince.' She had many friends but no serious male admirers. She shopped, went to parties, and enjoyed two years of freedom and anonymity. She drove her Metro, week-ended in the country and played practical jokes with her flat-mates. One of their favourite pastimes was to telephone people whose names they discovered in the directory and which they found amusing. Doorbells were rung at dead of night and car locks interfered with: Andrew Morton tells us that, after some minor disagreement with Diana, her friend James Gilbey found his cherished Alfa Romeo covered in a solid 'pastry' of eggs and flour. In this, Diana was scapegoating others for the pain she had suffered in childhood. Her 'jokes' were hurtful, aggressive and, as practical jokes often are, sadistic. Her adolescent acting-out, however, excluded sexual activity. It is not easy to give love if it has not been received. Diana's later interest in Aids emphasizes an unconscious conviction that sexual activity is contaminating and flawed: Diana Spencer had seen how sex had influenced the breakdown of her parents' marriage. Her flatmate, Carolyn Bartholomew, remarked that Diana was 'surrounded by this golden aura which stopped men going any further'. Diana herself has said, with hindsight, which must, none the less, preclude any suggestion of a sense of destiny, 'I knew I had to keep myself tidy for what lay ahead.' Tidy, in her vocabulary, meant good, well behaved – but, above all, virginal.

Diana entered her relationship with Charles sexually and emotionally naïve, without even one serious relationship or former boy-friend with whom to compare him. Charles, on the other hand, knowing perhaps that the stop-watch was ticking away and that pressure for him to marry could only increase, embarked upon his relationship with Diana having had no fewer than three intimate friendships with women in the previous year. Althorp is in Northamptonshire, but the Spencer family has property close to Sandringham and when Diana was at home during school holidays she was a frequent visitor there. She is the same age as Prince Andrew, whom she had known as a child, and had been considered a potential bride for him. She was sixteen when she again met Charles, who was twenty-nine. When he first took an interest in Diana she was working at the Young England kindergarten in Pimlico. An enterprising press photographer was responsible for the picture of her that captured the imagination of the world: a simply dressed, natural-looking Diana was caught with two small children, the sun behind her, and the silhouette of her legs clearly visible beneath her lawn skirt. The picture showed everything that the public wanted in a bride for the Prince of Wales: maternity, responsibility, beauty (albeit naïve) and sex appeal.

Diana was nineteen at the announcement of her engagement in February 1981. Her marriage took place just after her twentieth birthday in July. She lost a considerable amount of weight, partly due to stress and partly because as the royal dressmaker, Elizabeth Emanuel, remarked, 'All brides lose weight.'

Most brides need their mother's support while preparing for their wedding. Diana needed her mother but, like all other children, would have been angry with her for having left her. She would have identified with her mother as a defence against separation – identification in this context means a reluctance to lead a separate life and a wish to remain at one with her. Later, as a mother, she was also to leave her husband. This inner conflict contributed later to bulimia being diagnosed. Diana's therapy may have helped her to realize that vomiting symbolizes both a rejection of what the mother could not provide in the first place, and the need to retain a slim elegance to encourage the admiration and approval of others. She had visited her mother in Australia while considering Charles's proposal. During her stay, she may have been giving her mother an unconscious non-verbal message that, however worthless and unlovable she had felt as a child, the Prince of Wales wanted to marry her and all the world would love her. She would also have been reminded of the first commitment of all, the primary love affair between mother and child, which had been such a disappointment to her. In that first commitment Diana had learnt that nothing lasts and that the one who claims to love you will ultimately leave you. This was all too painfully borne out in December 1992.

Responsibility for Diana Spencer's confusion during her engagement cannot rest entirely with her ambivalent relationship with her mother. The girl who, as photographs suggest, was pleasant enough looking but no great beauty, was now expected by the tabloid newspapers and their readers to fulfil the public desire for a 'fairytale princess'. She was never an 'ugly duckling', but few overweight girls have achieved her swan-like elegance with such spectacular speed. The engagement was publicly celebrated, and basking in this mass approval would have encouraged her to acquire the image the public so ardently desired.

Little can have prepared her for her relationship with Charles, even though she had known the Royal Family peripherally all her life. Although she had had no serious boyfriends she knew that none of her contemporaries had to address a boyfriend as 'sir' until an engagement was announced. She might have hoped to hear more often from Charles during his visit to Australia and to be greeted on his return with more than a bouquet of flowers delivered to Clarence House from his office. From the beginning Charles played a distant role, familiar to her in childhood and reminding her of the often unavailable parent of the opposite sex. Diana's early life experiences were beginning to repeat themselves.

It is hard to avoid concluding that Charles was not in love with Diana when he married her. He had not severed his friendship with Camilla Parker-Bowles, and had, indeed, established that since Diana did not hunt he and Camilla would be able to meet, at least, on the field. The child who had depended on two 'nannies' was, as a man, unwilling to enter marriage without another available 'nanny' in the background.

Diana has described herself as being 'as thick as a plank'. She makes such remarks with confidence and humour, which suggests that she knows them not to be true and hopes that she will be told so. Affection surrounds her everywhere: the press, the public and her children supply her with the unqualified devotion, admiration and acceptance that she needs. She and Prince Charles were attracted to each other because their needs were similar. Charles's mother had 'deserted' him – not permanently as had Diana's, but intermittently, by her comings and goings. Each time she left him she reinforced his sense of being abandoned. Diana's popularity attracted love and attention to them both, while her husband's status gave her the platform upon which she would flourish. But while he has continued to seek the flattery and reassurance of other women, she has had to make do with a loving but distant admiring world. Charles hoped to find the love he missed out on as a child yet simultaneously penalized the 'mother' in Diana who had become the scapegoat for his own mother. Diana came to recognize that her marriage could only disappoint her and that once again she would be experiencing 'loss'. Her despair and anger, previously turned in on herself, would now be directed at her husband.

Up to a point, Diana must have expected Charles to be sparing with his affections. Arm's length involvement was, after all, what she had been accustomed to. Feeling neglected and lonely within her new family she took, as Andrew Morton claims, to the attention-seeking devices of the psychologically desperate and several episodes of non-fatal deliberate self-harm occurred at this time. Throwing herself against the glass of a show cabinet or attempting to cut herself with a lemon-juicer may be thought of as attempts to draw attention to herself, but the unhappiness that encouraged such actions cannot be denied. It is unlikely that Diana wished to kill herself: no mother as devoted as she would choose to deprive her sons of the depth of care that she had lacked. Her ongoing 'affair' with the people of Britain and the world and the support of her friends and children have been her only consolation.

She is known to have received advice and counselling, but has rejected suggestions that she takes tranquillizers, perhaps belatedly accepting that comfort taken by mouth is illusory, and cannot solve problems. Diana's devotion to her children may have saved her, but it could not save the marriage which she had said was over when her second son was born. Since then she has been neglected by her husband who, now that she has ensured the succession, sees her as far too much of a mother to interest him sexually. Diana is in danger of becoming, like Alexandra of Denmark, too smothering a mother for her sons' good. 'I hug my children to death and get into bed with them at night. I always feed them love and affection. It's so important.'

It could be damaging to the young princes if Diana – like Alexandra – came to make demands of her sons that should more properly have been met in the first place by her parents and later by her husband. That Charles chose to go hunting without her during their first New Year at Sandringham as newly-weds, causing Diana to hurl herself down the staircase, indicated his indifference to or unawareness of his wife's needs. Ten years later he was still hunting, leaving Diana to look for emotional input from her sons and from friendships outside her marriage. There was little attempt from either Charles or Diana at reconciliation: like Victoria and Albert, they each sought the opposite-sex parent in the other, but, unlike Victoria and Albert, they acted out their needs elsewhere.

When Diana was a child and was asked what she wanted to be, she is said to have answered that her ambition was to become the Princess of Wales. At that time the Royal Family was an example to Diana of all that was perfect about family life. Her fantasy of participating in a fairytale family came true at one level, but at another, more realistic, level, she realized that her present lifestyle was no different from the one she had in childhood, which had cheated her of unconditional ongoing love from both parents.

Diana has always been preoccupied with her appearance: she wants to look attractive and therefore lovable and goes to a great deal of trouble to achieve this. She has obsessional character traits related to cleanliness and tidiness and tries to impose order upon a life that brought her to the height of happiness as a royal princess and to the depths of sorrow as a cheated wife. As with her eating problem, she is either 'too full' or 'too empty'. She uses washing rituals to 'wash away' the guilt feelings she believes she has caused. She knows she is valued not by her worth as a wife but by the role she plays in public life. Her desire to please has led her to become a chameleon. Her self-esteem is so low that she only feels she exists when she takes on the colouring of her surroundings, identifying with whatever company she is in. She is a princess in Kensington Palace, a Sloane ranger in Knightsbridge, and an 'Essex girl' when in conversation with a second-hand car dealer.

The Princess of Wales, like her sister-in-law the Duchess of York, is an 'exhibitionist'. She has sought and receives massive photographic attention, and has received the approval of the public for her extensive charity work, which underlines the differences between her and her husband. While she concerns herself with human suffering, she knows that he is concerned with form and structure in inanimate objects. When their elder son was seriously ill in 1991, after an accidental blow to the head which could have been fatal, Charles did not stay with his wife at the child's bedside. He had an engagement. The hours which Diana described as being among 'the worst of her life' were dismissed by Charles in the interests of duty. He had an engagement, just as his parents had had many engagements that prevented them from being with him when he needed them. Charles was scapegoating another mother for the parental neglect that had left his 'head' problems unattended.

Friends of the Princess told Andrew Morton that any recent show of support or solidarity from Charles 'is simply a PR exercise to improve his increasingly threatened public image'. It was Charles, they asserted, who insisted that he flew home from Switzerland with Diana against her wishes after the death of her father, and Charles who left her alone with her grief once they arrived in England. The photographers were shown the supportive husband, but not his hasty departure to Highgrove. The Prince of Wales showed little concern about the loss which his sons might have felt at the death of their grandfather, Earl Spencer. It almost echoes the death of his own grandfather, George VI, in 1952 when Charles was four and his parents were in Kenya and therefore unavailable to him.

To maintain her high profile, Diana invariably adopts the trendiest haircut, the most sensational outfits and the latest fashions (a wardrobe on which she is said to have spent £1 million over the past twelve years), while at the same time touchingly maintaining her 'street-cred'. In all this she is photographed, copied and reported. 'I am lovely' *ergo* 'I am loved.' She may be trying to please the camera by looking glamorous and enchanting in the same way that, as a child, she had hoped to please her mother and latterly her husband. Her strongest desire, after caring for her sons, is to be pleasing and dutiful. She has been brought up to expect only conditional love, which was further reinforced by her schooling: the ethos of a boarding school is based on performance and competitiveness, both of which are rewarded. Diana would have worked hard for approval in the early days of her marriage: that she was not to receive it must have led to frustration and a sense of helplessness – Charles, ever in search of recognition of his own worth, had learned to look for it from other women. Diana soon came to realize that the person from whom she had expected the rewards of obedience and duty was too involved with his own needs to recognize hers. As in her childhood, she found herself once again being cheated of the ultimate reward from the care-giver to whom she had committed herself. 'Nursery puddings' once more became her consolation and, in her frustration, she again blamed herself for love having been withdrawn, attacking herself frequently. It was several years before she could rid herself of her guilt and depression by turning her anger outwards and blaming Charles who, she now knew, had rejected her.

Both Charles and Diana are said to have sought advice and, perhaps, consolation, from marginal advisers. Both look for some meaning in the stars, yet it 'is not in our stars, but in ourselves' that we find answers. Her hoped-for destiny, which should have developed out of love, proved to be based on indifference and hostility. While Charles continued to re-enact his anger with Diana – the 'mother' who neglected him – she attempted to find some satisfaction in caring for those whose circumstances were far worse than her own. As part of a self-fulfilling prophecy, Charles seemed to have created a situation in which Diana could not be other than indifferent to him.

Diana is one of life's victims, and finds it easy to identify with other victims. Her concern for Aids sufferers and leprosy research underlines this. She sees herself, like the leper, as an outcast or, as the Aids sufferer, the victim of a socio-sexual disease of our times, in her case, parental divorce. She hopes that she may influence the prejudiced, by her example, to empathize with those who suffer from these disorders. She is unafraid of contracting the Aids virus, seeing it as less damaging than the 'divorce virus' with which she is already infected.

Her work for Barnardo's, Birthright, and other children's charities reflects a concern for the disadvantaged child. As one herself, she can understand how children from broken homes feel. She works with them enthusiastically and with compassion, tuning into their needs and feeling at one with them. Her work as patron of Relate (formerly the Marriage Guidance Council) reflects another problem with which she is familiar: the failed relationship.

Diana will readily order a new outfit (although she is at pains to point out that most of her clothes are altered, adapted, recycled and worn time and again, as if self-adornment makes her feel guilty) if a photograph of herself in an eye-catching dress will help to raise awareness for child victims, sexual victims, or marital victims.

No one would deny that she is genuinely caring and devoted, but it is common for those who believe they have been given insufficient maternal affection themselves to redress the balance by being especially giving of love when they have children of their own. Alternatively, early patterns of emotional neglect may be passed on to the next generation. William and Harry are fortunate in having one parent at least who is anxious to ensure that they do not lack for love. William was taken as a small baby to Australia with the Prince and Princess of Wales in 1983. Nothing was more important to Diana than her new baby. When he was old enough to go to school, his nanny, Barbara Barnes, wanted to stay and look after him and his younger brother Harry. But it seems that Miss Barnes was dismissed because the Prince of Wales believed that she had not been strict enough with William, as if he wanted his sons to suffer withdrawal of affection as he had. Diana disliked Charles's attitude to their children: his mother had not been able to give him enough of her time and therefore he envied the boys Diana's attention, presumably because they were faring so much better than he did.

Diana has a wide range of personal interests. She not only enjoys pop music and disco dancing, shopping and lunching with her girl-friends, but she paints, takes photographs, goes to the ballet, does tapestry and plays bridge. She has belatedly realized that her hand of cards contained not only a king but a 'knave'.

Tensions existed within the royal marriage from the very beginning. Diana was blamed because members of Charles's household were said to have resigned because of her demands. By the mid-1980s royal-watchers were counting the number of days the couple had spent together, finding them to be few and already hinting at a rift. Birthdays and anniversaries were spent apart, holidays taken separately, and Charles and Diana did not look happy or comfortable together when photographed. In the twelve years since their marriage, Diana's character has developed while Charles seems to have become even more set in his ways.

Diana is thought not to have the best of relationships with the Queen Mother. This, again, is understandable since she must inevitably be suspicious of 'mothers'. Although the Queen Mother is particularly close to Charles, she is said to have done little to promote understanding between her grandson and his wife. A friend of Diana's told Andrew Morton that the Queen Mother 'drove a wedge' which helped to sustain the special closeness that has always existed between her and her grandson.

Another friend confirmed that Diana has no friends within the 'firm'. 'The whole royal business terrified her. They gave her no confidence or support.' Both the Queen Mother and Diana were 'commoners'. Clearly, by long association, the Queen Mother has now become royal while Diana, like any newcomer to a closed society, has been resented.

While Charles supports many causes and campaigns, enjoys polo and his gardens and also his other friendships, Diana has her charities and her children, the adoration of her public and the occasional arousal that fast driving brings. When behind the wheel of a car, she is, for a moment, in control of her destiny but this was not so on the road that she and Charles travelled together. Other forms of risk-taking such as illicit sex and dangerous games have previously been unavailable to her but more recently, perhaps as a retaliatory gesture, she has made token phone calls satisfying her expectation that the one who loves her, like her mother, must be at a distance from her. There was little to relieve her obvious sadness.

Diana's collection of porcelain frogs may recall for her the fable of the girl who kissed the frog who turned into a prince. But the Prince she kissed has turned into a frog.

CHAPTER TWELVE

Princess Anne

'I've always accepted the role of being second in everything from quite an early age. You adopt that position as part of your experience. You start off in life very much a tail-end Charlie, at the back of the line.'
PRINCESS ANNE

Princess Anne has seldom been a trend-setter. Despite journalistic attempts to associate her with the 'swinging London' of the 1960s, her half-hearted attempts with the mini-skirt, her back-combed hair, and the sporty caps she adopted as a teenager were ridiculed by the fashion pundits and other girls of her age.

During her teenage years, Princess Anne was expected by the public to identify with the mores of her contemporaries, as was her older brother, Charles, but this did not come easily for either of them. Princess Anne was a late maturer, as far as looks are concerned, and her distinctive appearance, which has come into its own in early middle age, did not do her justice in her youth.

Anne, like her grandfather and aunt before her, married a commoner: the marriage to Captain Mark Phillips took place in November 1973. The couple lived at first in married quarters near Sandhurst, to which Anne's husband was attached, and four years later the Queen presented them with Gatcombe Park in Gloucestershire, a large house surrounded by lands which were to be successfully farmed by Captain Phillips. The Prince of Wales, by contrast, had earlier been given a house in Sussex, followed, after his marriage in 1981, by Highgrove in Gloucestershire.

Princess Anne and Captain Phillips separated in 1989, and were subsequently divorced. At Anne's insistence neither of their children, Peter and Zara, had been given titles. Princess Anne's divorce, having been preceded in 1978 by that of her aunt,

Princess Margaret, was not the first within the present Royal Family, but the manner in which it was handled, in keeping with her democratic marriage, reflected the changing times. How was it that Anne, a princess of the Blood Royal, came to contract such a marriage in the first place?

To be a second or subsequent child in any aristocratic family is to occupy a second-class position. In the Royal Family this distinction is magnified. Princess Margaret experienced the same disadvantages as other second-born royals, but Anne's was a special case in that her invidious position as 'the spare' – and a female one at that – was exacerbated by the later arrival of her two younger brothers. Even before Princes Andrew and Edward were born, Anne was acutely aware of her status within the family, particularly in the light of the affectionate bond which had developed between her older brother and their grandmother, the Queen Mother. 'There is a rather special relationship,' she said, perhaps ruefully, 'between the eldest grandson and a grandmother, I think, which is not true of granddaughters.'

Holding fast, perhaps, to her one claim to distinction within the family, Anne said that she was delighted that she did not have a sister, and later declared that she had 'no sympathy' with 'women's lib'. She clearly felt she was both the 'odd one out' and under-privileged in that as a girl she was denied the special love which her brother received from their grandmother. Her unconscious envy of her brother (a male) might have led her to devalue the contribution of women to society.

As the only girl among three brothers, and constitutionally the least important of the siblings, Anne might have felt the need to distinguish herself so that it looked as if her 'separate' and 'different' position was self-imposed rather than dictated. This may explain her decision to marry a commoner, as it may be her resolution to deprive her children of the titles which would have been automatically bestowed on them had she allowed it. She, perhaps, was passing on to them the lack of privilege which she may have felt was characteristic of her childhood.

As Anne's constitutional importance dwindled, she perhaps made a statement through her aggressive competitiveness as a world-class horsewoman about her worth and her gender. She has spoken with admiration of the Amazon women, who were able to demonstrate on horseback their 'virility', worth, and power. 'It's the one thing that the world can see I do well that's got nothing whatsoever to do with my position, or money, or anything else. If I'm good at it I'm good at it – and not because I'm Princess Anne.' Her determination and courage in this field – as well as her competitive spirit – suggest that she would have been a success whatever stable she came from.

Princess Anne's close relationship with horses and children can be traced back to her childhood. Her involvement with Save the Children suggests she is making an unconscious identification with the cause. While she was free to lend her support to any charity, her choice indicates a particular empathy with children who, like herself, have suffered. Looking at the causes with which they identify, other members of the Royal Family (Princess Margaret and the Migraine Trust, the Princess of Wales and Birthright) also reveal something of themselves. Princess Anne's work for deprived children may appear wholly altruistic, but is it not possible to see her statement that 'If you don't invest in people at the earliest point of their lives you miss an opportunity – and you never get the chance again' as an unconscious side-swipe at what she perceives as her treatment by her parents? And also as a perceptive and intuitive understanding of what children really need. Nevertheless, like her own parents she has spent a great deal of time away from her own children.

When Anne was asked what she would have done with her life, had she not been born a royal princess, she said that she would have chosen to be a long-distance lorry driver. A more revealing remark about herself could scarcely have been made: the image of the long-distance lorry driver, isolated in his cab, proceeding from point to point with his heavy load, is essentially a masculine one. While he relies on the instruction of others, he has the freedom of the road, the ability to set his own pace, power, independence, and a sense of adventure. The lorry, with its illusion of freedom, is paralleled by the Princess's horse, the control of whose destiny, strength, phallic power, and energy, is in the hands of its rider.

As a baby, Anne had reason to feel short-changed by her mother, and was forced to seek the approval and attention of her father. She was successful to the extent that Prince Philip responded to her needs and appreciated her qualities more readily than did her mother. But his devotion to her was qualified, and his absences were frequent. It is Anne's spirit which has enabled her to take the upper hand, to control her horse in response to, or in revenge for, the limited paternal attention she might perceive herself to have received. Like many another small girl she was in love – entirely appropriately – with her horses. The horse has a strong masculine image. Little boys are seldom 'in love' with their horses, but if they are they may be looking for the man who was not there for them during childhood, which may be a first faint indication that later in life some confusion may arise as to their sexual orientation. It can be no coincidence that homosexuality is common among head stable lads and jockeys.

She has been romantically associated with one of her body-guards (a protective father figure) and has recently married a naval officer more clearly identifiable with Prince Philip, Commander Tim Lawrence. That Anne chooses men of rank inferior to her own is a reflection of how she sees her own status within the Royal Family.

Princess Anne was born in August 1950, fifty years after her grandmother, twenty years after her aunt, and when her brother, Charles, was a little under two. While Anne enjoyed a better relationship with their father, Charles's uneasy relationship with Philip was probably exacerbated by his position of greater consti-tutional importance than his father would ever have, and by the Oedipal rivalry felt by all sons towards their fathers. No such restraints prevented Anne from forming an early alliance and bond of mutual admiration with her father, particularly since she was endowed with many of the characteristics which Philip would have liked to see in her brother. After an unsuccessful attempt to kidnap Anne, in 1974, Prince Philip said admiringly, 'If the man had succeeded in abducting Anne she would have given him a hell of a time in captivity.' Both father and daughter possibly thought of themselves as outsiders: Prince Philip as a 'foreigner' and 'consort', Princess Anne as second in the family, and a girl who acted like the boy he would have preferred. Pressure on Anne to excel was always less than that which was imposed on Charles. To attract the attention she had earlier lacked, she was impelled to succeed at something of which her father would approve.

Perhaps, too, it is easier to succeed if pressure is not exerted in excess.

Despite not having a mother who was around all the time, a father who was absent on naval duties for much of her early childhood, the lack of a 'devoted' grandparent, and her unenviable place in the family pecking order, Anne appears *bien dans sa peau* in her self-confidence and uncompromising attitude to her public and private lives. Force of circumstance has made it necessary for her to plough her own furrow, develop self-reliance early, trust and depend upon few people. 'I don't reckon I've many good friends but that's partly the life one leads – one doesn't stay still for terribly long,' she once remarked, defensively. Her self-sufficiency, her suspicious nature, and the barrier she has erected between herself and the world, have contributed to her image of being cool, remote and, frequently, antisocial.

Anne fitted in well at school (Benenden), but made no special friends while she was there. She considered doing a degree at the University of East Anglia but shared neither Charles's intellectual bent nor his awkward interest in student diversions. She had been held back by him in the nursery, and, sharing lessons with her slower brother, she developed less of an interest in learning than she might otherwise have done, and set out to prove herself in ways which were different from his. In 1960, when Anne was nine, she was faced with the arrival of her second brother, Andrew, to be followed by a third, Edward, four years later. That she was a girl was her only claim to distinction within her immediate family. Even more so with her two younger brothers the focus of media attention, Anne had to think of other ways to make her mark.

She had always been encouraged to excel physically, particularly by her father, who taught her to shoot and to drive (on private land) before she was ten. It probably pleased him that his daughter appeared to have more aptitude for such skills than his eldest son. Princess Anne was a competent sailor at an early age, and was coached in tennis by the late Dan Maskell. She was given her first pony when she was three, at a time when her parents set off on one of their lengthy tours abroad. Her equestrian skills also reflect a desire to gain the approval of her mother, who is similarly keen on horses. Her attachment to horses became more 'hands-on' than that of her mother and grandmother, who are primarily associated with breeding, training, and racing. Princess Anne's achievements as a horsewoman – at Burghley, in the Olympics, and in European championships – have proved her mastery of her sport and also indicated the intensity of her desire as an individual to shine, to win, and, most of all, to be applauded. The pressure on all children, particularly royal ones, to be obedient, is strong. Anne rebelled against this through her riding: it was only on horseback that she knew that she literally had the whip hand.

Princess Anne inherits more from her father than his restless energies: she shares his volatile, impulsive, blunt nature, and, like him, she has endured long spells of unpopularity with the press. Determined not to conform to the image of 'fairytale princess' as which, at one time, the media were keen to portray her, Anne, as a young woman and through her own doing, came to be regarded as graceless and churlish. 'I didn't match up to the public's idea of a fairy princess in the first place. The Princess of Wales has obviously filled a void in the media's life which I had not filled, but I never had any intentions of filling it. I had already made a decision that it wasn't me in any way.' Here, defensively, Anne was protesting too much, in this case that she was not troubled by the glamour and overwhelming popularity of her new sister-in-law. Anne's difficulties with the press were apparent in the frequent and acrimonious brushes she had with them during the 1970s and 1980s. Her most celebrated public remark, 'Naff off,' was directed at some journalists whose intrusions she resented at a horse show. For whatever reasons, Anne has ensured that her children grow up with the minimum of the media attention she so despises.

Anne has, of course, been able to enjoy the privileges of being royal, but at the same time she has shown little sign of wanting to be fêted simply because of the accident of her birth. The lonely child still craves solitude as an adult, probably on the basis that 'if you cannot beat them you join them'. It may also be wondered if the Princess is expressing her own anger and resentment in her support of blood sports. The same violent impulse which inspires a competitive rider impels others to follow the hounds.

Even though Gatcombe Park is close to Highgrove, visits between brother and sister are few and far between, and Princess Anne is not thought to be close to either Charles or Diana. Diana has usurped her sister-in-law's position as the foremost young woman in the Royal Family, and, although Anne has shunned publicity as much as Diana has embraced it, it seems likely that some rivalry exists between them – Anne did not attend Prince Harry's christening. She knows that she will always remain in the background except within the context of her work and sporting achievements where her natural aggression and competitiveness stand her in good stead.

In 1987, when she was created Princess Royal by the Queen, she seemed finally to have gained recognition and reward from her mother, and in recent years, Anne has gradually begun to receive a more favourable press. Her charitable work has been recognized and applauded, and the dignified way in which her marriage to Mark Phillips was dissolved was greeted with approval.

By virtue of her upbringing, Anne has found it hard to demonstrate the softer side of her nature. She was obliged to become independent at an unusually early age. Care-givers often encourage 'do-it-yourself' activities in their charges, by emphasiz-ing and rewarding these virtues long before the children are ready for them. An arrogant self-sufficiency – 'I can do it myself, thank you' – replaces the interdependency on which mature and mutually satisfying adult relationships depend. Anne's relation-ship with her father may now be a fond and relaxed one – indeed, it probably always was – but his eking out of attention, and his frequent absences when she was young ensured that as an adult she was destined to seek father substitutes.

The loneliness of her childhood must be continually re-enacted. She may be less concerned these days with performance-related displays of self-worth and competitive activity, and a greater level of public acceptance will have bolstered her self-esteem. But early conflicts are not easily resolved and those who pursue blood sports may be unconsciously re-enacting childhood hostility that can never be fully assuaged. A wish to take life may be seen as a statement about feelings towards the life-giver, the mother. In many of her adult activities Princess Anne has made unequivocal, if unconscious, comments about how she felt dealt with by her parents when she was a child. Her early jealousies and disappointments are revealed time and again in her adult behaviour, from the 'peasant' style headscarf she adopts when visiting famine or disaster areas (in contrast to her mother's 'county' knotting of the scarf under the chin), to the choice of a wedding dress designed by the firm of Susan Small. She has always felt belittled, and whether on official duties abroad, or dressed for her marriage, she has made unconscious statements which confirm this.

When she said, 'I am the Queen's daughter, and as a daughter I get less involved than the boys. I doubt if the next generation will be involved at all', Princess Anne was being both prophetic and wishful, and expressing, once more, her resentment and pain at her neglect. Like her aunt, Princess Margaret, she has been labelled as 'difficult' by the press and by royal watchers. Both Princess Anne and Princess Margaret have had much to overcome and they both deserve – as Princess Margaret seems to be achieving – some emotional respite in the second half of their lives. With the dissolution of her marriage (long before that of the Prince and Princess of Wales came under serious threat), Princess Anne detached herself from the dictates of a monarchy that may, as she has done, have to adapt to survive.

Anne has developed her full potential and has not relied upon the Royal Family and her place within it to meet her needs or to provide her with the support which her family failed to give her.

CHAPTER THIRTEEN

Prince Andrew, His Duchess, and Prince Edward

The young ones.

Andrew, Duke of York, Queen Elizabeth and Prince Philip's second son, married Sarah Ferguson in 1986. Six years later, amid rumour and scandal, the marriage came to an end.

Prince Andrew Albert Christian Edward was born in February 1960. His mother was by this time coping with her royal duties with a calm and expertise that could hardly have been anticipated in 1952 when, as a young mother, recently bereaved of her father, with two small babies, she acceded to the throne. Prince Philip, who had long since given up his full-time naval command, should have been able to devote more time to his second son.

Andrew grew up with older, more experienced, and more tolerant parents than had his elder brother and sister. The near-ten-year age-gap between Andrew and his sister meant that he was less involved in nursery rivalry and enjoyed a more informal upbringing. He was allowed to watch television and to socialize with children of his own age. His parents spent less time away than they had when the two older children were growing up, telecommunication was easier, their absences were shorter and less disruptive.

In view of Charles's unhappiness at his prep school, Cheam, the Queen and Prince Philip sent Andrew, who, being apparently less sensitive and more outgoing than Charles, could probably have coped anywhere, to Heatherdown. Later, taking Gordonstoun in his stride, he met the physical and intellectual demands that were made on him more easily than his brother had. He graduated with reasonably good A levels in English, history, economics and political science, but did not want to go on to university. After enjoying a brief time at Lakefield College, Ontario, where emphasis was placed on outdoor activity, he began his naval training at Dartmouth. Andrew was lucky enough to grow up with several advantages: his father's athletic and leadership abilities came naturally to him, so there was little need for him to make a special effort to win Philip's approval; he was not under the same constitutional pressures as Charles; he was better looking than his brother and it was therefore easier for him to make friends; he was liked by the public and, being photogenic, popular with the press.

Although it has never been suggested that there is animosity between Andrew and his older brother, it is possible that during his upbringing Andrew suffered from the 'second son' syndrome. The good-humoured remark with which he greeted the discovery that he was an inch taller than Charles had been at a similar age, 'the happiest day of my life', may conceal an underlying resentment of his older brother. He later remarked, 'When I'm at sea I feel about six inches taller.'

There were few constraints on Andrew, and he was free to follow his chosen career of naval pilot. Brief, but well-publicized, participation in manoeuvres during the 1982 Falklands conflict enhanced his popularity, and in view of his macho image and lifestyle, with which the majority identified more easily than with his brother's cerebral interests, they were prepared to forgive the occasional social lapse. There was much public interest in Andrew's love life, which was followed keenly by the tabloids, and which he did little to discourage. Although other members of his family have had pre-marital relationships, none have advertised them as freely as Andrew has. He seemed to have been making a clear and unequivocal statement about his image.

Andrew's naval obligations spared him the heavy burden of State responsibilities and enabled him to travel the world as a serving officer on duty, and as a 'playboy Prince' off duty. In the wardroom of his ship he was known as 'H', an abbreviation of HRH. (It is tempting to wonder, in view of the collapse of his marriage, to what extent he has been married to the wardroom rather than to his wife.) A portrait of a well-adjusted, unpretentious, and personable young man appears to emerge.

But Andrew's youthful 'flings', his choice of bride, and the subsequent problems within his marriage, suggest that, despite apparent advantages, he is – in the long shadow cast by Queen Victoria, his great-grandfather and his grandfather – another victim of emotional deprivation. The Queen's first duty is to the Crown, her second is to its heir. While Andrew's mother was certainly able to spend more time with him than many previous royal mothers had spent with their sons, he was not so high on her list of priorities that state commitments could be suspended or postponed in his interests, and, just as his brother and sister before him, he saw more of his nannies than of his mother. Andrew was not, as was Charles, particularly favoured by the Queen Mother, and saw little of Prince Philip's mother, Princess Andrew of Greece, who died in 1969 aged eighty-four, since her life had been devoted for many years to a Christian mission in Athens. His sister, Princess Anne, was nine years his senior and too old to be much of a companion for him in his childhood. When his brother Edward was born in 1964, and lessons began with Catherine Peebles, Andrew's reign in the royal nursery was over and he was forced to make way for the new arrival. His later attention-seeking activities – particularly those with his inexhaustible supply of willing girl-friends – are likely to be rooted at this point in time and the flamboyant lifestyle he adopted was faithfully recorded on camera.

Andrew's companions were frequently either actresses or models, both attention-seeking occupations, which reflected his own need for approval. The 'voyeur' is obsessed with the need to 'look' without physical contact, while the exhibitionist's desire to be 'looked at' colludes with this need. The 'flasher' is not so much interested in sexual activity, as he is in provoking a response to the sexuality which he does not believe he possesses. Those who want to be 'seen' must, of necessity, have someone to 'look' at them. There is empathy between the model and the photographer. They are both, in their different ways, 'flashers'.

Andrew and his young ladies all craved attention and admiration to fill the emptiness of an earlier vacuum. Andrew was, in effect, an only child until the age of four. Had his needs been properly satisfied during this period, he would have felt no need to gratify them before the cameras, or see them reflected in the eyes of those he hoped would love him.

Like Lord Snowdon and Lord Lichfield, Andrew also enjoyed

being behind the camera and often – having loaded and aimed – 'shot' his girl-friends: his photography became a metaphor for his hostility to women and provided him with scapegoats for the woman whom he had earlier perceived as failing to give him sufficient love – his mother.

Koo Stark, who had starred in soft-porn films and is now herself a professional photographer, was Andrew's most high-profile girl-friend. He may have hoped that their relationship might continue, but although Koo was intelligent as well as beautiful and the Queen liked her, the revelations about her past made this impossible. Katie Rabett, another actress, was not to last. He also had an affair with Vicki Hodge, a model some years older than he, but the relationship came to an end when her account of it was published in a tabloid newspaper. Andrew's remark, 'My only vice is women', indicates a strange equating of women with corruption.

Although it is fair to say that the Royal Family disapproved of many of Andrew's female friends, and that he was clearly encouraged to give them up, his partner-choice was invariably unsuitable, precluding any real possibility of lifetime commitment. It is difficult to be persuaded that Andrew likes women since he has always loved them and left them.

His philanderings, which earned him the nickname 'Randy Andy', were at first eagerly and rather admiringly recorded by the popular press. When he overstepped boundaries, however, his popularity waned and the sobriquet was used more pejoratively.

Sarah Margaret Ferguson was extrovert, upper middle-class, and well connected. She was approved by the Royal Family as a girl-friend for Andrew and their courtship and subsequent marriage were greeted with relief. Sarah is a few months older than the Prince. She had had previous relationships with men, but since the birth of two sons to the Waleses meant that her children were unlikely to succeed, this was not seen as a serious obstacle. She was born in 1959. Her father had known Prince Philip for many years, and managed the Prince of Wales's polo ponies. It was at Cowdray Park that his daughter was first introduced to Prince Andrew, by her friend the Princess of Wales.

The existence of Prince William and Prince Harry seemed to provide the Yorks with an excuse to behave, both together and separately, in ways not at all in keeping with the tradition and dignity of the Royal Family. Andrew had found in Sarah exhibitionistic tendencies which mirrored his own. They were attracted not so much to each other, as to what each saw of him or herself in the other. Andrew enjoyed Sarah's good humour, her playfulness, and the apparent maternalism inherent in her physique, which reflected aspects of nurturing of which he might have felt he had been deprived. Sarah, coming from a broken home and needing reassurance, was similarly attention-seeking, and realized that in marrying Andrew she would seldom be out of his sight – and, by extension, the public eye. It was not until she became a mother that the promise which had drawn them to each other in the first place was revealed as false.

Sarah was twelve when her parents divorced. Her father, Major Ronald Ferguson, whose traditional upbringing of nanny, prep school, public school, Sandhurst and nineteen years in the Army left little time for close relationships with women, remained in the Life Guards until his daughter was nine, and was not likely to have been around much during her childhood. She has an older sister, Jane. Sarah's mother remarried, to Hector Barrantes, an Argentinian polo player, who died recently. Major Ferguson also remarried. Her life was disrupted too by several changes of school. She attended private schools in Berkshire, near the family home, but finished without even the basic intellectual achievements of her future husband. Like Andrew, she grew up largely among her own sex and, like him, she preferred outdoor pursuits such as horse-riding and skiing.

When she left school she took a secretarial course, which was followed by a succession of undemanding jobs appropriate to the upper middle-class girl with private means. There is little to suggest that she then genuinely hankered for a career, but she worked in public relations, publishing, and an art gallery, jobs which reflected the same need for both exposure and approval which drew her to Andrew. Their relationship foundered because their unconscious requirements (like Queen Victoria and Prince Albert they looked to each other to make up for the losses of childhood) were identical, rather than complementary. An 'exhibitionist' would have much to offer a 'voyeuristic' partner. Two exhibitionists would be unable to satisfy each other's needs since they would be competing with each other for approval.

Sarah enjoys winter sports and followed the motor-racing

Grand Prix, especially when her boy-friend, Paddy McNally, was a competitor. She is attracted to older men. Given her background this is not surprising, and she seems to be making up for lost time now by enjoying a close relationship with her father which she did not have as a child. Her much-publicized, infantile behaviour while travelling by plane with him – throwing bread-rolls around and placing the sick bag on her head – suggests the attention-seeking antics of a child.

Sarah has a distanced relationship with her mother. Susan Barrantes still lives in Argentina. When she left her daughters it was without saying goodbye to them, with their father having to break the news. Mrs Barrantes made some supportive statements about her daughter during the Yorks' marital crisis in 1992, but it is doubtful whether they were of much help to Sarah. The manner in which her mother was obliged to leave would not have encouraged trust between them, and it is unremarkable that Sarah prefers the company of her father, who was at least visible during her childhood. Ronald Ferguson himself has remarked, 'It doesn't matter what the father is like or how much he takes upon himself, or what he does, there is no substitute whatever for a mother at that age.'

Sarah found some comfort in food. At the time of her engagement she was seriously overweight. Although she lost many pounds before the wedding, the new Duchess of York was still a large woman. Like the Princess of Wales – who also lost weight before her wedding and even more after the births of her sons – Sarah is now as slim as she has ever been, in spite of having had two children.

'Fergie's' exuberance, her 'hilarious' social gaffes (about which she is unrepentant), her touching lack of dress sense, and her obvious enjoyment of a good time, endeared her at first to the public. She was fallible, fat, unpretentious, reassuringly human and good-humoured. She even weathered a potential storm when the publication of her two children's books was greeted with some criticism and hostility. Her stories about a helicopter called Budgie displayed an uncomfortable similarity to some published earlier by a less prominent author. Suggestions of plagiarism were quietly dampened, and the episode was apparently forgotten. The suggestion that the Duchess was keeping her royalties for herself, rather than directing them to the children's charities to which they were said to have been donated, failed to make a permanent dent in her popularity. She was forgiven because her 'crimes' appeared human, and because it was still thought that she was a working girl from a broken home and could use a few breaks. This goodwill on the part of her public helped her to breeze through the scandal which ensued when her father was reported to have been seen in a club where male members were entertained by young women. Sarah was forgiven every folly. Although she did not realize it at the time, she was sailing close to the wind.

The Duchess of York's popularity began to wane after the birth of her first daughter, Princess Beatrice, when she was criticized for leaving the baby at home while she joined her husband in Australia. Although Andrew had failed to get leave of absence to be with his wife after her confinement, it was Sarah who was pilloried for being a poor mother, and not Andrew for putting duty before family. Sarah could well have gone to Australia, perhaps made anxious by his apparent neglect, in an effort to save what she may have perceived as her failing marriage. But even the birth of a second daughter, Eugenie, a year later, failed to redeem it. If anything, it must have made it worse, for Sarah was becoming even more of a mother figure with whom her husband could no longer identify sexually. She was the mother of two daughters who were fifth and sixth in line to the throne. In the late 1980s the behaviour of the Yorks became the target for much criticism of which the Duchess bore the brunt. Her official workload was compared unfavourably with that of the Princess Royal, and there is no denying that she had only one public engagement for every four of her sister-in-law's, although it could be argued that her children were very young and should have taken priority.

Her 'Dallas-style' plans for a new home in Berkshire, followed by pictures of the interiors in *Hello*, were openly derided as vulgar, ostentatious, and an erosion of green belt land. Although the Queen had given her permission for, and the means to build, the house, the planners had allowed the Duke and Duchess to construct their home on previously protected land. The responsibility for affronting public taste was as much the Queen's and the Duke of York's as Sarah's.

In the spring of 1992, when Sarah took Princess Beatrice

skiing in Switzerland while she still had a rash but was in the non-infectious stage of chickenpox, she was criticized yet again. Every false move engendered a new barrage of harsh comment, and it seemed that the Duchess could do nothing right. Her holiday with Steve Wyatt, a Texan millionaire, while the Duke was at sea, coupled with some innocent group snapshots, became widely publicized and another furore blew up. The Queen insisted that the Duchess cancel her engagements and remain out of the limelight for several months. Rumours began to circulate, and in the early summer of 1992 it was announced that the couple were to separate.

Sarah's marriage, like that of the Waleses, had been solemnized amid a fanfare of goodwill, optimism, and affection. Even the Royal Family had welcomed her enthusiastically. 'My brother', said the Princess Royal, 'is a very lucky man.' 'I think she's wonderful,' agreed the Prince of Wales. When the marriage fell apart, however, the family closed ranks. Well before Sarah's climactic liaison with John Bryan, her 'financial adviser', the family's attitude shifted from amused tolerance to frosty recrimination. Her relationship with the press was now intolerable, and the extrovert personality, which had once been part of her charm, now militated against her. When photographs of her on holiday in North Africa with her Texan male friend among the party were released, even her public were reproving: they had had enough. The Duchess was 'grounded' by the Queen, and as a member of the Royal Family her end was in sight.

It is likely that, for Sarah, the rot set in with the televised showing of the undignified high jinks of *It's a Royal Knockout*, masterminded by Prince Edward. As far as the public was concerned, once she had proved to them, by her juvenile on-screen antics, now retrospectively deplored, that she was no different from them, she lost her right to hide behind her halo, or even to wear a coronet. In the past, other members of the Royal Family have proved themselves equally human, but Sarah Ferguson did not have the absolution of royal birth. She was a commoner, and was disappointing her admirers by behaving like one. She had become a scapegoat not only for troubles within her family but for those who had placed her on a pedestal.

It cannot be said that Sarah Ferguson was anything but honest. On the day of her engagement she announced, 'I'm not going to change. Why should I?' A little later she said, 'I will just have to think slightly more, but I will not change when I go out. I'm just going to be me.' It was some time before either her public or her new family objected.

In the absence of outstanding British economic or intellectual achievement, the monarchy, until recently, remained the one area in which Great Britain still led the world. Firstly the Duchess of York and then later the Princess of Wales drew attention to the flaws in their respective marriages which were the first steps towards illuminating the cracks that became all too obvious. Sarah could have been the catalyst that allowed her sister-in-law to follow the same course to disclosure. While pomp and ceremony, visible extravagance, and regal behaviour are tolerated, even encouraged, the Royal Family must not be 'vulgar'. The Duchess of York was unable to make this distinction, and the direct result of her unthinking behaviour ('a silly girl' was a comment attributed to Princess Anne but later denied) is that the Royal Family has been dragged down to an uncomfortably low level.

She acted recklessly, testing, as it were, the security of her position, by sunbathing topless with a man friend in the South of France. The same recklessness informed her utterances, her choice of clothes in which to appear on state occasions, and her determination to fly. She even risked making public the announcement, in the early days of their marriage, that 'Andrew comes home on Friday, absolutely tired out. On Saturday we have a row. On Sunday we make it up but by then he has to go back to base again.' Her comments were honest but reveal a degree of naïveté and tactlessness which did not endear her to her in-laws.

There have been three Duchesses of York this century, all of whom have been remarkable women. Queen Mary embodied the dignities and constraints of the past, while achieving a certain 'modern' outlook. She was in favour, for instance, of birth control. Queen Elizabeth the Queen Mother personified the warm and human face of royalty. Sarah Ferguson is a late-twentieth century woman who tried – and failed – to reconcile duty and motherhood with a self-seeking determination and an inflated ego. Her career as a duchess was short and anything but sweet. She is still young, though, and it is possible that, having learned her lesson, she will make a success of a future relationship which will, however, be something of an anticlimax.

Both previous Dukes of York came to the throne unexpectedly. It might be interesting to speculate on what kind of queen consort Sarah would have made, had circumstances been different. She has certainly shown little evidence of a sense of responsibility. She might, of course, have risen to the challenge and surprised her detractors, but it seems unlikely. While it is possible that the monarchy will survive for a few more generations, it is hard to imagine that the tax-payer would tolerate Sarah Ferguson as queen.

'Illusion' is one of the qualities which has allowed the Royal Family to survive – some would say to throw stardust in our eyes – for as long as it has. Sadly for some, the Yorks have dissipated the magic and left us with a rather ordinary 'first family' of fallible human beings. They have contributed to the 'demystification' which in recent years has been the greatest threat to the survival of the monarchy in its present form. Up to a point, the public are pleased to witness the human face of royalty. Beyond that point they are not prepared to go. Every ill-chosen remark uttered over the past few years by Sarah, and by extension 'the Yorks', has been paid for by the Waleses. While 'Fergie' was allowed to get away with murder, the Princess of Wales had to redress the balance through her dignity and discretion, until the Morton revelations when she must have felt that she could no longer play that part.

Sarah and Diana might be compared with Laurel and Hardy. Sarah, plump, extrovert, would always complain, 'That's another fine mess you've gotten us into', about one of the escapades that Diana had engineered. In fact it was Sarah's bumptiousness that more often than not caused them to come to grief, and the patient, long-suffering Diana who took the blame and got them off the hook. Sarah's commendable loyalty to her father, when Major Ferguson's association with the Wigmore Street club was the subject of speculation and criticism, displays a wish to retain the approval of a father whose army duties necessitated absences in her childhood. It is to be hoped that, for the sake of their daughters, the Duke and Duchess of York will remain on good terms and be able to achieve the apparently civilized friendship maintained by Princess Margaret with Lord Snowdon.

Like earlier royal risk-takers, both Andrew and Sarah have a passion for action and physical challenge. Both are aroused by high speed, flying, and social risk-taking. The latest 'flight' for both of them is from each other, with the challenge of new horizons which, hopefully, will provide them with the happiness which they were unable to find together. The Duke of York's horizons are still predicated by the destinations to which his naval career will take him. In command of a ship he may seem able to control his own destiny and to chart a course to search for what his mother was unable to supply.

The Duchess of York, who will probably retain her title unless she remarries, is likely to remain in the public eye. This will bring her the attention she craves, combined with freedom from the responsibilities of being 'royal', and therefore allow her the best of both worlds.

With the decline of the Yorks' popularity, the public appetite switched from a wish to applaud them for their common touch, to a similar desire to berate them for it. Overnight Sarah and Andrew changed from being good news to being bad news and it was the Duchess, not always deservedly, who was castigated. If it was thought that the 'Fergie' débâcle would buy time for the Prince and Princess of Wales, Andrew Morton's timely (or untimely) *Diana: Her True Story*, which blew the whistle on the Waleses' marriage, put paid to any such idea.

Prince Edward, the Queen's youngest son, escaped public scrutiny until 1987, when at the age of twenty-three, he resigned his commission in the Royal Marines. Prince Philip's anger at this was well documented, as was Edward's decision, shortly after-wards, to join Andrew Lloyd Webber's Really Useful Theatre Company as a production assistant, where he was sometimes referred to as 'Barbara' Windsor. Edward later formed his own theatre production company and now seems totally committed to his work, his royal duties and his family. If scandal has as yet barely touched his private life, it is not for want of journalistic prying.

Edward has found little to attract him in the marriages within his immediate family, and he has not yet made any such emotional commitments himself. Other than gravitating towards the public domain of the theatre, he has avoided personal publicity. As third in line of succession until the birth of Prince William, his childhood was respected. His liking for privacy is genuine, and in unassumingly performing his official duties he does little to court publicity. Perhaps Edward was his mother's favourite, as is often the case with the youngest child. At twenty-nine, it is still too early to calculate the cost of his self-imposed isolation.

The balance of the Royal Family is delicate. It is unable to survive in the absence of the limelight, but will wither and die if the glare is too focused or too strong. If the monarchy survives, it will be in the shadow left by Queen Victoria which seems still to be firmly attached to the heels of the young royals. The present generation is possessed of neither the charm of Edward VII and Queen Alexandra, nor the dignity of Queen Mary and George V. It does not even proclaim the family virtues extolled by George VI and Queen Elizabeth.

Will the future life of Sarah Ferguson inspire the speculation and gossip which dogged that of the Duchess of Windsor? When Prince Andrew finds another woman, will it hit the headlines? There are, for the moment, no more unbloodied young royals to satisfy the appetites of the tabloid editors, or of their readers. It will be at least ten years before William and Harry, Zara and Peter, Beatrice and Eugenie are old enough to be considered fair game for the press. How the curious will survive the absence of speculation and misinformation about the Royal Family has yet to be seen.

EPILOGUE

An understanding of one's childhood is the key to the understanding of one's adult life. Conflicts which are best resolved in the nursery but which, for one reason or another, have never been addressed may not only refuse to go away but will be passed through the generations domino fashion. A child's feelings towards its parents are nearly always ambivalent. While acknowledging our parents' best intentions on our behalf, we simultaneously resent what we perceive as their 'old-fashioned' ways, react with anger to their apparent lack of empathy with us and their inability to understand our problems, and are jealous of siblings whom we believe to be preferred to us.

When the time comes for us to leave the parental home in search of a new partner, we generally look for one who is either completely different from, or exactly the same as, our own parent of the opposite sex. Often, making a barely understood competitive point, we may have twice as many children as our parents, and then relate to them in precisely the same way as our parents related to us. We use the same phraseology, echoing words and using admonitions that, only a short time before, we objected to when they were used with us, and sometimes even re-experience the jealousy we had for a brother or sister with one of our own children.

For the most part we are unaware of the origins of these feelings and actions. We are, none the less, driven to repeat the childhood patterns which our parents acted out with their parents, and their parents with our great-grandparents. To become conscious of our individual past (and also our collective past) would be to ensure that that which we ourselves found disagreeable would not be repeated. The passage of time can play tricks, however, and our memories of the way in which we were brought up may be either incorrect or incomplete.

It is necessary to find out more about this lacuna in our understanding of why we behave as we do, why we treat our children the way *we* hated being treated, why we insist that they do what we say, rather than what we do, why we pass on our own suffering to those we love best. It is helpful to realize that repetitive and compulsive patterns of behaviour in adult life are a reflection and an echo of our own childhood. By becoming aware of and scrutinizing these patterns, we may be able to prevent the infliction of further damage upon successive generations.

Throwing a light upon the Royal Family, with its high public profile, enables us to understand its members and, by extension, our own family dynamics, about which we are all curious. The 600-millimetre lens of the paparazzi has replaced the keyholes of our childhood and provided us with important research material. Universal curiosity concerning the activities of the Royal Family reflects the child's feelings of exclusion by the adult world and in particular, should he confront it, by his parents' incomprehensible and frightening sexual involvement.

Both parents have an essential part to play in the development of their children. The role of the mother is biological and distinctive from the moment of birth, while the father's contribution is more detached and less obvious.

A 'good' mother allows her child to develop in a friendly, structured and secure environment in which care and understanding are not confused with discipline and restraint. Her child will then grow up feeling grateful and appreciative, a continuing re-enactment of what was provided for him in infancy. By remaining in touch with these good and positive feelings, his inner resources allow him to develop genuine independence and to make commitments as an adult. A 'neglectful' mother, on the other hand, provokes hostility in her child which he is obliged to suppress until it surfaces in later relationships.

Until recently the royal mother has had to choose between the duties imposed upon her by the Crown and the needs of her children. The demands placed upon her to travel (often for weeks or months at a time), necessitating the engagement of nurses and governesses, have taken precedence. Victoria, Mary, and Elizabeth II have all emphasized their royal duties at the expense of their duty to their sons who have grown up either to reject their mothers – as they themselves were rejected – or to scapegoat other women. Edward VII's apparent love for women covered his hostility to them, as he turned from one to another, always rejecting the previous one in the process. Edward VIII's behaviour was similar, until eventually he found a woman who he believed would compensate him for the love he had been denied in the nursery. His hostility then switched from women to the Crown.

In upper-class families of the 'virtuous' Victorian era, heavy emphasis was laid on obedience and duty during a child's upbringing. Freedom of expression was not permitted, the belief that 'children should be seen and not heard' was paramount, and this ideology persisted well into the twentieth century. A male child learns security and trust in his relationship with his mother. If he feels safe with her he will acquire self-confidence, self-worth, and self-esteem. If he knows he can trust her, he will be able to love other women and to entrust them with his feelings, when he is an adult. He will only be able to be strong, supportive and faithful to his partner in later life, if his first partner (his mother) has earlier been strong, supportive, and faithful to him. Even when he acquires brothers and sisters, he will need to believe that *he* is loved, uniquely, as if they did not exist, just as they will also need to feel that they are loved, uniquely, as if he did not exist. This is also true of the female child's relationship with her father. In the absence of a good relationship with him, she will seek a father in all men to the detriment of satisfactory non-incestuous sexual activity.

Jealousy is natural and will surface when the child becomes aware that others are sharing the love that his mother had previously given exclusively to him. If breast-feeding is withdrawn too early he may become envious and believe that something of value is being withheld from him. This is appropriate and normal and an essential part of development. If the child is allowed to express his jealous feelings at the time, these will soon be replaced by the ability to share. The Queen, as 'mother' of her people, might have invited greater envy than other mothers; her children had to realize that they must share her not only with their brothers and sisters but with millions of surrogate siblings. Love should be freely available as of right to the infant. If it is not, he may believe, as a deprived adult, that 'symbols of love' which do not belong to him are his by right. Queen Mary's compulsion, as an adult, to steal 'love' by acquiring the prized possessions of others, is a sad echo of her feelings of worthlessness as a child, when she was denied the love that should have been hers as of right. If Sarah Ferguson had not found herself the victim of a broken home at the age of twelve, as an adult she might have learned to rely on, and trust, a partner of the opposite sex. The one-on-one relationship with her father, which she was entitled to expect, could not, in her case, have been completely fulfilling. Since her father had remained a regular soldier until she was nine years old, it was probable that she saw very little of him even before her parents were divorced. Both Sarah and her mother suffered from the consequences of the all-male lifestyle of her father's army background. Sarah's husband (Prince Andrew) was, like her father, away from home for long periods of time in the course of his naval duties. He became a constant reminder to her of her own absent father, subconsciously precipitating the search for a better and more available 'father' outside the marriage. Both her father and her husband served their country well, but at the inevitable expense of their wives' needs. Did the Duchess of York feel that Andrew loved the Navy (as her father had loved the Army) more than he loved her?

Unlike Sarah Ferguson, her sister-in-law, Diana, was not also deprived of a father when her parents divorced. It was, on the contrary, her mother who went away, leaving her daughter's upbringing in the hands of her ex-husband. Yet Diana, it seems, was doubly disadvantaged. Her mother had, to all intents and purposes, loved her and left her, while her father, having to fill the role of both parents, found it impossible to achieve. It was natural for Diana as an adult to look for love from an 'older man'. A prince and 'would-be' king, and the potential 'father' of his people, must have seemed an ideal candidate. What Diana was not aware of was her need for the nurturing on which she had missed out. This need was unlikely to be satisfied by Prince Charles whose own mother had been insufficiently available to him as a child. By the time Charles and Diana realized that it was mothering *and* fathering that they both needed, it was too late. Because of the maternal absence in their childhoods neither was able fully to satisfy the needs of the other.

If only pleasing behaviour is permitted in childhood, the adult is likely to develop as self-effacing and with little or no self-esteem. In his turn he may be able only to offer 'conditional' love to his children, to whom he will look for the love which he was himself denied.

It is the child's good relationship with the opposite-sex parent which will enable him to make successful commitments, such as marriage, later. When this role-model has been unavailable, or uninterested, then resentment, rage, disappointment, and retaliation may be inappropriately acted out with the adult partner. A partner with similar childhood experiences to one's own will often be unconsciously chosen, and with that person the rejections experienced in childhood will be re-enacted and perpetuated.

Someone prone to fall repeatedly in love will readily recognize the miraculous feeling that each new partner – who is immediately acknowledged – has been 'known' to him all his life. What he is unaware of is that what attracts him to these 'soulmates' in the first place is the instant identification in them of aspects of himself. The sense of 'oneness' and 'sameness' which results is frequently mistaken for true transactional love. It is, in fact, much more likely to be self-gratificatory. A permanent relationship formed on this inadequate basis may soon break down, as the partners realize that what each is looking for in the other is something which neither of them has had in the first place, and which, in the second place, it is doubtful that they will find.

A man who has been deprived of his mother's love (for whatever reason) will be condemned to search for it in future relationships. Making one conquest after another, his hostility towards his mother will lead him to disappoint and reject all women in the same way that he was disappointed and rejected by his first 'love'. His unconscious hostility towards women may also take such forms as sexual coldness, which may sometimes lead to potency problems.

Queen Victoria is a typical example of the 'neglectful' mother. Not one of her nine children (except possibly Vicky who was doted on by Albert like a mother) experienced maternal love. It was probably this neglect that led Edward, her heir, to spend his adult life in promiscuous sexual activity as he vainly sought the approval, attention, and reassurance, which had been denied him by his mother.

Queen Mary also had little or no time for her children, and was happy to leave them with nursemaids. It is hardly surprising that her heir, Edward VIII, as Prince of Wales had one affair after another with married women (as did his grandfather Edward VII) as he sought compensation for what his mother had denied him; in a supreme and final act of hostility he turned his back on his 'mother' country (the Crown).

A woman whose father has been unavailable at critical times in her early development will similarly seek a substitute for him in her mate. An unconscious wish to punish the father who never loved her as a child may lead her later to turn her back on her husband (when he has become a father) and form extramarital relationships with other 'fathers' in an attempt to satisfy her unfulfilled needs for paternal love and attention. Hostility to the new partner will inevitably occur as this partner once again becomes the scapegoat for the absent parent. Signals are given off by the 'unloved' which others with similar feelings readily home in on. As happened with Victoria and Albert, a woman neglected by one or other parent in infancy will unconsciously find herself drawn to a similarly deprived man, and vice versa.

Identification, or feeling at one with another person, is a powerful defence against fears of separation. If a child's separation from the mother who has enclosed him in her loving arms has been gradual, this will have prepared him to cope with inevitable losses later in life. The degree of independence he ultimately achieves will depend on the quantity and quality of the mothering he has received.

The Duchess of Kent certainly failed Victoria as far as quality love was concerned. Victoria remained so reliant upon her mother that she was unable to separate from her. She could not sleep alone, and shared the Duchess's bedroom until she became Queen at the age of eighteen. Her desperate need for a caring partner led her to confuse her utter dependence upon her husband (whose needs she was similarly unable to fulfil) with true, unconstrained love, and to a bleak and unsatisfying marriage.

A smothering mother who is unable to let go of her son may prevent him from making a commitment to another woman, as mother and son remain perpetually in love with each other. If her son does reject her for another woman, she experiences this as an act of infidelity and the guilt that this engenders may result in his turning away from women altogether. Albert Victor, Duke of Clarence, Queen Alexandra's eldest and favourite son, died at the age of twenty-eight probably from an opportunistic infection, having spent his short adult life promiscuously in search of his true sexual orientation. Alexandra's second son, who became George V, affected by his mother's possessiveness, turned in on himself with his lonely habits and hobbies, and survived a marriage to Mary who enjoyed ceremony more than she did sex.

A bad mother is insensitive to the messages her infant sends to her conveying his need for her attention. The interaction so essential to the child's healthy development is aborted. He fails to receive the responses he needs for the growth of his intellect, becomes discouraged, and learns to send out only the more obvious signals such as crying (the reaction to pain or hunger) that can be picked up by the most insensitive and non-stimulating mother. Intelligent and sensitive mothers encourage the child's burgeoning intellect and in their creative attitudes to nurturing will often produce gifted children. Quality mothering is an all-important factor in the child's later achievements.

There are many ways in which gratification is sought to compensate for an unsatisfactory childhood. If there has been lack of stimulation in early life which has been experienced as regi-mented and routine, excitement – such as that which is found in gambling or dangerous sports – may later be looked for. Feelings of deprivation may also be covered up and denied under the influence of addictive drugs which have been described by Bruno Bettelheim as the 'instant nurturing mother'. Both George VI and his brother, Edward VIII, turned to alcohol as an illusory substi-tute for the love which neither perceived himself to have received from their mother.

Edward VII found some consolation in gambling, but any activity which is compulsively carried out to compensate for deprivation may only lead to further feelings of loss. To 'lose out' becomes a self-fulfilling prophecy which is fulfilled at the gaming tables.

Gratification may also be sought in sexual activity, or in the acquisition of possessions more commonly found in the nursery. These transitional objects, a piece of cloth, a beloved toy, a teddy bear (Prince Charles), or a reliance on 'Lady Luck' (Edward VII), from which solace is derived, are unconsciously experienced as being a part of the mother which the child cannot let go and are an extension of his need to be at one with her. 'Toys', such as cars and boats, are compulsively acquired by the bored and lonely adult who, as he did in the nursery, rapidly tires of them.

Promiscuous sexual activity serves a dual purpose. There is a need for conquest – winning love to compensate for its absence from carers – but at the same time one partner is rejected for another in retaliation against earlier parental renunciation. Edward VII chose women with children (mothers) as mistresses. He was thus able to delude himself that he had finally found a mother's love, and at the same time to take revenge on the cuckolded husbands (fathers) in retaliation for what he saw as the purloining of the mother-love, which was rightly his, by his own father.

Family life, which is heavily dependent on the role played by the nurturing mother, is complemented by a powerful, upright, and just father who will make his own contribution to it. As the male with whom his daughter forms her first relationship, a father influences the expectations and attitudes which will colour her opposite-sex relationships in later life. If her father reciprocates the love that she has for him in childhood, she will eventually be able to let go of him and transfer her love to another man. If he has failed to meet her loving expectations, she will be compelled to search in other men for what she was denied, and when she has a child herself she will very likely regard her husband as the loving 'father' whom she herself never had. A cruel irony then overtakes her. Sexual activity with the replacement 'father' (with whom, until their child was born, she has had a good relationship) may suddenly become repugnant to her as the psychological barrier of incest reappears. Her father's 'image', now superimposed on that of her husband, may rapidly bring the once promising marriage to an end. Symbolic replacements for ineffectual fathers are often sought by their daughters. The horse, traditionally a metaphor for strength and leadership (and therefore the monarchy), is a respected symbol frequently unconsciously chosen for its upright, powerful, and thrusting masculine image. A strong, caring and, above all, available father is as essential to the development of a male child as he is to a female. Fathers who are passive or absent at a crucial stage of their sons' development may lead their sons to turn to alternative males by way of compensation as did the Duke of Clarence, elder brother of George V, whose father Edward VII – because of his own defective upbringing – was unable to provide him with positive, paternal input.

In some cultures of the ancient world it was considered the duty of a father to initiate his son into manhood through ritual pederasty. Although this died out, the theme of dominance and submission (the kneeling position, the bared head, the bowed back) is still echoed in the granting of accolades and the conferring of titles by the British monarch.

It could be argued that the Royal Family, born to wealth and privilege, is a special case. But it is the right of every infant, irrespective of rank and privilege, to be loved and cared for, and to have its needs gratified, until such time as growing independence allows for a gradual, anxiety-free separation from its parents. This love must be freely given and unconditional and should not be regarded as an investment by the parents on which the return will be the child's gratitude and obedience. To *demand* love from a child is the first step to child 'abuse'. A girl who pleases her father by being good may, one day, be obliged to please him sexually. Counselling must be available for children whose appropriate feelings of rage, jealousy, and other negative emotions have been cruelly, if unwittingly, repressed by parents, to pre-empt their inappropriate recurrence in adult life. By the time that stealing the 'symbols of love' (jewellery, money) has offended society, or the denial of deprivation (drug and alcohol abuse), with its resultant self-damage, has been acted out, it is too late.

The rights of the child are paramount. The healthy family is a unit in which all members are equal, no one is victimized or scapegoated, and paternalism (the worst form of tyranny) does not exist. This has seldom been the case in the Royal Family where there has often been a combination of both neglectful mothering and harsh fathering. Queen Victoria's long depression affected all her children, although none more so than Edward VII. Victoria envied her eldest son the 'father' she had been denied, and later blamed him, incorrectly, for contributing to his own father's death. Edward's need for love and approval from his parents fell upon deaf ears, and it was no coincidence that he married Alexandra, herself deaf, who could hear neither him nor their children.

Edward's children, the Duke of Clarence and George V, had

not only a deaf mother, but an absentee father. Edward was to compensate for his own inadequate mothering by his sexual promiscuity, while his son George became introspective, heavily over-dependent on himself, cold, angry, and lonely, and married his mirror image.

George V and Queen Mary relived *their* experiences of childhood in their dealings with their sons Edward VIII and George VI. They were distant and formal towards them, failed to give them adequate emotional or intellectual stimulation, and did not provide satisfactory care-givers. As a result, their eldest son, Edward, later found the idea of commitment to a woman frightening until he eventually met a 'nanny' whom he could trust (Wallis Simpson), whereupon he left the stage to his younger brother.

George VI played the 'favourites' game with his elder daughter, Elizabeth, just as Albert had done with Vicky. Both of them sought to replace the love which they had been denied by their mothers, with love from their daughters. Elizabeth's younger sister, Margaret Rose, disadvantaged as a child in her relationship with her father, was to repeat her disappointment with men as an adult. At this point the family's recurring patterns might well have changed. Elizabeth had felt loved and wanted. She was her parents' golden girl and could have provided 'golden' caring for her own four children. But this time fate intervened. Elizabeth's uncle abdicated, her father died, and suddenly she became the Queen. The available prince was a man with a fragmented background, whose narcissism and inability to acknowledge the effect of his disturbed past led him to turn away from the emotional and spiritual to the material and physical.

Neither Elizabeth nor Philip was able to provide constancy of care to their four children. Elizabeth, as Queen, was preoccupied with affairs of state which led to frequent absences abroad without her children. Philip's emotional need to maintain a naval officer's *sang-froid* (a defence against his early losses) distanced him as a father. As a consequence of this unsatisfactory childhood, both Charles and Andrew married girls from broken homes, Anne divorced, and Edward experienced problems with his sexual orientation.

Many of the difficulties involved in bringing up children are well illustrated by the Royal Family. Although it is better to have absentee parents than cruel or negligent ones, the duties of royalty should ideally be correlated with the requirements of their children. The Queen, 'mother' of her people, fulfils an important role in Britain and her time is taken up by the many demands made upon her by her public engagements both at home and abroad. In common with other working mothers she has had to find her own solution to the problems of child rearing. Providing there is constancy of care, and the child is old enough to realize that when the mother leaves home she is not abandoning him and will reappear at the end of the day, an available grandmother or a suitable nanny will often be the answer. These surrogates, however – no matter how good – do not *provide* the child with security, they can only *reinforce* what the child has already learnt during the early bonding process with his mother for which there is no satisfactory substitute. The working mother commonly takes maternity leave which entitles her to stay at home to look after her baby. The fatal flaw which appears to run through the monarchy might well be eradicated if royal mothers were permitted to do the same.

Where the family unit is a democratic one, children's rights are of paramount importance. In an autocracy, where 'blind obedience only' rules, their rights are few. Every child has a 'right' to security, to constancy, and, above all, to be listened to. Too often parents form a united front against which a child is powerless. He or she will have been robbed, not only of the right of appeal, but also of an advocate to present his or her case. Suppression of a child's basic prerogative leads him to search for the 'understanding parent' – inappropriately and almost always unsuccessfully – in the relationships he or she makes in adult life.

The publicity given to the Royal Family's marital problems, and the realization that maternal bonding is so vital to the well-being of children, has already begun to influence the present generation of royal mothers. Both the Princess of Wales and the Duchess of York are loving and caring towards their children, although their own needs cannot be fulfilled at home. In satisfying the needs of the young princes and princesses, however, and in considering their feelings, they will have gone a long way to ensure that these same healthy attitudes are handed down to their grandchildren.

The understanding of a child's needs, precluding the repeating of patterns laid down by parents influenced by the flawed child-rearing techniques of their day and now known to be dangerous, is essential.

In *Inheritance* I have considered how the conditional upbringing of the Royal Family has contained within it the seeds of its own destruction. I am indebted to this high-profile family for providing us with a clear insight into aspects of our own negative behaviour which we unwittingly pass on to our descendants.

Recurring patterns are neither irrevocable nor written in stone. It is up to each one of us to take responsibility for the 'happy families' of the future by loving and understanding our own children.

SELECT BIBLIOGRAPHY

In the preparation of *Inheritance* many books have proved invaluable sources of reference and I am indebted to all their authors and publishers. In particular I would like to acknowledge the debt owed to the following:

Ronald Allison and Sarah Riddell (eds), *The Royal Encyclopaedia*, Macmillan Press, 1991.

Marion Crawford, *The Little Princesses*, Cassell, 1950.

Frances Donaldson, *Edward VIII*, Weidenfeld and Nicolson, 1974.

Anne Edwards, *Matriarch*, Hodder and Stoughton, 1984.

Robert Lacey, *Majesty*, Hutchinson, 1977.

Elizabeth Longford, *Victoria RI*, Weidenfeld and Nicolson, 1964.

Philip Magnus, *King Edward VII*, John Murray, 1964.

Andrew Morton, *Diana: Her True Story*, Michael O'Mara Books, 1992.

Kenneth Rose, *King George V*, Weidenfeld and Nicolson, 1987.

Giles St Aubyn, *Queen Victoria*, Sinclair-Stephenson, 1991.

Philip Ziegler, *King Edward VIII*, William Collins, 1990.

OTHER IMPORTANT SOURCES

Georgina Battiscombe, *Queen Alexandra*, Constable, 1969.

Michael Bloch, *The Secret File of the Duke of Windsor*, Bantam Press, 1988.

Charles Carlton, *Royal Mistresses*, Routledge, 1990.

John Chandos, *Boys Together*, Hutchinson, 1984.

Lewis Chester, David Leitch and Colin Simpson, *The Cleveland Street Affair*, Weidenfeld and Nicolson, 1976.

Jilly Cooper, *Class*, Eyre Methuen, 1979.

Elisabeth Darby and Nicola Smith, *The Cult of the Prince Consort*, Yale University Press, 1983.

Leslie Ebbetts, *The Royal Style Wars*, Sidgwick and Jackson, 1988.

Encyclopaedia Britannica, 1957.

Jonathan Gathorne-Hardy, *The Rise and Fall of the British Nanny*, Hodder and Stoughton, 1972.

Princess Alice, Duchess of Gloucester, *Memories of Ninety Years*, Collins and Brown, 1991.

Tim Heald, *The Duke*, Hodder and Stoughton, 1991.

   Networks, Hodder and Stoughton, 1983.

Christopher Hibbert, *The Court at Windsor*, Longman, 1964.

Charles Higham and Roy Moseley, *Elizabeth and Philip*, Sidgwick and Jackson, 1991.

Anthony Holden, *Prince Charles*, Weidenfeld and Nicolson, 1979.

Paul James, *Margaret*, Sidgwick and Jackson, 1990.

Susanna Johnston and Anne Tennant, *The Picnic Papers*, Hutchinson, 1983.

Denis Judd, *The Life and Times of George V*, Weidenfeld and Nicolson, 1973.

Penny Junor, *Charles*, Sidgwick and Jackson, 1987.

George III and the Mad-Business, Allen Lane, 1969.

The Selected Melanie Klein, Penguin Books, 1986.

Elizabeth Longford (ed.), *The Oxford Book of Royal Anecdotes*, Oxford University Press, 1989.

Alice Miller, *Prisoners of Childhood*, Basic Books, 1981.

Sally Moore, *The Definitive Diana*, Sidgwick and Jackson, 1991.

Ann Morrow, *The Queen*, Granada Publishing, 1983.

Penelope Mortimer, *Queen Elizabeth*, Viking, 1986.

Diana Mosley, *The Duchess of Windsor*, Sidgwick and Jackson, 1980.

John Parker, *Prince Philip*, Sidgwick and Jackson, 1990.

Lance Selway, *Queen Victoria's Grandchildren*, Collins and Brown, 1991.

Morton Schatzman, *Soul Murder*, Random House, New York, 1973.

D. G. M. Schreber, *The Harmful Body Positions of Children, Including a Statement of Counteracting Measures*, Leipzig, 1853.

John Van der Kiste, *George V's Children*, Alan Sutton, 1991.

John Van der Kiste, *Edward VII's Children*, Alan Sutton, 1989.

Thorkil Vanggaard, *Phallos. A Symbol and its History in the Male World*, Jonathan Cape, 1969.

Letters of Queen Victoria, Vol. I, John Murray, 1908.

Judith Viorst, *Necessary Losses*, Simon & Schuster, 1988.

Christopher Warwick, *The Abdication*, Sidgwick and Jackson, 1986.

Audrey Whiting, *The Kents*, Hutchinson, 1985.

Donald Zec, *The Queen Mother*, Sidgwick and Jackson, 1990.

INDEX

Adeane, Sir Edward, 157
Aird, John, 93
Airlie, Mabell, Lady, 89, 99
Albert, Prince: children, attitude to, 21–2; corporal punishment, believing in, 34–5; death of, 10, 24, 43; diarist, as, 16; distanced behaviour, 21; drains and sewerage, interest in, 20; economies, 20; father, as, 18; interests, 16; Lehzen, resenting, 8–9; marriage, 15–16; mimicry, talent for, 17; mother, banishment of, 3, 15; mother, yearning for, 19, 24; Prince Consort, as, 23; sexual indifference, 18–19; shyness, 16; social reform, efforts at, 23; subsidiary role, 17–18; Victoria, meeting, 14–15
Alexandra, Princess, 140
Alfred, Prince, 38
Allen, Gertrude, 160–1
Altrincham, Lord, 129
Anderson, Mabel, 147
Anne, Princess, (Princess Royal): attitude to life, 178; birth of, 124, 147, 177; Charles and Diana, seeing little of, 178; children, lack of media attention, 178; constitutional importance, dwindling, 175; early jealousies and disappointments, manifestations of, 180–1; education, 178; emotional respite, 181; father, inheritance from, 178; first marriage, 174; friends, 178; horses and children, involvement with, 176; kidnap attempt, 177; outdor interests, 126; parents, time away from, 126; Philip, relationship with, 126, 128, 149, 176–7; physical pursuits, 178; Princess Royal, becoming, 180; Save the Children, involvement with, 176; second child, as, 175; second marriage, 177; separation and divorce, 174; trend-setter, not, 174; world-class horsewoman, as, 175, 177, 179
Armstrong-Jones, Lady Sarah, 142

Baldwin, Stanley, 96
Barnes, Barbara, 172
Barrantes, Hector, 186
Barrantes, Susan, 186–7
Bartholomew, Carolyn, 165
Beaton, Cecil, 135, 137
Becker, Dr, 37–8
Bernhardt, Sarah, 51
Bill, Charlotte 'Lala', 75–6, 79, 83, 98
Birch, Henry, 36–7
Blunt, Sir Anthony, 20
Brown, John, 27–9
Bruce, Colonel Robert, 40
Buerger's disease, 101
Butler, R. A., 129, 157

Cadogan, Lady Sybil, 88
Camillagate tapes, 146, 156
Cartland, Barbara, 162–3
Channon, Chips, 107
Child, rights of, 2–5, 203
Childhood: understanding of, 195–6; unsatisfactory, compensation for, 201
Children, jealousy of, 197
Churchill, Winston, 59, 98, 113, 128–9
Clarence, Duke of, (Eddy): death of, 57–8, 62, 200–1; description of, 53, 58; George, separation from, 60–1; haemophilia, 58; homosexuality, 53, 61; intellect, lack of, 59; Jack the Ripper, association with, 61; Klinefelter's syndrome, having, 58; May of Teck, engagement to, 63; Navy, in, 59; proclivities, 61; tattoos, 60; women, attitude to, 61–2
Clarendon, Lord, 10
Coke, Lady Marian, 88
Comfort eating, 12
Conroy, Sir John, 5–6, 8, 11
Coward, Noël, 76, 140
Crawford, Marion, 115–17, 120, 135
Curzon, Lord, 121

Dalton, Reverend John, 59–60
Delors, Madame, 131
Diana, Princess, 46
Disraeli, Benjamin, 27, 29
Dudley Ward, Freda, 91, 94
Dupuch, Etienne, 96

Edinburgh, Duke of, (Prince Philip): absences from home, 126; Anne, relationship with, 126, 128, 149, 176–7; Charles, rivalry with, 177; children, attitude to, 127–8; education, 122; Elizabeth, meeting, 120; engagement, 124; family, 120–2; German connections, 121, 123–4; homes, 122–3; interests, 127; marriage, 124–5; mother, deafness of, 121; nanny, 121–2; naval career, 125; parent, as, 204; paternal instincts, poor role model for, 126; public opposition to, 125; separate identity, maintaining, 128; tactlessness, 127; tolerance, lack of, 127; Townsend, opposition to, 140; women, interest in, 125, 130
Edward VII, (Bertie): absentee father, as, 203–4; adolescent, as, 39; affairs, 199; army, in, 42–3; Bertie, known as, 34; birth of, 21, 32–3; Brown, resenting, 29–30; charm, 42; children, attitude to, 56; compensations, 55; death of Albert, scapegoat for, 27, 43–4; description of, 41; diet, 39–40;

209